Sue Turner

''139.

£2

THE WORLD'S GREATEST **BRANDS**

THE WORLD'S
GREATEST
BRANDS

Edited by Nicholas Kochan

MACMILLAN
Business

Interbrand

First published 1996 by
MACMILLAN PRESS LTD
Houndmills, Basingstoke, Hampshire RG21 6XS
and London
Companies and representatives
throughout the world

ISBN 0–333–66419–1

A catalogue record for this book is available
from the British Library.

This book is printed on paper suitable for recycling and
made from fully managed and sustained forest sources.

Designed and typeset by Jim Weaver Design, Basingstoke
Repro by Ocean Colour Ltd, Shoreham-by-Sea

Printed and bound by Jarrold Book Printing, Thetford, Norfolk

FOREWORD

In 1990 Interbrand published its first choice of the *World's Top Brands*. Now, under the title *The World's Greatest Brands*, we present our second review. During the intervening six years much has happened to test the mettle of brands. The world's leading economies have suffered the ravages of a deep and sustained period of recession. Most have now recovered but many smaller, dependent economies – particularly those in Africa and Latin America – continue to be affected. At the same time there have been profound political and social changes in eastern Europe and dramatic economic growth in the Far East. And almost everywhere there have occurred fundamental changes in the balance of power between manufacturers and retailers.

So how has this affected brands? Arguably they are stronger than ever. But it would be wrong to say that major players like McDonald's, Coca-Cola, Marlboro and Mercedes have emerged unscathed from the experiences of the last few years. Each has encountered problems: health scares, supermarkets' private labels, over-ambitious pricing and excessive costs of production have all threatened their competitiveness. These challenges have represented a sort of nemesis, an almost inevitable consequence of the hubris of the late 1980s. That each of these brands remains amongst the most powerful in the world is a great tribute to the underlying quality they possess.

Perhaps it is this quality – unwavering consistency in a rapidly changing world – that best explains the extraordinary influence of brands. When political systems crumble, long-standing geographical and ethnic boundaries change (seemingly) overnight, and the verities of the major religious faiths are called increasingly into question, who can blame people if they cleave to the more constant icons of civilisation? This may seem fanciful, but brands, by default, now supply many of the qualities of reliability, trust and emotional and physical fulfilment that were once obtained from other, loftier, sources. It is right, therefore, that we should recognise the social as well as the economic significance of brands.

This book contains Interbrand's choice of the world's greatest brands. Because it is Interbrand's choice it is of course idiosyncratic, and we shall no doubt be criticised for its peculiarities. But that most idiosyncratic of Englishmen, Samuel Johnson, was taken to task for his great *Dictionary* as much for what he had left out as for what he had put in. When asked by a lady friend why he had defined the word '*pastern*' (the area between a horse's fetlock and hoof) as '*a horse's knee*' the good doctor replied 'Ignorance, madam, pure ignorance'. If similarly challenged we will offer no more robust a defence.

We hope that you enjoy our choice of *The World's Greatest Brands*.

CONTENTS

PREFACE

This book is the result of a collaboration between a large number of people. I would like to thank all of them, but have only enough space here to name a few.

First, I would like to thank Interbrand, and in particular Interbrand's founder and former chairman John Murphy. John wrote and edited the first edition of this book in 1990, and I owe a lot to his work then and to his encouragement and support in the creation of this book. Then I would like to thank Paul Stobart, former Chairman of Interbrand's European businesses, who has also contributed greatly to this volume.

My colleague Keith Gray has lent me his extraordinary powers of administration for handling a project of considerable complexity. Keith has stuck at it when the going got tough and I am indebted to him. I also owe thanks for the contributions of Miriam Kochan, Robert Dwek and Nicholas Jones and for the administrative support of Karen Hayward.

Finally, I would like to thank the staff of Interbrand and Macmillan for their assistance in the long gestation of the World's Greatest Brands.

Nicholas Kochan   Editor

ACKNOWLEDGEMENTS

The publishers would like to thank all those brand-owners and their agents and associates who have supplied information and illustrations for this book. It should be noted that virtually every product or corporate name mentioned in the book is a registered trademark and virtually every logo reproduced in the book is the specific property of a company.

INTRODUCTION

What do Marlboro, Nike, Levi's and Michael Jackson have in common? They are all heavily promoted, all owned or sold by large companies, and each has a carefully developed set of 'values' which appeals to a specific audience. In short, each is an extremely powerful brand.

A powerful brand frequently provides the source of a company's wealth for many generations. The best brands improve with age, developing clearly defined personalities, as well as the affection and loyalty of the public. The best become parents to sub-brands and brand extensions, which give the owner a chance to exploit their values and names in new areas.

Brands impact enormously, not only on the company which owns them, but also on the wider society in which they operate and in which they are enjoyed. Brand values are of course designed to appeal to consumers and thus to sell products. But brand owners should not forget that they are dealing with a powerful emotional tool. For their own as well as society's good, brand-owners need to be aware of the responsibility inherent in managing these powerful properties. The creation of groups of nations, the globalising of the world economy, the expansion of massive companies across borders – all these factors make the brand increasingly powerful. Increasingly, the brand is becoming a cultural emblem in a shrinking world.

This book explains the origins of some of the greatest brands in the world. Readers will find many object lessons in brand-building as they proceed through this book, though they should be aware that, for every great brand described, there are numerous brands that failed. Brand-building entails vast risk as well as holding the promise of vast reward.

THE ORIGINS OF BRANDING

Asserting one's right to ownership through making a mark on one's goods is as old as the earliest farming. Branding, as this book will show, is at its simplest a way of saying that something belongs to me. When the Norse farmers branded their cattle, they were saying: "I have the right to this possession". When today a business seeks to build a brand it is asking the consumer to pick that company's product and not another. Thus ownership is still at the root of the brand.

When companies wanted and were able to sell their products to large numbers of people, brand building began in earnest. Such mass-selling was spurred by developments in communications. The speeding up of distribution in the United States and in Europe began in the second half of the nineteenth century with the arrival of the railways. Suddenly products could travel, more consumers could be reached and the salesman was on his way.

This was the era of some of the greatest entrepreneurs and brand-builders of all time; of Messrs Procter and Gamble, Kellogg, Cadbury and Rowntree. There are numerous examples cited in this book of men and women who had a bright idea for a product and were lucky and clever enough to have the funds to exploit it. Critically, they also had the customers to buy it and the intelligence to build an organisation to exploit it.

Today, although there are still entrepreneurs building their own brands, the task of the majority of brand-builders is to take the legacy of existing brands and adapt them to suit the requirements of more sophisticated consumers. They must embrace the increasing possibilities for the communication of brand values and acknowledge the growing financial pressures on brands to make a return.

These pressures have given rise to the massive growth in recent years of the advertising industry. Advertising agencies are the communicators of brand values and many are very effective. But some brand owners have occasionally allowed their agencies to create not just the message but also to modify for essentially tactical reasons the core brand values. The brand owner who does this will run into difficulties. Brand values are greater than the transient need of a particular market in a particular country or at a particular time. Brand values need to be nurtured, developed with great care and then communicated with clarity, conviction and consistency.

VALUES AND VISIONS

The brand starts as a product and a name. But much can be built on that name. In fact, a brand name can be best described as the foundation stone for an elaborate edifice. Without it, there can be no brand but on its own it has little interest. Branding shapes a wealth of perceptions, beliefs, attitudes, and experiences to turn a product and name into something to which the consumer relates.

The brand-building process begins by understanding and anticipating the needs and desires of consumers and the key attributes of the product. Products do not exist in a void, they are bought because consumers have found something they relate to in them, something which they value. These values will be communicated through every medium, from the shop shelf to advertising to comments in the newspaper to word of mouth, and there will be many different values within each brand.

Coca-Cola, for example, has become lodged in consumers' minds because of the shape of the bottle, the colour of the can, the script of the name, the host of youthful messages, the taste, the advertising and so forth. Not all brand values are equal, and the wise brand-builder will select those that are most compelling.

There are three tiers of brand values: first, "functional" values; second, "expressive" values; and third "central" values. Functional values govern the performance of the product. So Coke refreshes its drinker, Volvo gives its driver a safe ride, the IBM PC provides quick computing. Functional values do not differentiate the product from its rival since

Pepsi also refreshes, Mercedes is as safe as Volvo, and Apple is as quick, or quicker, than IBM. These values underplay the product's true strength because the technology of production is now so sophisticated that every manufacturer either makes excellent products or goes out of business. With increasingly sophisticated communications, one brand-owner's bright idea can now be copied almost instantaneously in every continent.

The brand-builder must therefore search for other values. Expressive values say less about the product and more about the consumer. Consumers buy Marlboro because they appreciate its masculine values, they buy Armani because they appreciate its status and fashionable values, and Apple computers because they appreciate their creative and human values. These values reflect and enhance the consumer's sense of him/herself and provide a key source of brand differentiation.

However, it is central values which are the most enduring and go right to the core of the consumer's system of beliefs. Central values, at their purest, are embodied in religious, national or political persuasions. Product brand values can command comparable power when they embody mass movements or cultural trends. Coke, for example, had great central values when it joined in with 1960s style fervour for love and peace in the Coke theme song, "I'd like to teach the world to sing..." One wonders if Coke will ever find a central value again to compare with that.

In today's more cynical world, the irreverence associated with Virgin and its founder, Richard Branson, or with Nike, is perhaps more powerful, while the highly individual Michael Jackson cult contains a central value for today's younger generation

These values are essential but they need to be harnessed and honed before they assist in the creation of a brand. The force guiding the harnessing of values is the brand-builder's vision for the brand, what might, in layman's parlance, be called the "big idea". The big idea infuses the entire presentation of the brand; without it, a brand will lack conviction. The vision is, in a sense, the brand's

DNA; it is present everywhere, it is formative and it can only be revoked or reversed with great difficulty.

Brand visions can be extraordinarily powerful. They can allow you to redefine the marketplace and so marginalise competitors. One has only to look at the way Virgin revolutionised air travel, Pizza Hut home delivery and Direct Line the UK insurance market to see the degree of change a vision can effect. Some of the most impressive visions adopted in recent years are those of Apple, Volvo, SKF and Benetton. Each of these visions seeks to bring man (or woman) closer together with the product, with his fellow man and with his wider environment. However technical and even boring the product, the vision is humane and appealing.

Apple's vision was to eliminate the chasm between man and technology by emphasising the product's simplicity. Volvo promotes a better environment by eliminating the wasteful and the glitzy. Benetton desires to bring mankind closer together by espousing racial harmony through the matching of colours. Brand visions may also be held by industrial or business to business brands. SKF, the Swedish ball bearings maker, eradicates friction (the literal purpose of the product) by linking the product with the elimination of friction in human and work relationships. "We ease friction to move the world forward," says SKF.

The brand vision lifts the brand above the mundane and functional to appeal to the expressive and central values that the owners would like to see lodged in consumers' minds. This process creates a bond with the consumer and ultimately, it is hoped, long-term brand loyalty.

The 350 brands in this book have passed the acid branding test. They have won customer appeal by delivering and fulfilling a promise that the branded product or service is of distinctive quality and pedigree. Making brands work is as much art as science and successful brand-building is achieved by a combination of specialist talent and a long-term vision. Excellence in organisation, market sensitivity and long-term commitment underpin every great brand; if this mix is not right, brands fail and a great deal of money is wasted.

At its best, branding is founded on a brand strategy which understands and reflects the functional, expressive and central values of a brand and its vision. Brand management also encompasses the design and presentation of the product; marketing and selling the brand; brand extension and building new sub-brands.

The key to developing a brand vision is to assess the values of the organisation, distil them into a vision and not tamper or interfere with the vision's simplicity and power. Consistency and clarity are all-important. The brand manager may want to tweak his message to keep in touch with his consumer, but the tweaking must stay in touch with those underlying values. Without those, the brand is lost. Coke seemed to forget the strength and simplicity of its existing product values when it tried relaunching its much loved product under the banner of 'New Formula'. Conversely, Mars understood perfectly its existing product values when it launched Mars ice cream on the back of the Mars bar.

Design and presentation of the product flows from the values. Coherence is once again the name of the game. The presentation of the packaging, the use of the logo, the typeface all need to accord with the brand values and be internally consistent.

The next question for the brand-builder is to gauge the geographical potential of his brand. How far will it travel while retaining values that still mean something to the customer? The brands most admired but hardest to copy are global brands. The Americans are master builders in this regard. American brand values transcend national cultures by emphasising concepts such as classlessness, service and consistency. Coke and McDonald's, the world's greatest brands, demonstrate this most clearly.

International brand-builders have experienced important social changes in their favour. The downfall of communism has spurred the expansion into Eastern Europe of American products. And the globalisation of the world economy has produced a group of wealthy consumers who desire Rolex watches, the best Scotch whiskies and the most sophisticated Mercedes-Benz cars wherever they live. These brands are strictly niche players, but they cross borders and are very valuable. Global brands like these will sell on the strength of their social status message. But this global approach is not the only route for expansion. Far from it. Many brands listed in this book – Chomel in the Pacific Rim, Fielmann in Germany, Hershey's in the United States, for example – extend little outside their own country, or their region, but they still have powerful groups of extremely loyal local customers.

Some brand-owners have expressed disappointment over the absence of many truly 'European' brands within the European Union. They complain that the distribution and advertising media in Europe have largely retained national identities, that there are no popular European newspapers, and that Europe-wide satellite television is still a minority taste. Those who complain may be seeking a European consumer that does not yet exist. They might well do better to sell their national brand values to the world, in the footsteps of Perrier, Guinness, Louis Vuitton or Braun, than tilt at European windmills.

An important feature of international brand-building is consistency from market to market. There are some famous exceptions (Green Giant is presented in France as Géant Vert) but Mars could not live with Marathon in the UK and Snickers in the United States and brought the two together under the Snickers name.

Different markets will have slightly different expectations of a brand's image, so the up-market Johnnie Walker Black whisky will be presented as a luxury drink for the romantic Mediterranean or South American but will be sold as a powerful drink to the very masculine consumer in America. In each case, however, the core values of masculinity and prosperity are emphasised.

There is another way to make the brand work harder without forcing it into countries that do not appreciate it. That is to extend its product range and create sub-brands or brand extensions. Betty Crocker started as a friendly face on the side of a packaged cake mix. Today the name appears on the side of 200 products. Life Savers started as a single mint with a hole in the middle but today has numerous flavours. The makers of Tide and Coke have successfully applied the original brand values to new products like Liquid Tide and Diet Coke. Richard Branson's Virgin has voyaged across more product areas than probably any other brand: from records and record shops to air transport, publishing, vodka and financial services. His exploitation of a brand personality embodying rakish, youthful rebelliousness has proved immensely fertile, and this is a harbinger for brand-builders of the next millennium.

The other option for the brand-owner is to leave all his existing brands alone, and set about creating a whole new brand. This is the riskiest and potentially most lucrative option. Six or seven brands out of every ten launched fail, making the cost of the exercise huge. There are some recent notable successes. Take, for example, Derwent Valley Foods, which was set up in 1982 to sell quality snacks into the crowded British food market. The founders called their product Phileas Fogg to help express the brand proposition of intriguing new snacks from around the world and differentiate it from other snacks, and they gave it distinctive packaging to show its quality. Phileas Fogg entered the market at a time when consumers wanted more interesting snack brands and had the money to pay for them. The sale of the business 10 years later for between £26 and £27 million shows how quickly brand value can be created from zero.

We hear a lot about the successes of branding, and less about its failures except when the brand-owner falls from a very great height. Unilever's nightmare with its Persil Power detergent, Perrier's problems with benzene or Intel's trouble with the Pentium chip show how much can go wrong if product quality does not live up to the brand promise.

BRANDS FOR THE NEXT CENTURY – FUTURE TRENDS

We believe that in the future the brands that succeed will not be those that sell specific products but those that communicate clear values which stretch across a number of products. The brand will not attach to the group of products but to the buyers, to the consumers themselves.

Products will be increasingly aimed at the individual. "We have become so good at targeting individual lifestyles that in due course there will be a brand for the professional gay man living in the centre of a cosmopolitan city. It will cover not only his car, but his supermarket and his travel insurance," says Interbrand's Raymond Perrier.

This approach affects the entire marketing and selling process. So where advertisers once mounted blockbuster campaigns costing millions and treated the public as a homogeneous group, they will in future try to reach individuals.

One international foods group heeded the call for greater segmentation when it launched a new pasta not through television, but through the post! They decided it was cheaper to develop a database of the right socio-economic profile of pasta eaters and send them all a letter and sample than to spend millions hitting a random group of television viewers.

The developers of 'brand clubs' are taking a leaf out of the direct marketers' book by trying to pinpoint their purchasers ever more precisely. They are collecting more information by getting buyers to fill in questionnaires and by setting up specialist media that will appeal to the niche. In the next few years we will see more and more companies putting information on the Internet for their customers and then distributing magazines developed for their precise tastes.

This personalised approach to branding has put the big 'corporates' on their guard. To attract and communicate with today's consumer, they need to portray themselves as reliable and ethical. The new personalised marketing approach means that the slightest damage in one corner of the product empire can rebound throughout the company and its product range. This can apply as much to a Hoover-style fiasco where a marketing department slips up, as it can to a corporate public relations disaster as with Shell, or a production crisis such as hit Perrier. The brand takes all the consumer "flak", and the subsequent company must suffer the damage to its share price in the stock markets.

Branding hyperbole aside, the global brands will march further and faster as we reach the millennium. Satellite television, for example, breaks down boundaries and spreads supranational culture with an ease never before possible. This has led, say the marketers, to a convergence of taste. New interactive technology will help manufacturers like Daewoo, which makes products as diverse as cars and washing machines; come the day when you sit in your armchair and use your television for buying or selling, Daewoo could be supplying all your needs!

The spread of the global brand has been helped by improving production and the removal of border controls and tariffs. Fast-moving consumer goods companies have driven production costs as low as possible and are now looking at distribution and marketing costs. Companies like Coca-Cola and PepsiCo are now looking for reductions in the cost of their advertising, packaging and marketing. They will rationalise this in due course by combining global brand development with local production.

The global brand can also make the distribution chain more efficient. Once they have standardised their pack, local manufacturers will find it increasingly difficult to tamper with the global look.

While the mega brands will continue to march into every corner of the world, the chance that they will be followed by new global brands recedes. As we have already said, building a worldwide brand is extraordinarily expensive owing to the cost of advertising and marketing, and failure rates are so high that only the bravest companies attempt it.

There are likely to be many casualties over the next five years as, by Darwinian branding logic, the weak go to the wall or are subsumed by larger brands. Particular devastation will be visited on food manufacturing and financial services, already the scene of considerable merger and acquisition activity. Newcomers will probably include the automotive sector where differentiation is currently limited and consumer interest is not sated.

Finally, but perhaps most importantly, as the value of branding grows so brand valuation, already established practice in many countries, will grow in the next millennium. Sophisticated companies will include a "statement of value" addendum to the balance sheet to include intangibles such as the value of the brands and the value of their technology and databases.

ASSESSING THE WORLD'S GREATEST BRANDS

The world's greatest brands have been the subject of numerous assessments of brand equity and brand value in the past. Interbrand has been at the forefront of developments in brand evaluation and has assessed the world's top brands in the pages that follow.

The assessment is of *Brand Power* – the fullest possible view of each brand's strength and potential as a marketing and financial asset. The assessment is based on Interbrand's 20 years of experience in branding and brand evaluation around the world. Brand Power is evaluated according to four dimensions:

Brand Weight The influence or dominance that the brand has over its category or market (more than just market share)

Brand Length The stretch or extension that the brand has achieved in the past or is likely to achieve in the future (especially outside its original category)

Brand Breadth The breadth of franchise that the brand has achieved both in terms of age spread, consumer types and international appeal

Brand Depth The degree of commitment that the brand has achieved among its customer base and beyond. The proximity, the intimacy and the loyalty felt for the brand

Few brands indeed attain power quickly and last for ever, and some famous brands may be omitted from this book if they are perceived as waning. Everyone can think of a brand in consumer goods that has shot to fame only to collapse just as quickly.

The people who have built the brands listed here are committed brand-builders; they have stuck by their brands and nurtured them, they have guided them through changes and they have seen the potential latent in their brands. Most importantly, they have spent money on their brands and their brands have repaid this care by delivering profits year after year.

THE WORLD'S TOP 100 BRANDS

Position	Brand	Score
1st	McDonald's	856
2nd	Coca Cola	849
3rd	Disney	840
4th	Kodak	821
5th	Sony	811
6th	Gillette	802
7th	Mercedes-Benz	799
8th	Levi's	797
9th	Microsoft	794
10th	Marlboro	790
11th	IBM	
	Nike	781
13th	Johnson & Johnson	747
14th	Visa	746
15th	Nescafé	741
16th	Kelloggs	737
17th	Pepsi-Cola	736
18th	Apple Computer	733

Position	Brand	Score
19th	BMW	732
20th	American Express	730
21st	Tampax	724
22nd	Nintendo	719
23rd	Lego	718
24th	IKEA	714
25th	Sega	713
26th	Harley-Davidson	712
27th	Intel	711
28th	Body Shop	704
29th	KFC	701
30th	Heinz	700
31st	Toyota	699
32nd	Xerox	692
33rd	CNN	689
34th	Adidas	688
35th	Pillsbury	686
36th	Reebok	685

Position	Brand	Score
37th	Cadburys	684
38th	Camel	683
39th	Chanel	682
40th	Swatch	681
41st	Harrods	680
42nd	Colgate	679
43rd	Toshiba	678
44th	Mars	675
45th	Ford	673
46th	*Time*	671
47th	Barbie	670
48th	Rolex	669
49th	Lucky Strike	668
50th	BBC	667
51st	British Airways	666
52nd	Mastercard	665
53rd	Mitsukoshi	664
54th	Fedex	663
55th	AT&T	662

Position	Brand	Score
56th	Persil	
	Heineken	661
58th	Campbells	660
59th	Fisher-Price	
	Marks & Spencer	
	Motorola	659
62nd	Porsche	
	Reuters	658
64th	Shell	657
65th	Mattel	656
66th	Honda	654
67th	Pizza Hut	653
68th	Compaq	652
69th	Fuji	651
70th	Duracell	
	BP	650
72nd	Johnnie Walker	649
73rd	Polaroid	
	Louis Vuitton	648

Position	Brand	Score
75th	Volvo	
	Hewlett Packard	647
77th	Boeing	646
78th	Zippo	645
79th	Casio	643
80th	Volkswagen	642
81st	Ray-Ban	641
82nd	Smirnoff	640
83rd	Budweiser	
	Philips	639
85th	Sears	638
86th	Pampers	637
87th	Schweppes	
	Nivea	
	Reader's Digest	636

Position	Brand	Score
90th	Kleenex	635
91st	Canon	
	Virgin	634
93rd	*The Financial Times*	633
94th	Haagen-Dazs	632
95th	Braun	631
96th	Samsung	
	Gordons	630
98th	Benetton	
	Sainsbury	629
100th	Dr Martens	628

THE WORLD'S TOP BRANDS BY SECTOR

ALCOHOL		
Position	Brand	Score
1st	Johnnie Walker	649
2nd	Smirnoff	640
3rd	Gordons	630
4th	Martini	614
5th	Bacardi	597
6th	Jack Daniels	580
7th	Moët & Chandon	573
8th	Bailey's	554
9th	Dom Perignon	526
10th	Southern Comfort	511

AUTOMOTIVE AND OIL		
Position	Brand	Score
1st	Mercedes-Benz	799
2nd	BMW	732
3rd	Harley-Davidson	712
4th	Toyota	699
5th	Ford	673
6th	Porsche	658
7th	Shell	657
8th	Honda	654
9th	BP	650
10th	Volvo	647

BEER		
Position	**Brand**	**Score**
1st	Heineken	661
2nd	Budweiser	639
3rd	Guinness	627
4th	Carlsberg	579
5th	San Miguel	550
6th	Tuborg	548
7th	Steinlager	518
8th	Tiger Beer	512
9th	Castlemaine	499
10th	Beck's	486

NON-ALCOHOLIC BEVERAGES		
Position	**Brand**	**Score**
1st	Coca-Cola	849
2nd	Nescafé	741
3rd	Pepsi-Cola	736
4th	Schweppes	636
5th	Perrier	598
6th	Maxwell House	579
7th	UCC	571
8th	Sunkist	534
9th	Lavazza	521
10th	7-Up	512

TOBACCO AND ACCESSORIES		
Position	Brand	Score
1st	Marlboro	790
2nd	Camel	683
3rd	Lucky Strike	668
4th	Zippo	645
5th	Winston	622
6th	Rothmans	607
7th	Samson	590
8th	Rizla	582
9th	Benson & Hedges	577
10th	Davidoff	566

FASHION AND LUXURY GOODS		
Position	Brand	Score
1st	Levi's	797
2nd	Nike	781
3rd	Adidas	688
4th	Reebok	685
5th	Chanel	682
6th	Swatch	681
7th	Rolex	669
8th	Louis Vuitton	648
9th	Ray-Ban	640
10th	Benetton	629

FINANCIAL SERVICES		
Position	**Brand**	**Score**
1st	Visa	746
2nd	American Express	730
3rd	Mastercard	665
4th	Thomas Cook	621
5th	Diners Club	577

FOOD		
Position	**Brand**	**Score**
1st	McDonald's	856
2nd	Kelloggs	737
3rd	KFC	701
4th	Heinz	700
5th	Pillsbury	686
6th	Cadbury's	685
7th	Mars	675
8th	Campbells	660
9th	Pizza Hut	653
10th	Haagen-Dazs	632

HOUSEHOLD		
Position	**Brand**	**Score**
1st	Persil	661
2nd	Duracell	650
3rd	Kleenex	635
4th	Post-it	624
5th	Elastoplast	612
6th	Dulux	610
7th	Andrex	606
8th	Fairy Liquid	602
9th	Tipp-Ex	600
10th	Alessi	598

LEISURE / TRAVEL		
Position	**Brand**	**Score**
1st	Disney	840
2nd	British Airways	666
3rd	Club Med	589
4th	Hertz	588
5th	Singapore Airlines	587
6th	Hilton	586
7th	Virgin Atlantic	576
8th	Holiday Inn	569
9th	The Ritz	561
10th	United Airlines	564

MEDIA		
Position	**Brand**	**Score**
1st	CNN	689
2nd	*Time*	671
3rd	BBC	667
4th	Reuters	658
5th	*Reader's Digest*	636
6th	*The Financial Times*	633
7th	*Wall Street Journal*	613
8th	Yellow Pages	596
9th	*Newsweek*	584
10th	Penguin	540

PERSONAL CARE		
Position	**Brand**	**Score**
1st	Gillette	802
2nd	Johnson & Johnson	747
3rd	Tampax	724
4th	Colgate	679
5th	Pampers	637
6th	Nivea	636
7th	BiC	618
8th	Durex	615
9th	Ivory	609
10th	Palmolive	607

RETAIL		
Position	Brand	Score
1st	IKEA	714
2nd	Body Shop	704
3rd	Harrods	680
4th	Mitsukoshi	664
5th	Marks & Spencer	659
6th	Sears	638
7th	Sainsbury	629
8th	Tesco	620
9th	Hamleys	616
10th	Conforoma	581

TECHNOLOGY		
Position	Brand	Score
1st	Kodak	821
2nd	Sony	811
3rd	Microsoft	794
4th	IBM	781
5th	Apple	733
6th	Intel	711
7th	Xerox	692
8th	Toshiba	678
9th	AT&T	662
10th	Motorola	659

TOYS		
Position	**Brand**	**Score**
1st	Nintendo	719
2nd	Lego	718
3rd	Sega	713
4th	Barbie	670
5th	Fisher-Price	659
6th	Mattel	656
7th	Hornby	584
8th	Monopoly	571
9th	Subbuteo	562
10th	Scrabble	559

TOP BRANDS LISTED BY
WEIGHT, LENGTH, BREADTH & DEPTH

WEIGHT (Dominance)	
Rank	**Brand**
1	McDonald's
2	Coca-Cola
3	Kodak
4	Gillette
5	Microsoft
6	Tampax
7	Levi's
8	Kelloggs
9	Mercedes Benz
10	Disney

LENGTH (Stretch)	
Rank	**Brand**
1	Disney
2	Johnson & Johnson
3	Harrods
4	Virgin
5	Sony
6	McDonald's
7	Samsung
8	Camel
9	Sega
10	Harley-Davidson

We have awarded brands a score for **weight** that reflects their dominance over their particular category or market. This is a key component of a brand's power. A high score for dominance tends to reflect a dominant market share (brands which score well in this category are usually clear market leaders), but other factors are taken into account as well. Through innovation and clear brand focus, a brand that is a standard-setter in its market can have as much influence over that market as the market leader (Apple in personal computing, for example). All the brands shown above exert clear dominance over their respective markets.

The **length** of a brand refers to its stretch and stretchability into new categories and markets. As the cost of brand support and new brand launches becomes prohibitive, a brand's ability to be extended into new areas is increasingly important to brand owners and has become an important element in most brand equity analyses. The brands shown above have proven ability to break into new categories and cross product boundaries – their 'area of competence' is the widest of the brands studied for this book.

BREADTH (Franchise)	
Rank	Brand
1	Coca-Cola
2	McDonald's
3	Kodak
4	Sony
5	IBM
6	Visa
7	CNN
8	Pepsi-Cola
9	Microsoft
10	Gillette

DEPTH (Commitmente)	
Rank	Brand
1	Apple Computer
2	Disney
3	Body Shop
4	Harley-Davidson
5	BBC
6	Mercedes-Benz
7	Nike
8	McDonald's
9	Marlboro
10	Camel

A brand's score for **breadth** reflects the breadth of franchise that it has achieved in terms of age spread, consumer types and international appeal. A 'broad' brand has proved that it can cross social, cultural and national boundaries – a testament to its strength as a marketing asset. A good score for breadth can also indicate a lower risk profile for a brand; its broad cultural and geographic spread can make it less vulnerable to local developments such as changes in taste, legislation and financial instability.

B

A key aspect of any brand's power is the degree of commitment that the brand has achieved among its customer base and the proximity, intimacy and loyalty they feel to the brand. Brands that have a high score for **depth** have developed intimate relationships with their customers, usually on the basis of shared 'central' or 'higher' values. The brands shown above may not always have dominant market shares, but they have real power to influence their customers.

D

THE BRANDS

AA

With 8.4 million members and 13 million customers, the Automobile Association is the UK's biggest motoring organisation.

Formed in 1905 by a group of motoring enthusiasts concerned about public antagonism towards the car, the AA has consistently campaigned for improvements in road safety and it has also been committed always to "courtesy and care".

Today the AA provides the leading assistance service for motorists, offering emergency breakdown and recovery services and its publishing and information services assist drivers with up-to-date global travel information. Other services include a legal aid service to motorists involved in accidents and a range of motor insurance products.

Offering 'courtesy and care', the Automobile Association is best friend to 13 million drivers in the UK.

ABB

Building the brand ABB – formerly ASEA Brown Boveri – has involved nurturing sound and reliable management, international presence and technological sophistication. This most modern of engineering and electronics companies presents itself to its numerous audiences as a highly decentralised company with a concern for the environment and excellent relations with stockholders and with communities in the many countries where it operates. In this sense, ABB is arguably the quintessential up-to-date corporate brand.

The extent to which ABB has succeeded can partly be gauged by the high regard businessmen have for the company. In fact, they voted ABB – the 1988 merger of Sweden's ASEA and Switzerland's Brown Boveri – the most respected European company in both 1994 and 1995. ABB has also been voted the European company with the best management of technology and innovation.

The implementation of a carefully worked out management plan is at the core of this approval rating. The electrical engineering group owes its success to a three-stage development strategy. The first phase, begun shortly after the formation of the newly merged business, was to cement market share by acquiring Combustion Engineering and Westinghouse Electric, both of the USA.

The second phase, consolidation, involved a reduction in overheads with much of ABB's production being moved to lower cost countries. This then allowed the now highly cost-competitive company to concentrate on the third phase – growth.

Growth has allowed ABB to build up businesses in the emerging markets of Asia and to merge its transportation division with the AEG division of Daimler-Benz of Germany, creating the largest supplier of railway equipment in the world.

ABB, the most modern of engineering and electronics companies, projects an image of a highly decentralised company concerned for the environment and with excellent relations with stockholders and communities wherever it operates.

ADIDAS

Few branding devices are more distinctive than the three stripes on an Adidas sports shoe. Adi Dassler, founder of the internationally known concern, realised from the start the value of observers being able to recognise the brand of shoe an athlete was wearing, while in action or from a photograph. Today Dassler is regarded as the founder of the modern sporting goods industry.

The three stripes were born when the brand name Adidas was registered in 1949, but athletes at the Amsterdam Olympic Games in 1928 were already wearing shoes made by the humble Herzogenaurach shoemaker. At the 1936 Olympics in Berlin, Jesse Owens won four gold medals in Adidas shoes. Today Adidas is an inseparable ingredient of major sporting events, with the brand having dominant presence at events such as the Winter Olympic Games in Lillehammer and the Soccer World Cup in the USA.

Adi relied heavily on the assistance of his wife Käthe and their five sons to develop his business and it was his eldest son, Horst, who raised recognition of the brand in the 1960s by

introducing sportswear bearing the three stripes. Later, the device of three leaves with three stripes running across them appeared on textile goods and the company also expanded into soccer balls. In 1970 the Adidas "Telstar" ball was the official ball at the Soccer World Cup. Horst also recognised the potential of sports promotion as a tool to build a brand. For example, he introduced basketball to Europe with the Streetball Challenge.

Through a widespread network of subsidiaries, distributors, licensees and agents, Adidas products are available in almost every country of the world. The company prides itself on its constant innovations. In recent years the three-stripe brand on trainers has become a mark of fashion for teenagers everywhere. The "retro" movement's reassessment of products from the 1970s has made the Adidas three stripes almost cult objects.

The three stripe hallmark of Adidas sportswear is known in all varieties of sporting events.

AGFA

In a hundred years Agfa has not only become a name which immediately means photographic film but also one of the world's leading photographic and imaging companies and a leader in all sectors of modern technology.

To amateur photographers worldwide, the name Agfa instantly conveys photographic film. The firm cannily retains its name as a prefix to virtually all new products, as with Agfacolor HDC, the new generation of colour negative films, and Agfachrome CTx for new slide films.

The firm has had a hundred years to refine its image. Its factory in Berlin-Treptow, the Actien-

Gesellschaft für Anilinfabrikation, released its first photographic material for sale to the general public on 12 May 1894: a gelatine dry plate. Agfa has come a long way since then. Today the Agfa-Gavaert group is among the world's leading photographic and imaging companies and well to the fore in all sectors of modern technology.

Agfa concentrates on three main areas. The photographic products group deals with films, photographic papers and laboratory equipment. The graphics group deals with office copying systems and photochemical products for the prepress sector and the technical imaging systems group is mainly involved with medical imaging and industrial radiography.

AGFA Agfa

Akubra is the quintessential Aussie hat, worn by heads of state and stockmen alike.

STICK TO
AKUBRA HATS

AKUBRA

Akubra is an Aboriginal word for a headcovering and today it is a brand name for a cowboy-type hat which is quintessentially Australian. The brand appeals to all sections of Australian society, and is worn by Australian politicans and heads of state, by the Australian Olympics team, by city dwellers, by farmhands and of course by stockmen. Bob Hawke has one, and golfer Greg Norman and the singer Slim Dusty have models named in their honour. Australian troops wore Akubra slouch hats during both world wars and the chances are that a foreign tourist to Australia will bring one back as a memento.

Although the brand name Akubra was only adopted in 1925, the business is now in its fourth generation of family ownership, and even though it is Australian to the core, Akubra's roots are in fact in England, as the company was founded by a Briton, Benjamin Dunkerley, who set sail for Tasmania in 1874 to check out hatting prospects there. He was later joined by another Englishman, Stephen Keir, who became his son-in-law, and a Keir still heads Akubra today – Steven Dixon Keir, great-grandson of the founder.

ALESSI

Alessi kitchen products have gained international acclaim for their chicness, simplicity and contoured lines. Founded in 1921 by the Italian Giovanni Alessi, the company has made an artform as well as a very successful business out of creating metal objects for the table and the kitchen. Alessi's coffee pots and tea sets are now world famous and their distinctive shapes and colours have made them a must for the design-conscious house-owner.

Since the 1950s Alessi has worked with top international designers and architects – such as the renowned Philippe Stark – to position the brand as a premium market leader in its field. Such is Alessi's reputation today that many of its products take pride of place in permanent collections in museums around the world. Over the last 10 years, Alessi has experimented with materials and product lines other than metal, its former speciality, using product names such as Twergi and Tendentse.

A notable and critically acclaimed recent design of Alessi's was a figurative corkscrew, which exhibited the brand's continuing finesse and wit, as well as giving a further twist to its brand positioning.

ALETE

The first food, other than mother's milk, consumed by nearly half of the babies born in Germany is that produced by Nestlé's Alete factories. The name Alete now stands as an outstanding example of high-quality baby and infant food. Alete, founded in Munich in 1934, is now a tightly focused brand which, in the minds of purchasers, embraces high-quality, safe baby food products which meet the highest dietary and legal standards.

ALPINE ELECTRONICS INC.

As early as 1976 Japan-based Alpine Electronics saw the potential for car audio products and started to focus on providing superior sound within the complex acoustic environment of the car. Today it is a leader in the field of car electronics with eight plants in seven countries, and the simple motto, "hearing is believing".

Alpine's image is bolstered by its association with the luxury Italian sports car Lamborghini and by the slogan "sonic excellence", as drivers worldwide, especially Alpine's younger, music-loving customers, instantly recognise both the world's fastest production car and Alpine as pinnacles of high performance. This close association coincides with one of the company's goals – to further the consumer's passion for music by transforming the motor car into a moving concert hall that enriches the experience of car owners around the world.

The company's logo of five stripes preceding its name symbolises the five areas of excellence that Alpine strives for: product, marketing, service, engineering and manufacturing. More recently, the brand's market franchise has been expanded to include car security systems and mobile phones as well as innovative products such as the world's smallest CD changer, the first in-dash 3-CD changer and car navigation systems – which combine audio, visual and telecommunications technologies into a multi-media package.

Through its motto "hearing is believing", Alpine Electronics Inc., a leader in the field of car audio products, aims to make your car a moving concert hall.

AMERICAN AIRLINES

American Airlines is both a leading national American carrier and an international organisation which competes with the world leaders. American Airlines has succeeded in building a distinctive graphic identity around the silver bird symbol.

American has been winning its fight with low cost carriers by maintaining and building up its premium brands and business class accommodation. The airline has developed a system of hubs and spikes; routes begin at the hub and go to a large number of destinations in it. Travellers go from point to point changing at the hub, and this gives access to more destinations. American Airlines' hubs are at Dallas/Fort Worth, Chicago, Miami and San Juan.

As part of its bid for the premium airline brand position, the airline recently upgraded its first class and business seating in its McDonnell-Douglas and Boeing range. American also boasts one of the youngest fleets in the USA.

With one of the youngest fleets in the USA, American Airlines is a leading national carrier and an international organisation.

American Airlines

AMERICAN EXPRESS

To the public at large, American Express means first and foremost 'plastic money' – credit cards or charge cards – for wealthy people. Though many other financial institutions issue credit cards, American Express is an undoubted market leader, mainly owing to the prestige of the brand.

Introduced in 1958, the American Express Card was a logical extension of the company's existing interests in travel and financial services. However the origins of the company go back to the opening up of the American West and the need for safe and speedy transportation of goods, valuables, bullion and bank remittances and the company has links through its founder, Henry Wells, with both Wells Fargo and the Pony Express.

In 1882 the company issued the first American Express Money Orders, precursors of the postal order, and in 1891 it introduced American Express Travelers Cheques, a business which expanded rapidly after World War II with the increase in transatlantic travel. Now the company is involved in travel and holidays, freight handling, banking,

corporate finance and insurance, and it has achieved an enviable reputation for reliability and service, especially among American travellers. Indeed American Express offices abroad have often acted as a kind of unofficial embassy for American travellers, notably when they assisted in the evacuation of stranded nationals at the outbreak of both world wars in Europe.

The prestige of the brand makes American Express an undoubted leader in the field of plastic money.

AMORE

Amore is Korea's leading brand in cosmetics. The name is deliberately eye-catching, given the brand's oriental origins, but owners Pacific Corp have managed to build a sophisticated and exotic brand.

Amore's philosophy is typically oriental in its holistic approach to the individual and the larger world. It seeks "beauty for millions and affluence for society". The Amore brand has many sub-brands including Soon (hypo-allergenic for sensitive skin), Sammi (ginseng based cosmetics) and Twin-x for men. Amore is now widely exported and the largest overseas markets are France, Germany, Canada and Mexico.

Amore's typically oriental philosophy of "beauty for millions and affluence for society" has made it Korea's leading cosmetic brand.

AMSTEL

For 125 years the Amstel brand has represented top quality beer that gives people around the world a sense of friendship, honesty and pleasure as well as good value for money. Amstel started as an independent brewery by the River Amstel in Amsterdam. In 1968 the company merged with Heineken and Amstel became the Heineken Group's second international brand.

Amstel exploits its brand value to the full. It sells a wide range of beers, demonstrating the rich brewing and craftsmanship available, all bearing the Amstel prefix. They range from Amstel Malt (non-alcoholic) to Amstel Gold (7 per cent alcohol) and include

Amstel Bock, a dark-coloured season beer and Amstel 1870, a speciality beer with a rich hop taste.

Over 6·7 million hectolitres of the brand's products are sold in over 80 countries, the biggest markets being Greece, the Netherlands, South Africa and Hungary. In 1994 Amstel was introduced into the UK, Switzerland and Portugal and further expansion of the European market is expected to accrue following Amstel's sponsorship of the UEFA Champions League, a major European soccer tournament.

Amstel is a top quality beer, providing a sense of friendship, honesty and pleasure to drinkers worldwide.

AMSTRAD

The first home computer in many British homes and the first word processor in many British offices was probably an Amstrad. No surprise therefore, that the Amstrad brand carries with it a strong reputation for the design, production and marketing of a wide range of affordable electronic products, not just in Britain but in over 50 other countries. Typical of the brand was the PCW 8256, launched in 1985. Its market included people who had never bought a word processor before because of the high price. By paying close attention to component costs, quality control and packaging, Amstrad succeeded in delivering a particular product to a particular market at just the price the mass market consumer could afford.

Founded by Alan Sugar in 1968, Amstrad's policy of seeking out lower-cost production processes and passing the saving on to the consumer has been an inseparable ingredient of the brand from the start. Its first manufacturing venture in 1970 consisted of plastic hi-fi turntable covers produced

by a more efficient process which enabled it to undercut competitors. In 1971 manufacturing capacity was expanded to include audio amplifiers and tuners.

The association of the brand with computers began in 1983 when Amstrad identified the potential of the fast expanding computer market. In quick succession Amstrad launched its first home games computer, then a word processor and finally a personal computer, complete with monitor and software. Amstrad prices were always well below those of the established market leaders, making it a tough competitor.

Today Amstrad plc is Britain's largest consumer electronics company, manufacturing personal computers, facsimile machines, telephones and personal digital organisers, as well as a range of satellite and audio products. In 1994 it launched Amstrad Direct to sell its products direct to the consumer by mail order.

Amstrad is Britain's largest consumer electronics company.

AMTRAK

Railroads opened up America in the nineteenth century. Today the National Railroad Passenger Corporation, a quasi-public agency operating under the brand name Amtrak, provides an energy-efficient, environmentally benign alternative to congested highways and crowded skies.

It was not always so. Amtrak was formed in 1971 at a time when most American railroads had filed applications to abandon passenger services altogether. It was intended as an experiment to identify the importance of rail passenger services to a balanced national transportation system, and the experiment has clearly succeeded. Total passenger miles covered have increased 27 per cent to 6.1 billion since 1981 and on some routes

Amtrak is even the dominant public carrier; on the Washington–New York route, for example, it holds 43 per cent of the combined air/rail passenger market.

Amtrak is now one of the most widely recognised brand names in America and the luicidity and appeal of the brand and its red and blue logo have played a major part in the renaissance of American passenger rail transport.

Working against the tide of the movement away from rail travel, Amtrak successfully provides an energy-efficient, environmentally benign alternative to congested highways and crowded skies.

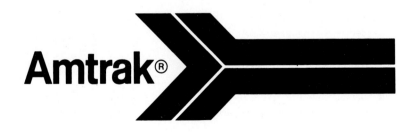

ANCHOR BEER

Anchor, a Pilsner beer, was first launched in 1932 by the Archipelago Brewery Company in Singapore, a Far Eastern subsidiary of the German brewer, Brauerei Beck and Co. It has had a chequered career.

In 1941, while war raged in the Far East, Malayan Breweries Ltd was able to add the Anchor brand to its brewery list by acquiring Archipelago for the princely sum of one Straits dollar. When the Japanese invaded Singapore, they took over the brewery and used it to brew Asahi beer for the Japanese troops, utilising the expertise of the expatriate staff who were placed under house arrest.

Today APB runs Anchor Beer as a strong second brand, retaining its centuries-old European process of brewing beer using three basic natural ingredients: malted barley, hops and Anchor's own exclusive yeast.

Anchor has had its ups and downs but the Singapore-based beer has ultimately benefited from its multi-cultural ownership.

ANDREX

Softness, strength and value are not the elements of a brand's personality one would usually associate with a mundane, rather embarrassing product like toilet paper. Yet Andrex has managed to transform the banal into the stylish, the rather private into the openly advertised.

Andrex achieved this transformation by bringing the Briton's favourite friend, his dog, into his home and onto his television. The Andrex puppy (the golden labrador) has appeared in over 80 commercials, and Andrex adverts consistently win the British public's plaudits. Some brand-owners have mimicked the Andrex advertisement, the most successful being Hamlet. Other brand-owners have used animals seriously and profitably, most notably Dulux.

Introduced by Bowater-Scott Corporation in 1956, Andrex gained market leadership in 1962, dominating a third of the UK tissue market. From the start, the brand was highly innovative, launching the first coloured tissue paper in 1957 and the first decorated paper towels in 1969. The brand is unique in having a royal warrant as the official tissue manufacturer for the Queen and Queen Mother. Andrex is now owned by Kimberley-Clark Corporation and looks set to have a secure future under its ownership.

Andrex, an excellent product which has received powerful, consistent promotion and support.

APPLE

Founded on April Fool's Day, 1976 by Steve Jobs, then 21, and Steve Wozniak, then 26, Apple both anticipated and benefited from the explosion in personal computer sales in the 1980s and 1990s. Based in California, the company was determinedly individualistic and anti-establishment while its identity was everything that the then bloated and conservative IBM was not: radical, in favour of the small private buyer over the big business customer, overtly artistic and in sympathy with technophobes.

The Apple logo epitomised this hard-headed, hippy mentality. It is organic, friendly, colourful, humorous, the perfect antidote to the cold and remote Big Blue (IBM), and success came in a big way for Apple with the launch on 24 January, 1984 of the Macintosh, a quirky, retro-shaped computer which featured a mass of extremely user-friendly "click and drag" icons on a simulated desktop. Technophobes everywhere were soon convinced this was a computer they could work with.

Shrewd marketing also played its part. Apple's advertising budget leapt dramatically, from $4.2m in 1980 to $100m in 1984, and the company gained a reputation for its innovative use of event marketing. The TV ad for the Macintosh used Orwellian 1984 imagery and it was aired during the Superbowl broadcast and replayed dozens of times over the following weeks by news and talk shows.

Apple is now pressing ahead with a global software licensing programme, which it believes will broaden its appeal without jeopardising the brand values. It is also developing multi-media products and voice-activated computers and, with the home computer market still less developed than the corporate market, Apple has scope for much further growth. The bigger challenge to these leading-edge computer boffins is less in making the advanced products than in managing growth. Problems here could puncture some of the brand's persuasive freshness and youth.

The Apple logo epitomises the mentality of a company which met the booming demand for personal computers.

APPLETISER

Appletiser, "the champagne of fruit juices", is a sparkling apple juice drink with a particularly successful brand image. It is marketed with an eye to the health-conscious drinker, emphasising that Appletiser is a 100 per cent pure light-coloured, clear apple juice made from concentrate, which has been lightly carbonated to give it a sparkle. It contains no added sugar, no preservatives and no artificial colouring.

Appletiser is marketed as a slightly dry and yet very refreshing drink, suitable for consumption on all occasions. The brand's across-the board appeal is encapsulated in the company's slogan:

> 'Made from apples but not like cider
> Pure fruit juice but not synthesised
> Soft drink but not a kid's lemonade
> Looks like champagne but not alcoholic
> Sophisticated adult drink but not a wine substitute'.

Appletiser was the brainchild of a visionary: Edmond Lombardi went to South Africa from Europe in the mid-1930s. He bought Applethwaite farm and settled into the fruit farming community of Elgin. There he conceived the dream of harnessing the golden juice of the abundant local apple crop. With the help of Swiss technology he developed and marketed a new, healthy, refreshing and pure fruit juice. In 1966 the Appletiser brand was launched in South Africa and today Appletiser is available in over 30 countries worldwide. In the UK it is known as Appletise.

Although South Africa–based, Appletiser Worldwide is an international premium beverage company whose dedication to developing, manufacturing and marketing high-quality sparkling fruit juices has made it a world leader in its field. The success of its products is achieved by the professional integration of growing, processing, blending and packaging skills and the company owns and manages a huge modern deciduous fruit farm to produce fruit for its needs and develop varieties suitable for its fruit juices.

Appletiser, "champagne of fruit juices", is the drink of the health-conscious.

Elimination of the superfluous and emphasis on comfort and elegance have made Armani a brand denoting fashion supremacy.

ARMANI

Giorgio Armani launched his business in 1973 and now heads an international fashion empire with estimated sales of over $850 million. Armani products are sold in over 2000 stores worldwide and brand licenses have been granted to 24 companies, while Armani also has two joint ventures in Japan. Armani started work as a buyer, fashion co-ordinator and freelance designer before building a world-leading clothes design empire. His hallmarks are a commitment to style, to the elimination of the superfluous and an emphasis on comfort and elegance.

Like Marks and Spencer, Armani watches his suppliers like a hawk and holds shares in a number of them, including Luxottica, which produces his eye wear and Antinea which manufactures women's clothing for Emporio Armani.

AT & T

The American Telephone and Telegraph Company (AT&T) traces its origins back to Alexander Graham Bell and his invention of the telephone in 1876. For almost 100 years AT&T's primary mission was to provide telephone services to the US market and manufacture telephone equipment. During this time the company enjoyed a virtual, though regulated, monopoly.

Through a government initiated divestiture on 1 January, 1984, AT&T gave up the Bell Operating Companies in return for the freedom to enter new businesses, such as computers. In one day, AT&T saw its $150 billion of assets reduced by 75 percent and its familiar logo (the bell symbol) taken away. Today AT&T is prohibited from using 'Bell' in its name.

Since divestiture, AT&T has faced a host of challenges. In particular it has had to make the transition from being a regulated monopoly to being a participant in highly competitive industries. In the long-distance telephone sector, AT&T has faced the added challenge of having to compete against rivals who are essentially unregulated, while AT&T remains subject to many of the regulatory burdens of its monopoly past. Also, AT&T has had to adjust to a market-place that is becoming increasingly global in nature.

The company has been generally successful in meeting these challenges and the brand is still the long-distance choice for millions of Americans.

No country has, or uses, a telephone system like America. AT&T has been largely responsible for America's love affair with the telephone.

AUDI

Audi is a brand which has no doubts about its identity and makes a virtue of unconventionality. Indeed the cars built by German-based Audi emphatically proclaim their own particular variety of prestige. The target customer for the Audi range is also clearly defined: an individualist who demands singular solutions, understands that satisfaction comes from refinement, not ostentation, and knows that technical excellence is worth seeking out and can make a difference.

Audi's founder, rally champion August Horch, indirectly gave his name to the car, as 'horch' is the German word for "hear", and that loosely translates in Latin to "Audi". An emphasis on technology and innovation is carried through into the German slogan in the company's British advertising: "Vorsprung durch Technik" (Progress through Technology) and Audi claims its policy of daring through innovation, of finding new and original solutions to age-old engineering problems, of creating new precedents instead of following accepted norms, while continually questioning the conventional, has changed general attitudes to cars and the way other manufacturers think when designing them.

A brand which makes a virtue of unconventionality, Audi is a car for the individualist.

AVON

Women not only use Avon brands of fragrances and cosmetics, they also go out into customers' homes to sell them and have done so since the company was founded in 1886, at which time the first "Avon lady", Mrs P.F.E. Albee of Winchester, New Hampshire, pioneered the company's direct-selling method, giving women their first opportunity to be financially independent at a time when their place was traditionally in the home. Today Avon aims to be the company that best understands and satisfies the needs of women throughout the world for products, service and self-fulfilment.

More than 40 million women (25 million of them in the USA) have at some time sold Avon products over the last 100-plus years and it is some 40 years since Avon first expanded outside the USA into Venezuela. Today Avon has nearly 1.7 million sales

Avon is the world's largest direct-selling company, selling fragrances and cosmetics to women for women by women.

representatives, in more than 120 countries, including Hungary, Thailand, China and Poland. It recently moved into the Czech Republic, Slovakia and Turkey.

Today Avon is the world's largest direct-selling company with more than 600 million customers worldwide and sales of $4 billion and the Avon brand stands for high quality beauty products at affordable prices.

BA

B

By concentrating on customer service and excellence in design and marketing, British Airways has established itself as a model for the best world airlines. All this is a far cry from the pre-privatisation days when the airline had a reputation for poor customer service and management. That said, the squeaky-clean image of "The World's Favourite Airline" took some blows after it lost the "dirty tricks" libel case brought against it by Virgin Atlantic Airways in

A model for the best world airlines, British Airways concentrates on customer service and excellence in design and marketing.

1993. It is perhaps a tribute to the soundness of the global brand that it is still extremely highly regarded in Asia and the USA as well as the UK.

To enhance the global brand further, BA has recently taken substantial stakes in various foreign airlines, including Qantas (a 25 per cent stake), US Air (24.6 per cent) and Deutsche BA (49 per cent). These joint ventures will enable it to capture the business of business customers making a complex series of short haul international flights. The alliances also put BA in pole position to take advantage of the 1997 liberalisation of European Union aviation regulations, which will allow an airline of one EU country to operate internal flights in another. To take itself forward into the twenty-first century, BA has launched "Leadership 2000", a programme aimed at improving management skills and placing customer service responsibility in the hands of front-line staff. By the turn of the century, BA hopes to be regarded as the UK's best-managed company.

BRITISH AIRWAYS

BACARDI

Once the drink of buccaneers and adventurers on the Spanish Main, Bacardi rum is now a sophisticated high-quality drink for discerning purchasers. Indeed Bacardi is the world's best-known rum and a leading international name among all liquors.

The brand's history began over 125 years ago when the world's first light, dry rum was developed by a Spanish immigrant, Don Facundo Bacardi y Maso, a wine importer and merchant in Santiago da Cuba. The local rum, scarcely changed since the sixteenth and seventeenth centuries, had a harsh, coarse bite to his refined palate, so Don Facundo made his new rum originally solely for his own use, though eventually he acquired a small distillery in Santiago. It started production on 4 February, 1862 in a tin-roofed shed housing a colony of fruit bats and these are the bats that still appear on the Bacardi rum label. Don Facundo clearly realised the value of an easily recognisable trademark in the light of the general illiteracy of the day.

Over time, Don Facundo perfected a process for distilling and blending from molasses a spirit so mellow, light and pure that it could be sipped straight. The Bacardi family still guard the secret of this process, passing it down from generation to generation.

Through war and revolution the business has continued to prosper, winning medals along the way. It also won favour with Americans visiting Cuba: one invented the daiquiri, an icy cocktail of white Bacardi rum and lime juice; another launched the Cuba Libre, mixing his Bacardi rum with Coke. The "mixability" of Bacardi rum is now virtually a global advertising theme and one of the marketing factors that has helped the brand achieve its worldwide leadership position.

BAILEY'S ORIGINAL IRISH CREAM

Establishing new spirits brands is notoriously difficult. The reason is not hard to see – drinkers are extremely conservative and rarely take to a new name or a new recipe. Yet Bailey's Original Irish Cream has in a couple of decades become a global brand. Its secret? Well, that is something its Irish forebears can answer more adequately than anyone else. But let us speculate that Bailey's has found the magic touch, the right degree of brand positioning, the apt traditional message, the superbly rich product formula, the most appropriate bottle and label design and just the right amount of Celtic heritage.

Taken together, these factors now account for the brand's current leadership in the world's liqueur stakes. It also ranks seventeenth in the top 100 spirit brands with sales of over 3·7 million cases and has helped make IDV, part of Grand Metropolitan, one of the world's leading consumer products companies.

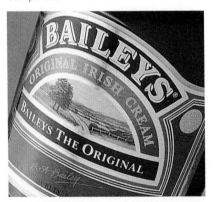

Within a couple of decades Baileys Original Irish Cream has conquered the world liqueur market to become a global brand.

The bats on the bottles of Bacardi rum are an easily recognisable trademark of a sophisticated high quality drink for discerning purchasers.

Ballantine's Scotch Whisky is the number one whisky brand in Europe (excluding the UK) and the third most favoured whisky brand in the world.

BALLANTINE'S

Ballantine's Scotch Whisky, which dates back to 1809, is the number one whisky brand in Europe (excluding UK) and the third most favoured whisky brand in the world. Originating from a small family concern in an Edinburgh grocery and continued under the family name by successive generations, Ballantine's has established itself as a major world player overseas. In Spain, for example, it accounts for a quarter of all Scotch whisky sales and it is brand leader in the growing Eastern European markets.

Ballantine's is available in four different varieties; the brand Gold Seal is popular in Europe, Latin America and the Far East, while Ballantine's "17 years old" is the market leader in the premium deluxe sector and is particularly strong in Japan and in major duty-free outlets. The ultimate and most expensive premium whisky available is Ballantine's "30 years old", while the roll-call is completed by Ballantine's "21 years old", launched in October 1991. This version is already an award-winner and looks set to follow its more established sister brands on the road to international fame.

BANG & OLUFSEN

Bang & Olufsen, 'the music masters', are renowned for their high performance music systems. Their expertise in speaker technology and the state-of-the-art design of their products have established them as a prestigious name in consumer electronics.

Bang & Olufsen began life in 1925 when two young engineers, Peter Bang and Svend Olufsen, began producing radios in the attic of a large country house in Quistrup, north-west Denmark. Whilst they have now progressed onto the high-street their image is carefully maintained through the thorough selection of dealers. Only those outlets that meet rigorous standards are allowed to become official suppliers and use the Bang & Olufsen signage above their outlets. The significance of the retail chain in conveying the image and values of the brand is reinforced by the emphasis that management places upon point of sale material and dealer training.

Bang & Olufsen, 'the music masters', are renowned for their high performance music systems.

For music lovers world-wide the sentiments and emotional appeal associated with the ownership of a Bang & Olufsen product speak louder than words.

BARBIE

Barbie, the teenage fashion doll, was born in 1959, wearing a sporty, zebra striped swimsuit. By 1995, as a result of skilful management of the brand, Mattel Inc., which owns Barbie and her associated trademarks, had sold well over 900 million Barbie dolls (and family members) in more than 140 countries round the world. Barbie, they claim, has become the most popular toy ever created. The typical American girl aged between three and 10 owns an average of eight Barbie dolls, her counterpart in Italy seven, in France and Germany five.

Apart from filling a gap in the doll market – hitherto dominated by baby dolls – much of Barbie's success comes from careful nurturing of the brand. In 35 years, Barbie has acquired a family and innumerable friends, some from different ethnic groups, and innumerable pets, including 16 dogs, 10 horses, 4 cats – even a giraffe and a zebra. She has also changed her appearance and her role to suit the taste of the day – one recent incarnation is Super Barbie in a bright pink body suit, with holographic arm and leg coverings, pink tennis shoes and pink stud earrings, topped by a holographic cape that lights up, with accompanying sound effects. Indeed some 120 new outfits are designed for Barbie annually, with accessories to match which are marketed separately.

The marketing of Barbie focuses on the educational benefits of the brand, because Barbie enables the child to experiment with the future from a safe distance through pretend play, an important element in growing up. She thus has a unique ability to inspire self-esteem, glamour and a sense of adventure, and serves as a role model for young girls, creating new dreams in her guise of astronaut, college graduate, surgeon, business executive and presidential candidate. So high is the brand's prestige that collectors place the value of an original mint condition Barbie doll at more than $4500. Inspired by this, Mattel is manufacturing Barbie dolls specifically for the collector, including porcelain recreations of some of the most popular dolls and fashions from the early 1960s.

Nurturing of the brand has made the Barbie doll the playmate and role model of millions of little girls worldwide.

BASS

The Bass red triangle is Britain's first registered trademark. Bass has been brewed since 1777, when William Bass established his brewery in Burton-upon-Trent, a century before Britain's first trademark act (1876). Mr Bass used the famous Burton well water, drawn from wells situated above the valley gravel beds, and insisted on using the best barley and hops, earning a reputation for quality not just in the UK but also as far afield as Eastern Europe and Russia, where the very dark, strong, sweet and heavily hopped beer was much appreciated. The beer was a huge export success even during the Napoleonic Wars when Bass had no less than 67 merchant importers in various countries.

Market development was not, however, always entirely conventional. In 1827, for example, a consignment of Bass Pale Ale on its way to India was shipwrecked off the British coast and 300 casks of the light, sparkling, pleasantly bitter drink were salvaged, sold in Liverpool and immediately acclaimed. Today Bass Brewers has a 23 per cent share of the UK beer market and is also Britain's biggest beer exporter, supplying some 80 overseas markets. In the USA, Bass Ale remains the leading imported draught ale and the best-selling British brand.

Bass Brewers' portfolio of brands now also includes Carling Black Label, Draught Bass, Worthington Best Bitter and a range of Tennent brands. It brews, markets and distributes over 60 ales and lagers and owns and operates eight UK breweries, producing over 8·5 million barrels of beer annually. (A British "barrel" is 288 pints or 36 gallons/163·7 litres – the British brewing industry is still determinedly traditional!)

Bass beers have travelled the world for more than two centuries but remain determinedly British.

BBC

The British Broadcasting Corporation – the BBC – is the world's best-known broadcaster. The most distinctive element in the BBC's brand personality is its independence and authority and central to this is the unusual nature of the BBC's funding.

The BBC is funded by all British viewers and listeners, who have to pay a licence fee, and this frees it from interference by advertisers or the government. However the license fee is increasingly an inadequate source of funds and some speculate that the BBC brand will wane as wealthier competitors consume the most popular programming.

The BBC's great brand values are strongly embodied in the BBC World Service, whose tradition for broadcasting without fear or favour is unmatched. The BBC World Service is a formidable marketing service for Britain, expressing powerful central values of trust and solidity. The service is also a lifeline to many living in countries where censorship or repression is active. However the BBC's core activity remains the production of high quality radio and television programmes for UK audiences, although the BBC is also following other broadcasters into new media.

The world's best known broadcaster, the BBC has a worldwide reputation for independence and authority, integrity and quality.

BECK'S

Beck's has one of the most up-market profiles of any premium lager, and is the drink for yuppies.

Today, Beck's beer is one of the leading lager brands in the world. Brewed in the German city of Bremen, it is the country's number one beer export. In fact, Beck's has been brewed in Bremen since 1874 and always in accordance with Reinheitsgebot – regulations introduced in 1516 to regulate the quality of all beers brewed in Germany.

The brand's packaging is clean, unfussy and understated and strongly reflects the brand's origins. Beck's has one of the most up-market profiles of any premium lager – 59 per cent of its drinkers are in the ABC1 sociodemographic group, while 68 per cent of its drinkers are under 35 and 30 per cent of its drinkers are women. This results partly from the brand's critically acclaimed arts sponsorship programme which gives Beck's access to many of society's opinion-formers on a regular basis.

BELL'S

Bell's whisky is currently the leading spirits brand in the United Kingdom, holding 17 per cent of the blended whisky market. Not content with this, the company continually develops its brand. In 1994, for example, Bell's stipulated that its blend would be eight years old and incorporated into the blend whiskies which are famous in their own right and which have names which read like a poem by Robert Burns: Glenkinchie, Linkwood, Oban and Blair Athol. Each lends its own character to the blend, giving the whisky more contrasts, textures and depths than many others.

In an increasingly competitive drinks market, Bell's is engaged in an active campaign to recruit young adult drinkers to Scottish whisky through using an adventurous advertising campaign. Bell's was acquired by Guinness in 1985, and is now a major constituent of the United Distillers brand portfolio.

Bell's whisky, the leading spirits brand in the United Kingdom, is currently aiming to attract young adult drinkers.

BEN AND JERRY'S

Ben and Jerry's homemade icecream was first produced using a hand-cranked icecream maker in a renovated filling station in Burlington, Vermont in 1978. Ben Cohen and Jerry Greenfield, "two fat nerdy guys with glasses" who had been friends "since they met at the back of the track in their seventh grade gym class", learned to make icecream through a correspondence course. Although their company retains the brand's folksy, trendy image, it has come a long way since then.

Ben and Jerry's icecream has kept its folksy, trendy image though it is now an international company with a worldwide clientele.

Today Ben and Jerry's is an international company distributing icecream and frozen yogurt products throughout North America. It has over 120 franchised scoop shops in 19 American states and four in Canada, a joint venture (Iceverks) in Karelia, Russia, and a licensee in Israel.

The brand covers super premium all-natural icecream made from fresh Vermont milk and cream, low fat and non-fat frozen yogurt, and icecream novelties. Although Ben and Jerry's produces traditional flavours, it is particularly associated with its innovations, its newest flavour being Chubby Hubby, a concoction of chocolate-covered peanut butter-filled pretzel nuggets in a vanilla malt icecream with a fudge and peanut butter ripple. As the publicity brochure says, "Wow!"

Ben and Jerry's distributes 7·5 per cent of its pre-tax profits to charity and other worthy causes providing grants to community-based non-profit organisations with creative programmes for progressive social change.

One of the world's most famous drinks, Bénédictine comes with over four centuries of religious history and traditional values.

Benetton, a powerful brand reputation in a difficult and changing market sector.

BÉNÉDICTINE

Bénédictine goes right back to 1510, when Benedictine monks living at Fécamp on the French Normandy coast put 27 herbs and spices together into a recipe and found they liked it. They continued making it until the French Revolution 280 years later when the monastery was dissolved, along with its famous drink.

In 1863, a wine and spirits dealer, Alexandre Le Grand, found the recipe and marketed the old drink. He emphasised its religious history and traditional values and quickly sold out his first production of 23 000 bottles.

Today, Bénédictine is one of the most famous drinks in the World. No fewer than five million bottles are produced annually and sold worldwide.

BENETTON

Benetton's knitwear, clothing and accessories brand has a worldwide reputation for quality and style. This is based partly on the care and attention the company gives to the colour and design and quality of its products and partly to Benetton's policy of continuous innovation. The group's research department keeps a constant eye on the evolution of styles and tastes in order to foresee global market trends and produce collections that encompass both an international fashion element and an individual Benetton character.

Benetton has communicated its brand values through some of the most potent and controversial advertising of recent years. Based round the theme of matching and conflicting colours, Benetton advertising emphasises a vision of harmony through colour co-ordination.

Established in Ponzano Veneto near Treviso in north-east Italy in 1965, the Benetton group is today an international concern, exporting not only its own products, mainly under the brand names United Colors of Benetton, Sisley and 012, but also production technology and know-how. Although Benetton principally operates from centres in Italy, France and Spain, its production and commercial network extends to 120 countries and 7000 retail outlets. In European markets, recent initiatives have included the opening of megastores carrying a full range of Benetton garments and accessories in the key shopping areas of major cities, and Benetton has also opened 50 stores in China and consolidated its presence in Japan.

By way of brand extension, Benetton has a joint-venture agreement with the American company Timex and the German Junghans Uhren group for the design, production and worldwide distribution of high quality watches, chronographs and alarm clocks to bear the United Colors of Benetton brand name. In Korea it co-operates with the Tae-Chang company in the production and local marketing of a Benetton intimate apparel line. A significant contribution to the brand's image has been the company's activities in sport sponsorship, particularly Formula 1 motor racing.

BENSON & HEDGES

120 years of continuous adaptation to changing smoking habits and production techniques has made Benson & Hedges today the leading trademark in Virginia cigarettes worldwide. The familiar gold packet of Benson and Hedges Special Filter was introduced in 1961 to reflect a move towards longer, more luxurious filter-tipped cigarettes while the royal warrant awarded by Queen Victoria to Alfred Paget Hedges in 1900 was emphasised in the pack design and in B&H's advertising.

Indeed Benson and Hedges has linked its products to royalty from the start, naming its first-ever brand "Prince of Wales Mix". This smoking tobacco was launched from the Bond Street, London, shop of William and Richard Benson. The switch to cigarette production came in 1883 when the Prince of Wales (later Edward VII) summoned William to Buckingham Palace to instruct him in preparing a blend of the then popular Egyptian tobacco. The new brand, Cairo Citadel, became one

of the first London-made Egyptian cigarettes. However Benson and Hedges Virginia, which first appeared in 1925 in a red and white tin, is the brand which to most consumers epitomises "Benson & Hedges".

Benson and Hedges began in Britain but is now the leading trademark in Virginia cigarettes worldwide.

BERLITZ

The renowned Berlitz method, which aims to teach students to think

in the foreign language they wish to learn, has made Berlitz International the world's leading language services company. Today Berlitz describes itself as a communications company, with the mission to "help the world communicate".

The Berlitz method was devised by a German immigrant to the USA, Maximilian D. Berlitz, who opened a school in Providence, Rhode Island in 1878 and quickly found that his pupils learned better by listening, repeating and speaking. His

method has stood the test of time. More than 31 million Berlitz customers have learned a variety of foreign languages, ranging from French and German to Arabic and Mandarin, through the Berlitz method. Today some 320 language centres located in more than 30 countries use the method and operate under the Berlitz name.

The brand has extended its success to Berlitz Publishing, an organisation which produces self-teaching books, audio tapes and CD-ROMs, while Berlitz Translation Services offers software localisation and interpretation services as well as document translation.

Berlitz uses its distinctive method to "help the world communicate", in some 320 centres in more than 30 countries.

BETTY CROCKER

The value of having an apparently real and reassuring face behind a brand is nowhere better illustrated than in the story of Betty Crocker. This extraordinary composite of the qualities of the American housewife first took shape in 1921 when The Washburn Crosby Company was promoting its flour. Following a competition, the company was deluged by thousands of questions about baking and decided to create a female signatory for the company's responses – no real Betty Crocker has ever existed.

The Betty Crocker name was selected for good-old fashioned reasons: the company thought 'Betty' sounded genial while 'Crocker' was the surname of a recently retired director of the company. The following years saw 'Betty Crocker' become a star. The name was used for national radio promotions on cookery spots on regional radio stations and later there was a 24-year stint on the NBC network.

During the Depression and then World War II, the Betty Crocker name appeared on nutritional health booklets and the brand's owners, by this time General Mills, finally built a product brand around it in 1947, when packaged cake mixes were introduced. Today the Betty Crocker brand line is huge: 200 convenience food products bear the name, and General Mills has licensed out the name for hundreds of houseware items, from dishes to kitchen gadgets and small appliances.

Through her long and eventful life, Betty Crocker has maintained a reputation for quality, helpfulness, trustworthiness and service to consumers. She also continues her initial role of offering them food information. The Betty Crocker image has also been updated over the years to ensure that her fashion and get-up remain appropriate to the period and the customer. This has ensured her longevity and continuing appeal.

The Betty Crockers brand conveys quality, helpfulness, trustworthiness and service.

Grandfather of today's everyday essential tool, Bic launched the first low-cost, disposable ballpoint pens in 1958, revolutionising the writing instrument market.

BIC

BiC is derived from the name of Marcel Bich, a Frenchman who ironed out many of the teething problems of early ballpoint pens and, in 1958, launched the first low-cost, disposable ballpoint pens on the French and British markets, a development which revolutionised the writing instrument market.

The first disposable pen was in fact invented by a Hungarian, Laszlo Biro, before World War II, when he settled in Argentina to escape Nazi persecution and patented his invention in 1943. The first commercially produced Biro pens appeared in the USA and the UK in 1945. Later the Biro and BiC companies merged and today BiC produces a complete line of writing instruments, including its Micro Metal, Clic Stic, 4 Color Pen, Brite Liner and Softfeel sub-brands.

Every BiC product is invested with the BiC philosophy – maximum service, minimum price – and produced with the most advanced technology. 15 million ballpoint pens and 3·5 million lighters are now sold every day.

BIRDS EYE WALL'S

Frozen food as we know it today owes its origins to an American biologist, inventor and fur trapper called Clarence Birdseye. Whilst on a hunting expedition in the frozen wastes of Labrador, Clarence met and ate with the Inuit (Eskimo) population. He noted that they left their meat and fish to freeze in the intense cold of the Arctic in order to preserve it and that, despite months of freezing, the food would be tender and fresh once defrosted.

On his return to the USA he set about trying to reproduce mechanically the extreme conditions under which foods could be frozen. In the 1920s the "Birdseye Plate Froster" was invented and in 1930 a group of shopkeepers began to sell frozen fish, vegetables and poultry under the brand name "Birds Eye".

Birds Eye, now owned by Unilever, has invested heavily in expanding the frozen food business throughout Europe and in many parts of the world. Birds Eye in Britain has become one of the largest frozen food manufacturers in the world – bigger than the original Birds Eye business in the United States with which the British company no longer has any commercial links.

BLACK & DECKER

Black & Decker high quality power tools are an indispensable item of equipment for the constantly growing number of DIY addicts.

Black & Decker do-it-yourself power tools have a worldwide reputation for innovation and the brand's owners are equally well known for their careful monitoring and development of the brand image. However, at times Black & Decker has been concerned because retailers use the brand as a loss leader, calculating that, by cutting the price of a top brand, customers will be enticed into their stores for similar bargains. The practice poses problems for Black & Decker as other major customers continuously suspect that the manufacturers must be doing 'sweetheart deals' with their competitors and therefore they will put pressure on Black & Decker to give them exclusivity, a sensitive requirement, given that in many countries it is illegal for a manufacturer to control the selling price or establish networks of willing retailers under the control of the brand owner. So heavy discounting of leading brands such as Black & Decker in price-led promotions has become almost routine and the price of brand leadership has become a brand which is often promoted on price rather than on its other many merits.

In 1984 Black & Decker acquired the household electrical appliances division of the American General Electric Company and the Black & Decker brand has been extended to a whole new range of domestic products, including hairdryers, irons, toasters and blenders.

Bob Birdseye picked up the idea of quick-frozen foods from native trappers in Northern Canada. In order to exploit the idea a retail distribution system and the widespread availability of domestic freezers were required.

BMW

BMW is the badge of refined engineering and sleek motoring. It exudes the powerful expressive values of exclusivity and class. The BMW, at least in the 1980s, was the marque of aspiration for the driver who wanted to be seen with an excellent and status-rich piece of machinery. The power of these values, as of the BMW technology itself, has ensured that even older BMWs are massively in demand.

BMW is based in Munich and has a worldwide reputation for advanced technology, excellent product quality and fine styling. Started in World War I, the company's origins as an aircraft manufacturer are still evident in its white and blue symbol, conceived as a stylised rotating propeller.

In the world of corporate identity, BMW is renowned for the attention paid to its brand image, that is to its corporate brand. For example, BMW showrooms or service centres anywhere in the world share the same BMW 'look' typified by messages of quality, efficiency and professionalism. BMW bought the Rover group in 1994, giving it a broader mass appeal to add to its top of the range prestige portfolio.

BMW has successfully transformed itself from a minor manufacturer with an ill-defined brand image to a major player on the world stage, renowned for its technical wizardry and commitment to driving pleasure.

THE BODY SHOP

Building global brands is becoming ever harder as media become more expensive and more diffuse. But growth of The Body Shop has shown that global shifts in consumer retail patterns, if sensibly tapped, can create brands quickly and internationally, and also that major international brands can be built without heavyweight advertising: The Body Shop has relied mainly on public relations, word of mouth and a powerful retail presence on the world's shopping streets. The Body Shop is little more than 20 years old, but it already has a global reputation and is firmly established in 45 countries, with over 1200 shops.

This pioneering company produces high-quality skin, hair and colour cosmetic products while retaining its core values based on the pursuit of social and environmental change through business. It has never compromised its fundamental values, namely environmental concern, animal welfare (including opposition to animal testing in the cosmetics industry), fair trade and the development of trading partnerships with communities in need. Its skin and hair care products and colour cosmetics are also sold without excessive packaging. The company also manufactures around 65 per cent of its own product range at its headquarters in Littlehampton, England and in Glasgow.

The Body Shop has survived recession, copycat competition and adverse criticism and is now set for a period of renewed global growth.

BOEING

If you are flying today, the chances are you will travel on one of the Boeing jetliners that take off or land somewhere in the world every two seconds. Boeing has built more than 6000 commercial airliners, making it the world's leading aircraft manufacturer. In 1995 the company estimated that its planes carried some 675 million people.

The brand's history reflects the history of aviation in the USA. It began in 1916, only a dozen years after the Wright brothers' historic flight, when a partnership between a young Seattle lumberman with vision, Bill Boeing, and a US Navy engineer, Lieutenant Conrad Westervelt, led to the first B and W, a twin-float seaplane. Made of wood, linen and wire, it was built by a team of shipwrights, carpenters, cabinet makers and seamstresses. It was a far cry from Boeing's newest streamlined twin-engined 777 jetliner.

In between, Boeing planes – trainers, fighters, bombers, including the famous Flying Fortress – have played their part in both world wars and in the Korean war. In 1943 it was in the Boeing Model 314, the "Clipper", that Franklin D. Roosevelt celebrated his birthday en route to meet Winston Churchill for the Casablanca conference. A B-29, *Enola Gay* dropped the world's first atomic bomb.

In the 1950s, the Boeing 707, with four turbojet engines, revolutionised commercial aviation, almost halving intercontinental travel times, while its reliability and relatively low operating costs brought air travel within the financial reach of even more people. Today these amenities are taken for granted and the Boeing brand has become synonymous with innovation based on advanced technology and efficient production.

The history of Boeing is the history of US aviation, but it is also the history of marketing: consumer awareness is much higher for Boeing planes than it is for any of the aircraft maker's rivals.

BOLS

BOLS today is a major international business with subsidiaries across Europe and South America and products which sell throughout the world. Not bad for a company that started life in a wooden shed.

The BOLS story starts in 1575, when Lucas Bols built his legendary wooden shed – Lootsje – at Rozengracht near Amsterdam. It was here that he formulated his first liqueurs using water drawn locally and simple copper kettles heated with turf. These early experiments resulted in the range of liqueurs and 'genevers' – the highly distinctive Dutch gins – that are now sold in over 150 countries.

The success of BOLS owes much to its ancient craftmanship and to its obsession with quality.

BOLS raw material buyers have for centuries travelled the world in search of the finest herbs, spices and fruits for the numerous products featuring the BOLS brand.

BOLS' perfectionist streak has served it well. Its excellent ingredients continue to ensure a loyal international following for the Dutch spirits brand.

BOOTS

Founded by Jesse Boot in Nottingham at the end of the nineteenth century, Boots The Chemist is the UK market leader in many areas of its business, including healthcare, cosmetics, toiletries, baby consumables, film and film processing. Boots' branding message is simple. It is a traditional, reassuring and honourable British retailer, of long pedigree and proven reliability.

Every week, over 30 per cent of the UK population visit one of the 1167 stores, ranging from community pharmacies to city centre department stores. Boots has invested heavily in an own-brand range, of which almost a third are developed and manufactured by Boots Contract Manufacturing. The 'No7' colour cosmetics range demonstrates the strength and flexibility that results from this vertical integration. Shapers foods, Soltan and the Natural and Global Collections are other successful own-brand marks.

"Boots the Chemist" is an appropriate brand slogan for a company which has the UK high street sewn up.

Engineering giant Bosch is an inspiring combination of hard-nosed marketing savvy combined with socially responsible behaviour – a perfect recipe for success in today's "stakeholder" society.

BOSCH

Bosch is a classic example of brand extension. First applied solely to automotive equipment manufactured in Germany for the German market, it has expanded to embrace a range of products, including household appliances, power tools and industrial equipment sold worldwide.

The automotive sector, which saw the company's beginnings, is still the largest in the powerful Bosch Group. The small "Workshop for Precision Mechanics and Electrical Engineering", which Robert Bosch opened in Stuttgart in 1886, soon started to specialise in ignition systems for all types of engines. But an advertisement the following year also already cited "telephones and private telegraphs" as a particular interest of the firm and Bosch today is very active in the growth area of communications technology.

The brand was already selling internationally at the turn of the century: the first distributor in Great Britain, for example, dates from 1898. Today the Bosch Group has subsidiaries, affiliated companies and foreign representatives in more than 125 countries and has over 120 production facilities in Europe, the United States, Latin America, Africa, Asia and Australia.

Robert Bosch was a man of conscience and a philanthropist. He introduced the eight-hour working day as early as 1906 and four years later abolished Saturday afternoon work. In 1916 he donated over 20 million marks for public use and in 1940 the Robert Bosch hospital was opened in Stuttgart. His will binds his company to this tradition, stipulating that the company's assets be administered for public benefit purposes. By the end of 1992 disbursements had reached some DM 477 million (approx. £207 million).

BOSTIK

Through innovation, skilful marketing and the continuous introduction of new products, the Bostik brand has become synonymous with glue and a leading international name in adhesives and sealants. It is a classic example of brand extension applied to variations of the same product. Whether it is simply a question of sticking one piece of paper to another or more complicated operations involving bonding pottery, metals, rubber or other materials, there is a brand of Bostik to do every job.

The success of Bostik's two main sub-brands – Easy Stik for the stationery market and Prostik for the DIY market – comes partly from the quality of the products, partly from careful attention to consumer needs and judicious packaging. Bostik adhesives come in a variety of easy-to-use containers, ranging from Gluepen's pump action pen and Super Glue's fine nozzle for precise application, to the paper glue stick of Sticky Stick and the sponge-tipped dispenser of Paper Glue. Safety is a major consideration. A picture of a cartoon character, Billy Bostik, appears on Bostik packs suitable for children. Those unsuitable have child-resistant safety dispensers (Super Glue 4) or safety collars (Super Glue). If all fails, there is Bostik Emergency Skin Release.

The Bostik Endangered Species Project, created in conjunction with the Whale and Dolphin Society, emphasises the brand's strong appeal to the education market, as well as its commitment to environmental conservation.

A glue for every purpose,
the Bostik brand embraces
the whole market.

BP

A dynamic international organisation, BP's newly painted green pumps showed, in 1927, its concern to "preserve the beauties of the countryside".

In a successful exercise in adapting a brand image, British Petroleum Company plc, one of the world's largest petroleum and petrochemical groups, launched a revised identity for the 1990s. The new style aims to project a new image of BP as a dynamic international organisation determined to be a leader in all its fields of business. It responds to fundamental changes in the company, which has a stronger, more competitive international presence than ever before.

The group logo, the traditional BP shield, has been modernised and the letters "BP" – regarded as a major asset and in use long before the parent company was officially named British Petroleum – italicised to create a new sense of movement. Fresh shades of green and yellow have been introduced to give a richer, more friendly feel. Green, compulsory background for the logo, has been adopted as the group's dominant colour, to produce a striking presence at all sale and service points.

The new shield is the latest version of a logo that has remained basically the same since it won a design competition amongst company staff in 1920. Showing "BP" in black within a red shield, it appeared on the tulip-shaped globes fitted to roadside petrol pumps. The well-known green and yellow were adopted in 1923 and, as the group grew and spread in the 1920s and 1930s, became internationally recognised symbols of the brand. In 1927 advertisements appeared in Britain urging motorists to buy from the newly-painted green BP pumps that "preserve the beauties of the countryside". A simplified system of company naming policy is a major part of the changed brand image, adding clarity to the organisation and a clear focus to the BP trade names. Short business names are now used internationally for all BP's commercial activities, stressing the thrust of the main business. Operating units in countries worldwide now use these business names rather than those of the local national associate. BP's three core businesses have thus become BP Exploration, BP Oil and BP Chemicals.

BRAUN

Braun is a worldwide brand and the global leader in electric shavers. Founded by Max Braun in Frankfurt in 1921, Braun A.G. initially manufactured radios and other audio equipment. From the start, Braun emphasised the importance of originality and design quality.

Early products were electric razors, and household appliances in the oral care and hair care sectors followed. In 1949 Braun introduced the world's first electric foil shaver and in 1957 it launched the multi-purpose kitchen food processing machine.

In 1967, Braun was acquired by Gillette, and it has linked up with another Gillette subsidiary, Oral-B, to launch the Braun Oral-B plaque remover, a world leader in oral care appliances.

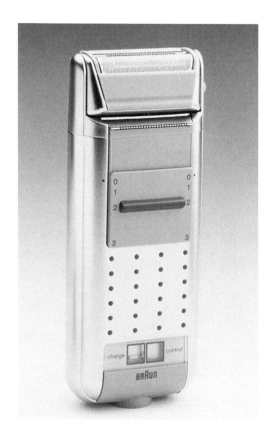

The inventor of the world's first electric shaver, Braun's highly original products are now as likely to feature in the kitchen as the bathroom.

BRIDGESTONE

The brainchild of an ambitious Japanese businessman, tyre giant Bridgestone has rolled its way into dominant positions in many markets and is now busy diversifying into other automotive and leisure areas.

The Bridgestone Corporation has risen to prominence in the last 20 years on the back of the success of the Japanese motor industry. Though still very much centred in Japan, Bridgestone has grown swiftly into the world's largest manufacturer of rubber and plastics, with factories throughout the world, including America and Europe.

Bridgestone was established in 1931. With an eye to foreign markets, its founder Shojiro Ishibashi took his own surname – literally, 'stone bridge' – and translated and adapted it. The name presented certain problems after the company's goods started to appear in the West in the mid 1970s. Customers tended to confuse it with the American tyre giant Firestone, a confusion which was finally settled in 1988 when Bridgestone bought out Firestone for $2·6 billion.

Though 75 per cent of Bridgestone's sales remain in tyres – one recent innovation is the studless snow tyre – the company is now diversifying rapidly, using its powerful technological and international marketing bases. It now makes a wide variety of motor components, including wheels and rubber belts and chains. Other products range from conveyor belts and rubber caterpillar crawlers, bearings and hoses to large-scale marine equipment. Its chemicals division produces building materials such as tiles and insulation and co-operates with leading designers in the manufacture of bedding and furniture centred on its polyurethane foam.

Company profile is enhanced by a number of domestic and leisure products such as tennis rackets and balls, golf clubs and balls, and windsurfing equipment. Bridgestone is still the largest manufacturer of bicycles in Japan. Its move into world markets is supported by a number of training programmes in less developed countries.

BUDWEISER

Budweiser is the largest and most powerful brand in the Anheuser-Busch stable of drinks products. Bud, the affectionate abbreviation amongst its typically youthful drinkers, has been brewed and sold since 1876 and is the largest selling beer in the world. In 1993, Bud outsold the next four competitive brands combined, and it has reached an unassailable position.

Many brand extensions have flowed from the original Budweiser brand. For example, in 1982, Anheuser-Busch produced Bud Light, which is now the top light beer in the USA. In 1990 Bud Dry Draft was rolled out nationally and, in 1993, Ice Draft from Budweiser was the first American draught beer to be ice-brewed, creating a rich and smooth taste. The Anheuser-Busch beer brands portfolio is the largest in the world, including Carlsberg, Busch Natural Pilsner and Michelob.

The world's biggest-selling and best-known beer brand, Bud has not rested on its laurels but continues to extend into new areas.

BUITONI

Acquired by Nestlé in 1988, Buitoni is now available in over 60 countries and is a world leader in authentic Italian food. Giulia Buitoni created the brand in 1827. Her home-made pasta had gained such a reputation in her home town of Sansepolcro that she was faced with an insatiable demand. So she opened her own pasta-making shop and enjoyed a flourishing trade. After her death in 1879, her five sons incorporated the company as "Giovani & Fratelli Buitoni". They started winning awards internationally: for example, a gold medal at the Paris International Exposition in 1886. Buitoni did not, however, open its first foreign manufacturing plant – in Paris – until 1934. The admonition of Mama Giulia, "Don't remain closed in your own home, even if that is where you feel most comfortable", became the driving force for further dramatic expansion.

Buitoni is now a key brand in the Nestlé portfolio. Its name stretches across a wide range of frozen, chilled, dried and even sterilised sauces as well as a variety of pasta products.

The founder's expansionist philosophy can still be seen today in Buitoni's commitment to conquering new markets and building consumer loyalty through direct marketing.

Get your burger's worth.

BURGER KING

Burger King is the world's second largest hamburger restaurant group. Designs emphasising the grilling of hamburgers have ensured Burger King a strong visual identity, although the brand has an unenviable task fighting an all-powerful and highly innovative market leader in McDonald's.

Burger King has an international presence and it has built up ties in the USA with the Walt Disney Corporation. In 1994 Burger King participated in its largest promotion with the highly successful film, *The Lion King*. The company, which is owned by Grand Metropolitan, operates over 7,500 outlets in 56 countries around the world. Burger King has franchised approximately 90 per cent of its outlets.

The world's second largest hamburger chain has used a string of third-party joint promotions to keep the pressure on McDonald's.

CADBURY'S

Cadbury's is synonymous with chocolate, particularly in the UK, its home market. Indeed it claims to have the biggest annual sales, around £1·3 billion, of any UK company built around just one product. As market leader in the UK chocolate confectionery industry, the brand has seen impressive and sustained growth over the years. Sales from Cadbury's Dairy Milk alone (a flagship brand for the parent company Cadbury Schweppes), are estimated at over £135 million for 1995.

Cadbury's started life as a small grocery business in 1824 producing a sideline of hand-produced cocoa and drinking chocolate. The company was officially founded a few years later, in 1831, when it relocated to a large warehouse. In 1878 Cadbury moved again to Bourneville, a town developed specially to cater to its new factory. It was here that the inimitable Cadbury taste was developed.

The Cadbury brand is now sold in over 150 countries, including Russia, India and China, and continues to produce innovative product lines. The company's most successful new brand in the 1990s is Time Out, a UK market leader and a top selling confectionery brand in Ireland. Fuelled by growing global aspirations, the company acquired Dr. Pepper/Seven-Up, marking the biggest single corporate move since the formation of Cadbury Schweppes in 1969.

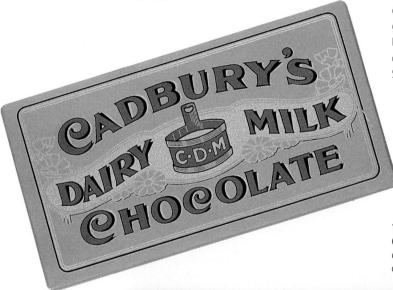

The purple and gold wrapper of Cadbury's Dairy Milk indicates one of Britain's best loved chocolate bars.

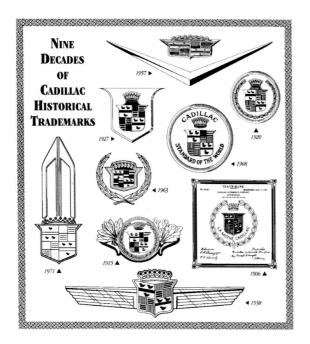

NINE DECADES OF CADILLAC HISTORICAL TRADEMARKS

1957 ▶
1927 ▶
1920
1908 ◀
1963 ◀
1971 ▲
1915 ▲
1906 ▲
1938 ◀

Once associated with the square-jawed, reliable, all-American "regular guy", Camel cigarettes are now favourites of smokers worldwide.

CADILLAC

No product represents the American dream more intimately than the Cadillac. To many Americans it is the ultimate status symbol. The marketing men have counted over a hundred popular songs containing references to Cadillacs – way ahead of any other make – a vivid testimony to the aspirational qualities of the classic American luxury motor car. In recent years this image has helped Cadillac to withstand fierce competition from European and Japanese marques such as BMW, Volvo, Mercedes Benz, Jaguar, Acura and Lexus. The owners, General Motors, still sell more than a quarter of a million Cadillacs a year, over a quarter of the entire luxury car market in the USA.

The Rolls Royce of US car marques, the Cadillac brand has seen off fierce foreign competition and remains a formidable marketing phenomenon.

The reputation for excellence goes back to the very dawn of the motor industry. The company was established in 1902 and as early as 1908 the Cadillac had won the Royal Automobile Club's Dewar Trophy for Automotive Excellence. It introduced the V8 engine in 1915. The famous wreath and crest symbol, based on the arms of the French founder of Detroit, even appeared on tanks during World War II.

The status that goes with the Cadillac name is jealously protected and exploited by a worldwide licensing programme. General Motors operates tight quality control on companies licensed to use the name, whether on clothes, leather goods, fragrances or toys. In line with its image, Cadillac is active in the sponsorship of golf and one of the largest brand extensions is in golf carts and golfing equipment.

CAMEL

Camel was introduced as the first major cigarette of R.J. Reynolds Tobacco Company in 1913. Four years later, Camel became the nation's best-selling cigarette. In the next half-century, it went on to become the most popular cigarette ever produced.

In large part, Camel's popularity is due to its brand image. Around 1920, a foursome of golfers, fresh out of cigarettes, sent for a new supply. While they waited, one of them said to to another, who happened to have been handling Reynold's outdoor ads, "I'd walk a mile for a Camel." That slogan was worked into a poster, using a New Haven, Conn., fireman as a model. In 1921, the famous slogan appeared on billboards and in newspapers and magazines.

For years following the war, Camel continued to hold first place in the sale of all cigarette brands. In the late 1960s, the famous "I'd walk a mile" slogan was reintroduced, which proved popular with nostalgic smokers.

The brand's image has been updated with the Joe Camel campaign, which was introduced in 1988 to celebrate the brand's 75th birthday. Despite the proliferation of cigarette brands on the market globally today, Camel remains one of the top 10 best-selling international brands in the world.

The original non-filter Camel is still available today, as are Camel Filters and Camel Lights, a low- tar version introduced in 1978. Camel Ultra Lights entered national distribution in December 1990, Camel full-flavour and lights in March 1992, and Camel Special Lights in April 1993.

Today, Camel is one of the ten best-selling international cigarette brands in the world, and its worldwide sales are growing. In markets outside the United States, the Camel cigarette brand is supported by various advertising campaigns. A campaign that stresses a sense of individuality and humour is used in some countries, while a campaign with an adventure theme is used in other markets.

CAMPARI

Campari dates back to the Italy of the 1860s when Gaspare Campari created the red aperitif and served it in his fashionable Caffe Camparino in Milan. Whilst the brand remains a relatively niche product in the UK it is one of Europe's largest spirit brands. As with other brands such as Coca-Cola and KFC the recipe for Campari is a secret and kept so by systems surrounding the herbs and spice store that rival Fort Knox. Even the ingredients are personally assembled by the President of the company.

A byword for canned soup and immortalised by Andy Warhol, Campbell's continues to exert an awesome emotional hold over consumers, especially in the USA.

CAMPBELL'S

Campbell's Soups has its origins in Camden New Jersey, where Abram Anderson and Joseph Campbell formed the Joseph A. Campbell Preserve Company to make canned tomatoes, vegetables, jellies, soups and minced meats. The company really took off when it developed its famous condensed soup in 1897. This eliminated the water content, and so cut the cost of packaging, shipping and storage. The company's 10·5 ounce can of condensed soup cost a dime – against 30 cents for a typical 32 ounce can of soup – and there were 21 varieties. In 1922 the company recognised the power of the soup brand and introduced "soup" into its corporate name.

Campbell's has built its success on value-added, competitively superior branded products, consumer repeat purchase and a very strong brand franchise. A tribute to its success was the fame of the remarkable representations that Andy Warhol made of its distinctive red and white tin designs in the 1960s.

Today Campbell's Chicken Noodle and Cream of Mushroom Soups have overtaken the tomato soup as the company's most popular brand, and these three soups are among the most popular of all American grocery products. Americans consume a remarkable 2·5 billion bowls of the three soups every year.

Canon amply demonstrates the 'bridging' at which Japanese companies are so adept. Originally formed as a camera manufacturer, Canon has used its technological base to become a leading manufacturer of business machines.

CANON

Canon derives its name from Kwah-non, the Japanese name of the Chinese Goddess Kwan-jin who brings grace and fortune. Kwanon became Canon in 1947, fourteen years after the company was first formed as a manufacturer of business machines as well as of cameras and other optical products. In addition to the wide variety of copiers, laser beam printers, bubble jet printers, memory systems, facsimile equipment, electronic typewriters, Japanese language word processors, DTP systems, calculators, cameras and other products marketed under the Canon brand name, Canon also markets both Apple and NeXT computers in Japan and the Far East. It also operates Imageland in the United States where customers can use colour laser copiers (CLCs) to produce original artwork.

Canon are now the major world competitors to Xerox in copiers and their technology is so advanced that the new Canon high fidelity colour copier is giving Governments around the world a major headache – it can produce colour photocopies of bank notes which are of such a high standard that a rush of forged banknotes is feared. Already the Bank of England is redesigning the currency with the Canon copier firmly in mind.

CANTERBURY

Canterbury clothes are multifunctional, stylish, fashionable, durable, comfortable and colourful. They are now sold worldwide, including countries such as Canada, the UK, the USA, Japan, Germany and Sweden.

In New Zealand, its home market, Canterbury has over 90 per cent awareness. This is largely because of a raft of high-profile sponsorships. The brand backs rugby (All Blacks, Australian Wallabies, the Fiji rugby team and so on), yachting (Whitbread Round the World Race, Admiral's Cup) and special events (Commonwealth Games, Brisbane Expo and so on). It is also an aggressive advertiser, heavily promoting its slogan: "The world's toughest activewear".

Canterbury stands for rugged, outdoors activity and has shrewdly exploited its sponsorship links with New Zealand's high-profile rugby teams.

CANTERBURY OF NEW ZEALAND

CARLSBERG

Carlsberg is the global byword for lager branding. The message used in the UK marketing – "probably the best lager in the world" – says it all. For many people, Carlsberg is lager.

But Carlsberg would not have attained this position of fame without the early resolution of its founders, J.C. Jacobsen and Carl Jacobsen, to aim for excellence: in their own words, "to develop the art of making beer to the greatest possible degree of perfection in order that these breweries as well as their products may stand out as a model". None can now deny that they have succeeded. Carlsberg has a passionate devotion to product excellence, enormous pride in the brand and direct and unswerving message and positioning.

Founded in 1847, Carlsberg began exporting beer from its Copenhagen brewery in 1868 and has since expanded into 33 Carslberg breweries worldwide. Carlsberg is also brewed under licence in 18 countries, thus bringing the brand to over 130 countries, making it a truly international brand.

The Carlsberg portfolio contains a number of brands which have all been successful in their own right. In addition to Carlsberg Pilsner, there are Carlsberg Export, Carlsberg Special Brew, Carlsberg Elephant Beer and the latest brand, Carlsberg Ice Beer, launched in September 1994 and already making a significant impact on the premium packaged lager market. The company has many high profile sponsorship arrangements, including the European Championships, the UK FA Cup and the internationally renowned English football team, Liverpool Football Club. These have kept Carlsberg in the forefront of international appeal and brand positioning.

CARNATION MILK

Nestlé has built the strength of its two milk brands around the nutritive properties of milk, the excellence of Swiss pastures for grazing cows and the company's ability to produce top quality milk products.

Nestlé Condensed Milk, claimed to be one of the first convenience foods, was first conceived by Napoleon to nourish his armies when fresh milk was unavailable. Invented as a substitute for fresh milk, the brand now places more emphasis on the uses of its products in the kitchen. Carnation Evaporated Milk is well known for its striking red and white packaging the world over.

In line with current dietary concerns the brand has been extended to include Carnation Lite, an evaporated semi-skimmed milk with no added sugar, and also the desert toppings, Tip Top and Simply Double.

The red and white packaging of Carnation evaporated milk means quality throughout the world.

Carlsberg's bold marketing has lived up to its high manufacturing standards and it is now recognised as a supremely powerful global beer brand.

CASIO

Companies need quick reactions to compete in the world of electronic technology. Things change fast and the demand for innovation, and behind it research and development, is ever-present. Those who cannot keep up with the pace fall by the wayside. But for the winners, the rewards are enormous. In less than 20 years Casio has grown from a specialist producer of electronic calculators to an international conglomerate with an annual turnover of $2 billion.

One factor has been the identification of niche markets. Casio did not try to compete with the giants of the computer and audiovisual worlds; it focused its attention on more personal items, such as watches and musical instruments. The key word has always been 'small' – witness innovations such as the electronic personal organiser and pocket television – though other lines include office machinery and cash registers.

Crucial to Casio's success have been its technical base and its worldwide distribution network. Allied to these, the company promotes heavily through advertising, public relations campaigns and point of purchase literature available in retail outlets. The cumulative result has been to establish a brand image which enhances the prospects and reputation of all its products.

Casio has grown very big by concentrating on niche markets, by building a global distribution network and by committing serious money to its marketing initiatives.

CASTLEMAINE XXXX

First brewed in Australia in 1916, Castlemaine XXXX became one of Australia's biggest selling brands – especially in Queensland where it instils great loyalty and dedication among its drinkers. XXXX is a classic Aussie lager brewed to an original Australian recipe, using authentic Aussie ingredients, such as Pride of Ringwood and Golden Cluster hops. It also uses original brewing techniques.

Castlemaine XXXX hit the UK in the early 1980s, attracting a new generation of upbeat lager drinkers. A key to the marketing success in the UK is the legendary television and poster advertising campaign which focuses on the Australian heritage, the Outback and the Aussie reputation for being "expert drinkers". The advertising has made the strapline, "Australians wouldn't give a XXXX for anything else", famous around the UK.

The brand's advertising and irreverent sense of humour, coupled with its strong Australian character, have made Castlemaine XXXX as much a success in the UK as it is in Australia. In the UK alone, an average of more than 18 pints are sold every second during pub opening hours.

Castlemaine XXXX, a classic Aussie lager, is the drink of Britain's upbeat lager drinkers.

CASTROL

Making the mundane and unexceptional look attractive and different is the objective of fine branding and nowhere is it better achieved than with Castrol. Castrol motor oil is no different from that of its other major competitors, but the company has succeeded in building a brand that identifies Castrol as the oil for the high-performance, sleek driver who only wants to buy the best. It is remarkable that such an apparently unattractive product can exude such powerful expressive values.

The branding power developed by Castrol and its GTX multi-purpose motor oil has made it the world's leading specialist brand for lubricants and allied products. The brand has a worldwide presence and Castrol lubricants are used across the range of industrial, marine, electrical, and automotive applications.

Castrol has managed its brand through three essential techniques. First, it has retained its corporate definition as a specialist, with tight focus and a rigorous emphasis on lubricants, benefiting from the recent preference for specialists who focus on a product and understand their markets. While major oil companies have much more broadly based brands covering a host of products besides lubricants, Castrol has stuck to its knitting.

Second, Castrol has invested heavily in product developments and in marketing including advertising, motorsport and other forms of sponsorship and promotions. The company has also taken care with its visual identity. This has been regularly updated since it first appeared in 1909, but the striking use of red, white and green has been retained and this has reinforced the brand's appeal.

Finally, it has nurtured a distribution chain to rival the oil majors. While most Castrol is sold through predictable outlets like motor accessory shops and workshops, the company has also experimented with sales through some of the more innovative parts of the retail chain, such as supermarkets.

Fine branding makes Castrol the world's leading specialist brand for lubricants and allied products.

You don't have to dig deep to discover the reason for Caterpillar's success: propping up the powerful brand image is a set of very down-to-earth factors that include price, reliability and after-sales service.

CATERPILLAR

Caterpillar Inc., headquartered in Peoria, Illinois, is the world's largest manufacturer of earthmoving, construction and mining equipment, industrial gas turbines and natural gas engines. Other major lines include agricultural and forestry equipment, diesel engines, engines for heavy-goods vehicles, ships and locomotives, solar power systems and generating systems such as back-up power supplies for hospitals and industry. Sales in 1994 were $14·3 billion, about half in the USA, and the workforce numbers over 50,000.

The company's early success was based upon the invention by its founders, in 1904, of the Caterpillar track – the modern generic term for the endless belt tracking system comes from the name of the company and rivals still have to use less familiar descriptions such as 'track machine'. This, in effect, enabled vehicles to lay their own roadbed and solved the problem of traction in muddy fields which hampered the large, heavy harvesters of the day. The trademark was registered in 1910 and shows the word written in the form of a caterpillar, clearly alluding to the tracking system and its ability to make good progress over difficult terrain.

People do not buy heavy plant on brand name alone. The key factors are price, specifications, reliability, delivery, after-sales service and financing. Nevertheless Caterpillar's long-established reputation for ruggedness and the ability to tackle daunting tasks efficiently and without fuss is enormously reassuring to potential customers. The name is a powerful and valuable business asset which often helps tip the balance when customers are faced with a choice between competitive brands.

CHANEL

The name Chanel is associated with elegance, style, sophistication and luxury. Whether it is clothing, cosmetics or perfume, the brand bestows its timeless appeal. Probably the most famous Chanel product is the Chanel No.5 perfume, created in 1921 by parfumier Ernest Beaux. Its name derives simply from the fact that it was the fifth sample submitted to Coco Chanel for her approval.

Chanel has a wide international appeal and owns a number of boutiques around the globe.

Chanel, shorthand for French elegance and *savoir faire*, is a brand whose timeless aura will stand it in good stead long into the future.

Though it is not widely known outside the US, to American sports car enthusiasts the Chevrolet-Corvette brand is a classic.

CHEVROLET-CORVETTE

Many sports cars come and go. Fashions change and their image dates quickly. Not so the Corvette. For two generations of Americans, the Corvette has been the prototypical sports car and its appeal remains as compelling as ever. Its distinctive styling, gutsy performance and colourful racing history have attracted a loyal, almost fanatical following.

A classic within its own country, the Corvette is surprisingly little known outside it. The image is bold, brash, and very American, enhanced by a series of high-profile owners from the worlds of music, film and sport. Above all, the Corvette epitomises the fun and freedom of youth – hence the nostalgia,

reflected in around 700 owners' clubs around the world and even a National Corvette Museum at the production plant at Bowling Green, Kentucky.

The Corvette is the flagship of the Chevrolet group, now part of General Motors. First produced in 1953, it has been constantly updated while retaining its classic features: the two-seater fibreglass body, manual transmission and the throaty roar of its massive 5·7 litre aluminium block engine. Production is only 480 cars a week, maintaining the tag of exclusivity, yet by 1992 the Corvette had passed its millionth sale, making it by far the highest selling sports car of all time. Despite increased competition, mainly from Europe and Japan, the Corvette still commands 36 per cent of the US high-performance market.

CHOMEL

Founded in 1979 by Mrs Kuok Cheng Sui, Chomel is a local Singaporean fashion brand which caters for the woman in her 20s to 40s. The name Chomel was chosen for its local roots: 'Chomel' is the Malay word for cute or pretty.

Chomel's brand philosophy stresses value for money and serviceability and the view that the right combination of clothes and accessories can assist those wanting to dress well and keep up-to-date, so Chomel creates affordable, well co-ordinated stylish, classic workwear and casual wear for the modern woman. In addition to apparel, Chomel also makes a wide and varied range of accessories, handbags, shoes and belts to complement its costumes.

Chomel's fashion collections, store design, visual display, advertising and promotions are created by in-house teams who meticulously maintain a high standard of quality. Chomel has attained an international retail presence, and its 16 chains make its products available in Malaysia, Indonesia, Thailand, Brunei, the Philippines and Saudi Arabia.

Affordable yet stylish, Singapore-based Chomel is likely to become well known as a fashion brand outside its existing markets in South-East Asia and the Middle East.

The Chrysler brand is associated with prestige, design and engineering innovation.

CHRYSLER

Today's price-conscious car-buyer is less interested in the added 'gimmicks' attached to the vehicle than he is in a vehicle's inherent qualities, such as a balanced blend of comfort, performance and style. So says one of America's largest and most successful car-makers, Chrysler.

Since its foundation in 1924, Chrysler Corporation and its Chrysler brand have been associated with prestige, design and engineering innovation. It has now outlined the qualities that make a true 'luxury' car for the 1990s: a well-appointed, comfortable interior with practical, unpretentious features that are easy to use; a stylish, provocative exterior design; a balanced blend of performance, handling and fuel efficiency; high value that exceeds customer expectations in every area.

In recent years, Chrysler has aimed its branding at a younger age group. The company has said that, since the beginning of the 1990s, the age of its average customer has dropped 15 years, and is now in his mid-40s.

CITROËN

Citroën's distinctive double-chevron trademark is synonymous with a certain Gallic flair in the world of motoring. The company's reputation for style, innovative engineering and sheer quirkiness has been fostered by promotional campaigns bordering on the bizarre: the trans-Sahara and trans-Asiatic expeditions of 1922 and 1931–32; epoch-making endurance marathons; the company name emblazoned in lights up the sides of the Eiffel Tower over the years 1924–34.

The Torpedo in 1919 was Europe's first mass-produced motor car. Since then Citroën has been responsible for most of motoring's most avant-garde technology and distinctive designs. Of the former, notable landmarks include front-wheel drive in 1934 and the unique hydropneumatic suspension system in 1954. Of the latter, there were the Traction, launched in 1935 and immortalised by Inspector Maigret and a thousand war films; the DS, rising from the kerb with a gentle sigh; and above all the 2CV.

The 2CV is the ultimate basic, no-frills motor car. Somehow it manages to be both cheap and chic at the same time – to say nothing of durable, notching up 6·5 million sales between 1948 and 1990. Typically for Citroën, not everybody loves the 2CV, but those who do would not exchange them for anything.

Responsible for some of motoring's most avant-garde technology and distinctive designs, Citroën is synonymous with Gallic flair in motoring.

CLUB MED

Founded as a non-profit-making organisation with a simple philosophy, Club Méditerranée today is a global tour operator with more than 140 different holiday villages in over 35 countries. It is a far cry from the collection of tents grouped around a bivouac kitchen in Mallorca originally set up by Belgian water-polo player Gérard Blitz in 1950. The philosophy, however, remains unchanged: to provide Club members with all-inclusive holidays and the chance to relax, by participating in sporting activities and enjoying good food in congenial company. Also unchanged is the atmosphere of international camaraderie, with Gentils Membres (known as GMs) coming from 40 different countries. Club Med aims to cater for GMs of every status from all age groups, but recommends certain villages as more suited to couples, singles or families.

The brand has been extended to other areas of tourism, such as villas, the Vienna City Club, and corporate and incentive travel, as well as cruises in the islands of the Caribbean and the South Pacific on the Club Med 1 or Club Med 2 yachts. However, the brand remains best known for the villages located in renowned beauty spots as far apart as the Gulf of Aqaba in Israel, the Swiss ski resort of St Moritz and Bora Bora in Polynesia. Typical perhaps is the village at Ouarzazate in Morocco, set in a spectacular oasis on the edge of the desert and surrounded by the Atlas mountains. GMs can relax by the village swimming pool, take mint tea with the Berbers or follow the amethyst trail into the mountains. Particular emphasis is placed on the friendly attitude of the Club's employees. Club Med has a core staff of some 25 000 "Gentils Organisateurs" (known as GOs) drawn from 52 nationalities.

An intriguing mix of convenience and culture, Club Med is an upmarket package holiday brand with romantic roots and a desire to cater to all kinds of holidaymaker: families, couples and singles.

CLUEDO

Cluedo, the murder mystery game where the players have to deduce 'whodunnit', has been extremely popular with home 'sleuths' since its launch in 1948. Today it embodies much of the traditional British brand: a sense of style and status, and nostalgia,

Invented by a British solicitor's clerk, Anthony Pratt, the game involves having to deduce who murdered Dr Black, in which room and by what means. With six characters, six weapons and nine rooms, there are a potential 324 different murder combinations. So popular is the game that its participants, Miss Scarlet, Colonel Mustard, Professor Plum, Reverend Green *et al.* have become household names.

Waddingtons, which was acquired by Hasbro in 1995, has sold over 100 million Cluedo games to date. The game is played in over 20 countries and the manufacturers sell just under three million sets a year.

Cluedo, a murder mystery board game played in over 20 countries, is based on the universal fascination with country house detective stories.

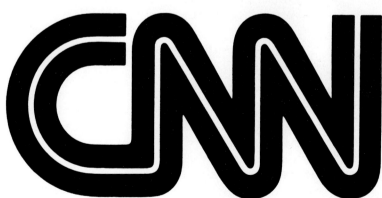

Based in Atlanta, Cable Network News broadcasts 24 hours news, features and current affairs 168 hours a week.

CNN

Based in Atlanta and owned by the Turner Broadcasting System, Cable Network News broadcasts twenty-four hour news, features and current affairs, one hundred and sixty-eight hours a week. Funded by Cable Subscriptions and advertising space CNN has sixty-eight million subscribers in the United States and its sister network, CNN International, has a further one hundred and ten million subscribers world-wide.

Since its formation in 1980, CNN has set up five other news networks, three private place-based networks, one radio network and three websites, all branded with CNN.

COCA-COLA

Few people in fewer countries can fail to react to the twin brand names, Coca-Cola and Coke, two of the world's most recognised trademarks. Today Coca-Cola is distributed to more than 195 countries through a unique bottling franchise system developed at the beginning of the century.

Coca-Cola is one of the dominant forces in world branding, exuding some of the core values of its generation. Coke's mission in the 1960s to represent the spirit of love was so successfully accomplished that it placed Coke at the heart of a generation, which loved it. Good branding has ensured Coke exhibits all the essential values of a consumer product. The expressive values of "the real thing" still excite the young and lively, while the central values of a product so intimately associated with American culture have ensured its success in every emerging and developed country. There is some suggestion that Coke, two of whose values are freshness and näiveté, is now struggling to find a new central value in a more cynical world; that is a strategic branding question undoubtedly being examined by the men in Atlanta.

The syrup on which Coke is based was created in Atlanta, Georgia, in 1886 by a local pharmacist, Dr John Styth Pemberton. His book-keeper, Frank M.Robinson, devised the name for the drink from its principal ingredients, the coca leaf and the kola nut, and wrote it down in his flowing copperplate. It remains the brand's logo to this day. The basic brand proposition, "Coca-Cola is a refreshing beverage with a great taste" has also gone unchanged for over a century.

The times were propitious for the brand to take off. Mass transportation was beginning to enable branded products to be marketed and distributed throughout wide territories. Many other leading brands, such as Kodak, Heinz, Quaker, Waterman, Sunlight and Sears Roebuck, can also trace their history back to the same period of rapid commercial expansion. But this circumstance only explains part of the brand's success. Early on, the company realised that branding was not mere labelling, but the creation of a distinctive personality. The Coca-Cola Company has sought constantly to reinforce the identity of the brand through powerful and consistent advertising campaigns and careful marketing and packaging.

The well-known Coca-Cola contour glass bottle was originally developed in 1915. The Coca-Cola "red disk" logo – featuring a prominent image of the original contour bottle – has been a core element of the global "Always Coca-Cola" advertising campaign.

The brand has been developed to suit changing tastes and market conditions. New forms of packaging for Coca-Cola, such as tins and plastic bottles, have been introduced over the years. Special versions of the Coca-Cola logo have also been produced in many languages around the world and the range of flavours has been extended to cater to changing tastes and life-styles. These include caffeine-free Coca-Cola, diet Coke, caffeine-free diet Coke, Coca-Cola light, caffeine-free Coca-Cola light, cherry Coke and diet cherry Coke.

Coca-Cola displays virtually every characteristic of a classic brand. To students, the marketing of Coca-Cola is a textbook case of meticulous brand management and development over more than a century. The company will need to draw on these skills in the future to meet the challenge of the many colas now on the market, especially own-label rivals.

Coca-Cola's global dominance in the soft drinks market shows no signs of abating, despite feverish activity from arch-rival Pepsi and the growth of private label copycats.

COCKBURN'S PORT

Skilful branding and marketing strategy enable Cockburn's to take full advantage of today's buoyant demand for port, which it partly created. 1994 was the second successive year when Cockburn's sales worldwide exceeded the growth in the world port market.

The leading brand, Special Reserve, specifically aimed to attract new, younger, up-market drinkers, was launched in 1969 in the UK to revive what was once the world's biggest port market. With packaging designed to appeal to that sector, the brand bridged the gap between younger, less expensive ruby and tawny ports, often drunk with mixers, and top quality vintage ports, perceived as prerequisites of upper class tables, gentlemen's clubs and Oxford colleges. Under the brand name "Reserve", invented to indicate a premium style port, it combines the robust quality of ruby port with some of the depth of flavour and complexity of vintage port.

Brand strategy focuses on the enjoyment of drinking Cockburn's port with friends. It is about being sociable, relaxed and savouring the taste of port.

Cockburn's, the sophisticated port for discerning palates, is investing heavily in marketing to broaden its appeal to a younger market.

COLGATE

Oldest of the three company components, Colgate began as a soap, candles and cheese business in Manhattan in 1806. In 1873 it produced its first aromatic toothpaste in jars. Today that toothpaste, sold in tubes and the innovative Colgate pump, is itself a major brand. In 1927 the company extended its production and distribution facilities by a merger with the Peet Company. The following year Colgate-Peet merged again, with Palmolive, founded by the B.J.Johnson Soap Company.

Benefiting from parent Palmolive's reputation for innovation and quality, Colgate continues to lead the toothpaste market despite the growth of private label copycats.

COMPAQ

Compaq Computer Corporation relies on brand definition to hold its position as a world leader.

COMPAQ

Compaq Computer Corporation's decision in 1991 to adopt a single brand for all consumers and price points tipped the scales in turning its first quarterly loss into profits of around $900 million in 1994. Today the company places heavy stress on brand positioning, what it calls the "Compaq soul", as smart in all it does, human and caring in its approach, reliable in all respects, and a source of useful innovation, as opposed to innovation for its own sake. This brand image reflects Compaq's change of direction from product-centred to consumer centred.

Founded in 1982 by three engineers, Compaq quickly built a reputation on product attributes. Sales boomed in a still young computer market. The company built the first 386-based PC, notebook and PC server. The climate of pervasive PC technology at the end of the 1980s made change essential. For Compaq the solution was brand definition, conveying the image of a leading brand that customers around the world would rely on to provide the products and services they needed to easily gain access to, use and manage information.

CONCORDE

It is somewhat ironic that a venture which proved to be for its sponsors (the British and French Governments) one of the most costly commercial failures of all time should have led to the development of an aircraft which, thirty years after it first flew, remains both the fastest and most prestigious means of international transportation in the world. Concorde carries a cachet that no other aircraft can match.

When the British and French Governments first decided to co-operate in the development of a supersonic passenger aircraft one early decision which needed to be made was what to call it. Resolving the issue almost led to the collapse of the project: the name Concord/Concorde was agreed on at an early stage, but the British wanted the English spelling, the French the French. Resolving this delicate issue, it is reputed, required diplomatic skills of the highest order.

CONFORAMA

Conforama is the leading specialist distributor of home furnishings in France, with a brand image based on discount prices and customer service. Offering a wide range of furniture, decorating materials, household appliances, electronics and micro-computers, Conforama has 161 stores in out-of-town commercial centres in France and French overseas territories, five in Switzerland, two in Spain, and one each in Luxemburg and Portugal. Established in 1967, the success of the brand lies in the availability of the large range of products as a result of warehouses located near the stores and the quality of the goods in relation to the prices asked. Service quality, including after-sales service, ensures Conforama's place as a retailer of excellence.

France's leading distributor of home furnishings, Conforama's success relies on discount prices and customer service.

DANONE

The French company Danone has one of the greatest European food brand portfolios. Its only rival of any substance is Nestlé.

The brand's origins are in Barcelona and a small family yogurt production concern. With the outbreak of the Spanish Civil War, the brand was to move to new markets via the founder's two sons, one of whom moved to France while the other went to to USA. Both sons set up yogurt production companies, respectively Danone and Dannon (due to American pronunciation – a spelling that remains today). The brand is owned worldwide by Danone of France (formerly known as BSN).

The company's success is ensured by the regular introduction of new quality products into specific national markets. Notable Danone successes include the launch of the Danone "Petit Gervais Croissant" range in France, of "Combi", a breakfast product consisting of separately packaged yogurts and cereals in Spain, and of "Obstgarten Joghurt" in Germany.

Danone, a brand principally sold in France, Spain and the USA is now expanding with a vengeance into Eastern Europe, especially into Poland, the Czech Republic, Hungary and Bulgaria. In Russia, Mos-Danone runs a shop in Moscow and there are more than 60 Mos-Danone minishop kiosks in food stores around the city.

From humble beginnings in Barcelona, Danone is now one of the greatest European food brands.

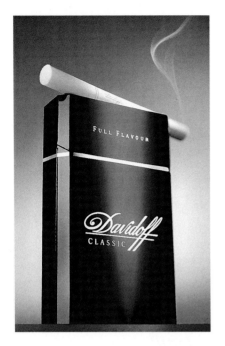

Firm belief in the importance of its brand has made Davidoff the cigarette for the discerning smoker worldwide.

DEL MONTE

The Del Monte name and shield are one of the world's oldest brands. Today the brand appears on a wide range of products all over the world, from canned fruit to fruit juice, ice cream and sorbets, tomato products and pasta sauces, fruit flavoured teas and fresh fruit.

The Del Monte identity is consistent throughout all world operations, thus ensuring maximum recognition and brand power to the consumer.

The brand Del Monte, founded in the early 1890s as the label for a co-operative of fruit canners, is today owned by several worldwide companies, who each have the right to use the name and logo. When Kohlberg, Kravis & Roberts took ownership of the Del Monte brand in 1989 with their takeover of RJR Nabisco, parts of the Del Monte empire were sold to investers in the USA, Japan and Europe.

Del Monte Foods, the largest processor of canned fruit and vegetables in the USA, also operates in the Philippines, Mexico, the Caribbean and Central America. Its fruit and vegetable products are one of America's most highly regarded and best known brand names. The fiscal sales figures for 1994 were $1·5 billion.

In Europe and South Africa the brand is traded by Del Monte Royal Foods. The brand has an exceptionally high brand share in its market: for example, it has a market share of over 20 per cent in canned pineapple. The company has also been innovative in launching pan-European brands such as Fruitini, and national products such as ice cream in Sweden, fruit-flavoured tea in Italy and chilled juice and dried fruits in the UK. Del Monte Royal Foods has recently expanded into Southern Europe, Eastern Europe and the former Soviet Union, taking the essence of the 1920s advertising slogan, "Not a label but a guarantee" to a new type of consumer. Other Del Monte brand producing companies are Del Monte Far East and Del Monte Fresh Produce.

DAVIDOFF

"Enjoy in moderation but only the best" are the words of Zino Davidoff, the patentee of Davidoff cigarettes. Born in Kiev, he emigrated to Geneva in 1911 and built up his business boasting that he only used the finest tobacco. Davidoff's vision was to create the most exclusive cigarette brands worldwide. Davidoff names include Davidoff Magnum, Magnum Lights, Davidoff Classic, Lights, Mild and Menthol, and most recently Davidoff Slims.

Such is the importance Davidoff has placed on its brand, it has protected by patent the Davidoff Magnum, the only cigarette so treated. In line with the parent company, Reemstma's, policy of worldwide alignment, Davidoff cigarettes have established themselves in the hotly contested premium cigarette segment in over 50 countries. Internationally, Davidoff cigarettes pursue a globally oriented marketing strategy with a uniform advertising campaign.

In addition to a presence in all important duty-free shops around the world, Davidoff cigarettes are successful in some South-East Asian markets. In Taiwan, for example, this cigarette range in the unusual octagonal pack has already overtaken Marlboro. The first steps towards the goal of international market leadership in the premium segment have therefore already been taken.

DEUTSCHE TELEKOM

As Deutsche Telekom, the German telecommunications company, moves towards privatisation in the largest stock issue in German economic history, it is transforming itself from dreary state enterprise into a bright new private sector company. As part of this change, the company is adopting a new visual identity, designed to create continuity, to stress its flexibility for customer requirements and to position it among the leading telecommunications companies in the world.

The Deutsche Telekom name has been compressed down to its initials, but the corporate colours of magenta, grey, white and black have been retained.

DHL

As ever-faster electronic communications transform the world into a global village, so the demand for speedily despatched packages and original documents increases. DHL, the bright idea of three entrepreneurial Californians in 1969, has pioneered the international express delivery industry. The company's first route was San Francisco to Honolulu and back.

With its corporate objective of "being there first", DHL uses a combination of speed, service and technological innovation to keep ahead of the pack. The DHL brand is truly global: its familiar terracotta logo is carried to the furthest flung climes. The company links more than 70,000 destinations in over 200 countries and carries more than 80 million packages a year. Spearheading the DHL service is a fleet of 165 aircraft. In addition, scheduled aircraft bearing DHL packages take off every 58 seconds. The DHL brand offer has developed from parcel despatch and delivery to a WorldMail system designed to be as 'user-friendly' and all-encompassing as a national post office.

DHL is an international delivery service that takes pride in being first with the post.

DINERS CLUB

When Diners Club was launched in 1950, the cashless society was a mere twinkle in an entrepreneur's eye. Some 45 years later, this vision has become – almost – a reality. The entrepreneur in question was Frank McNamara, who one day found himself without enough cash to pay for the restaurant meal he had just eaten. This sobering experience prompted McNamara to create his own charge card. He found 27 local restaurants that were prepared to accept his Diners Club card as payment, and 200 people who were prepared to pay him five dollars for the privilege of using it.

Within a year, the number of cardholders had grown to 42,000 and McNamara had found well-heeled friends wanting a slice of the action: Alfred Bloomingdale, for instance, who eagerly sank $25,000 into the operation. Diners Club soared in popularity during the rest of the 1950s, and was given huge boosts when motel and petrol companies agreed to accept it. By 1960 Diners Club was being accepted in over 50 countries.

Today the silver and blue card is promoted as the businessman's friend – an ingenious supplier of ready cash, reliability and quality, and accepted at 2·5 million outlets. Diners is now owned by US bank Citicorp. It has worldwide sales of $21 billion and boasts 6·4 million members.

Diners Club is the businessman's friend, an indispensable ingredient of business lunches everywhere.

DISNEY

The Walt Disney Company virtually invented the business of 'character merchandising' – licensing others to use your brand (usually a character from literature, television or movies such as Mickey Mouse, Kojak or Thomas the Tank Engine) on products not related to the business activity for which the character was originally developed. Thus Mickey Mouse and his friends are not just used in films, TV, records, videos, comics, books and magazines, but also on clothing, watches, toys, jewellery, lunch boxes, children's furniture and even food. For example, until 2002, Nestlé has the exclusive right to Disney characters on branded foods in Europe and certain other countries. Disney will earn $176 million in licence fees and Nestlé knows it has a winner – it successfully pioneered the concept in Germany with 'Mickey Mousse', a chocolate-flavoured dessert.

Disney and Mickey Mouse became household names in 1928. The company now has huge publishing interests, four theme parks (the latest just outside Paris), movie studios, record labels, stores, a mail order business, hotels and a television channel. Disney's philosophy is to build 'an integrated system in which each Disney property enhances and reinforces the whole'. Jealously guarding its brands, the company is an extraordinary example of the power which can flow from well managed brand properties.

DOMESTOS

Domestos is the UK's leading brand of bleach. Since its launch in 1929, the Domestos brand has typified high standards in home hygiene.

Domestos' success has a number of strands. Its owner, Lever Brothers, has established a set of consistent messages and a steadfast proposition (even with new variants or products) and the product performance always lives up to its promise. Second, Domestos has been innovative. The product has been constantly improved and reformulated over the years. Keeping pace with these developments, its family of products has grown to include Domestos Mountain Fresh and Domestos Glacier, both launched in response to consumer demand for perfumed bleach. Third,

Domestos has been given strong marketing support. Millions of people are familiar with the slogan "Kills all known germs...dead!" This was coined for an advertising campaign back in the 1970s, and it has helped establish Domestos's heritage as a "germ killer" in the hearts and minds of consumers.

The brand was drastically repositioned in the 1990s with the introduction of Domestos Multi Surface Cleaner, the first general purpose cleaner on the market to contain bleach. Specifically designed to clean surfaces as well as kill germs, its presence in the marketplace was further strengthened by the introduction in 1994 of Domestos Multi Surface spray.

Domestos is Britain's premier germ-killing bleach

DOM PÉRIGNON

Dom Perignon is a high quality vintage champagne produced by Moët et Chandon. It is named after the Benedictine monk who, as cellarer to the Abbey of Hautvillers until his death in 1715, reportedly composed the recipe for the sparkling wine that has now become known as champagne.

The Dom Pérignon champagne was first sold in the USA in 1921 and is only produced in those years when the grapes are particularly good. This means there is a very limited supply and what is on the market is highly sought-after by the cognescenti and fetches premium prices.

A champagne for the connoisseur, Dom Pérignon is named after the eighteenth-century Benedictine monk said to have discovered the recipe for champagne.

DOUWE EGBERTS

The Douwe Egberts 'D.E. Seal' has become one of the most famous trademarks in Holland and is used across the company's extensive range of coffee products.

The brand is a representation of the original wax seal which was used after the death of the founder in 1806. In those days the seal bore the letters W.D.E., an abbreviation for 'the Widow Douwe Egbert' who, with her sons, had taken over the running of the company. The seal was used on coffee and tobacco bags, on the labels of bottles of spirits and on the company's correspondence – a fine early example of co-ordinated branding!

A brand, of course, can only succeed as long as it continues to provide satisfaction. It says much for the high quality of Douwe Egberts' marketing and manufacturing, therefore, that the brand continues to satisfy an ever-growing diversity of consumer tastes and expectations. The Douwe Egberts 'D.E.Seal' may truly be said to represent excellence in relation to coffee.

Holland is one of the world's leading trading nations with strong early associations with the Dutch East Indies. It is no wonder that Holland has a wealth of powerful brands in such areas as tobacco, spices and coffee.

A part of almost every style trend and youth cult since the 1960s, Dr. Martens has entered everyday language, denoting its distinctive footwear.

DR. MARTENS

The famous air-cushioned sole was originally developed in the mid-1940s by a German doctor, Klaus Maertens, to help relieve the pain of an injury he sustained while skiing. The shoe was so effective that, working with a university friend, Dr Herbert Funck, Maertens developed the design commercially and sold shoes all over Germany to elderly women with foot trouble.

In the late 1950s, the two doctors decided to look for a manufacturer in the UK and eventually chose an established industrial footwear company, which was part of the R. Griggs Group in Wollaston, Northamptonshire. The name was anglicised to read 'Dr. Martens' and the first pair of black boots rolled off the production line on 1 April 1960. Called 1460s in deference to this date (1-4-60), these boots are still popular today.

Dr. Martens have been part of almost every style trend and youth cult since the 1960s, including the skinheads and punks of the 1970s and the "grunge and indie" movements of the 1990s. The profile of Dr. Martens customers is extremely diverse. They are worn by popstars and policemen, super models and street buskers; the brand is popular with people of all backgrounds and all ages.

The R. Griggs Group now exports Dr. Martens boots to more than 50 countries. The wide product range now includes sandals and shoes with high heels. Sales have grown impressively but, despite international success, the brand remains true to its roots: the original sole construction is unaltered and every pair of footwear is still made in the UK in Wollaston village.

DR PEPPER

The 1904 St Louis World Fair marked a milestone in American consumer tastes – the first hamburgers, the first hot dogs, the first ice-cream cones and the first large-scale promotion of what was to become America's favourite non-cola soft drink, Dr Pepper.

The drink originated in 1885 with an English pharmacist experimenting with flavours in a drugstore in Waco, Texas. The company is the oldest major manufacturer of soft drink concentrates and syrups in the USA and the fourth in market share. And a huge market it is – a third of all the soft drinks in the world are consumed by Americans, to a value of $50 billion a year. Of this market, the fastest growth is in the non-cola section, which now accounts for 34 per cent of the total, with Diet Dr Pepper, introduced in 1991, currently the market leader.

Dr Pepper has always cultivated an image of youth and informality. Like other soft drinks, it is heavily promoted, ranging from the sponsorship of the *American Bandstand* TV show in the 1960s to the painting up of Volkswagen 'Beetles' as part of its drive into European markets in the 1980s. Since 1995 Dr Pepper/7-Up has been part of the British confectionery and beverages giant Cadbury Schweppes and the company's avowed aim is to become the biggest non-cola manufacturer in the world.

With an image of youth and informality, Dr Pepper is America's oldest and most popular soft drink.

DRIZA-BONE

What an irony that one of the world's favourite raincoats originated in one of the world's driest continents! Even the name of this Australian caped oilskin riding coat (which is pronounced 'dry as a bone') refers to the parched and sun dried bones of animals in the arid Australian Outback. But the traditional Driza-Bone was first used for those plying the Great Southern Oceans on windjammers. When the sailors went ashore the coat was rapidly adopted by wealthy landowners and labourers alike.

Driza-Bone has retained its wide appeal: the coat is now worn as much as a fashion item as it is as a high performance workcoat. Driza-Bone conveys good, old fashioned, down-to-earth traditional values and a commonsense approach. The brand-owners pay attention to modern values by seeking to use natural fabrics, with the protection factors of naturally occurring wool lanolins or a well-guarded formula of oils and waxes.

Although renowned for its traditional caped styling and extra length, the brand now encompasses jackets, oiled leather bags, natural lanolined pure wool sweaters and hats for hail, rain and shine. Great care has been taken to ensure that each item carrying the Driza-Bone name reflects the core values of the brand. Driza-Bone is today exported to more than 20 countries, with sales outside its country of origin now exceeding its traditional domestic market, where it is a leader in its field.

Driza-Bone – the Australian coat that keeps you dry as a bone – is a fashion item as much as an efficient workcoat.

The Dulux dog, plus high quality and woman-directed marketing, make Dulux Britain's leading paint brand.

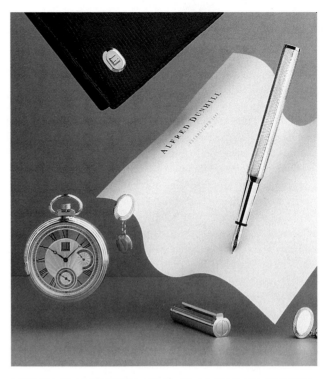

Less than twenty years ago Dunhill was a niche brand focused mainly on pipes and gas lighters. Now, it is a major international luxury products brand and its success is a tribute to careful, skilled brand management.

DULUX

Dulux is Britain's leading brand of paint. It is owned by ICI Paints, who operate in 24 countries and license to a further 17. Dulux has virtually universal recognition among adults in Britain.

Dulux is a successful brand for a number of reasons. It is a high-quality product, competitively priced, has strong marketing support and has directed product innovations. It has been particularly skilful in anticipating and influencing consumer tastes in colours and finishes. Its new Naturals range and wood effects Brushwood range have been particularly successful.

The introduction in 1961 of the Dulux dog – a memorable and lovable character – has helped to contribute to the brand's success. The old English sheepdog associated with the Dulux brand has become such a universally recognised icon that dogs of his variety are likely to be referred to as a 'Dulux Dog'. Dulux has also had the foresight to pitch its marketing at women, whom they recognise as often being the chief decision-maker on household issues. Not only is the woman of the house choosing when, where and in which colour the home should be decorated, but, increasingly, she is also the main purchaser and decorator.

The brand's major challenge is the rapid concentration of retail buying power in the hands of a few major do-it-yourself chains, including B&Q and Homebase. These massive chains have launched a plethora of own-label paint, enabling the retail owners to squeeze Dulux's margins.

Dulux's brand values over the years have proved as durable and consistent as its paint product. Dulux can be credited with pioneering the DIY paint sector which has become the most potent driving force in the DIY market.

DUNHILL (ALFRED)

Alfred Dunhill, the English name in luxury, specialises in a full collection of clothing and accessories for men.

The company was founded in London over 100 years ago in 1893 by Alfred Dunhill, grandfather of the current Chairman, Richard Dunhill. Alfred's maxim, which still holds true today and refers to the entire Alfred Dunhill collection, is "It must be useful, it must work dependably, it must be beautiful, it must last, it must be the best of its kind."

At the heart of Alfred Dunhill there is an English tradition and a commitment to superb quality and style. Richard Dunhill ensures that the legacy of his grandfather continues, with priority given to traditional values and contemporary requirements. Through all of its activities, Alfred Dunhill creates an expression of English style which is recognised the world over.

The Alfred Dunhill collection includes two seasonal menswear ranges, watches, jewellery, writing instruments, a leather collection, fragrance, pipes and cigar accessories, and eyewear, whiskey and cognac.

Today, the Alfred Dunhill collection is available in 21 countries, in over 100 retail outlets, 70 of which are Alfred Dunhill stores.

DUNLOP

Dunlop is the leading sports goods, tyres and automotive parts manufacturer employing 3,000 people world-wide.

The production of tyres has always been one of Dunlop's key strategic activities. The brand is associated with innovation and its involvement with motor sport has helped to raise awareness of their specialism in performance tyres.

Within the sporting arena Dunlop's four key brands are Dunlop, Slazenger, Carlton and Maxfli. The parent company is currently attempting to develop a distinct image for each of

The leading sports goods, tyres and automotive parts manufacturer employs 3,000 people world-wide.

these, beginning with Dunlop footwear who are relaunching their Green Flash brand. The cheap n' cheerful plimsoll, first released in 1933, soon gained credibility through endorsement by leading tennis players. In the 1950 Wimbledon tournament four out of five players wore them. The 1980s were barren years, with the brand unable to compete with increasingly high-profile brands such as Nike, Reebok and Adidas. The latest fashion trends, with their roots entrenched in '1970s retro', may provide Dunlop with the ideal environment in which to rejuvenate their brand.

DURACELL

Duracell has taken over from Ever Ready as the world's best-known battery brand. The rapid speed of its triumph was due almost entirely to its powerful promotion of alkaline long-life batteries, when its competitors were sitting on their laurels as market leaders, churning out the weaker zinc carbon products. Rarely have so many great names, like Eveready in the USA and BEREC/Every Ready in the UK, been humbled so quickly and so convincingly.

In fewer than 10 years long-life alkaline batteries accounted for 50–60 per cent of unit sales in the USA and over 70 per cent by value. Union Carbide, the American zinc carbon market leader, complained that "Duracell sneaked in on us". In fact the market leader saw little to gain from winding down zinc carbon production, as this would only emphasise their lack of preparedness to sell what the consumers now wanted, longer-lasting batteries. Britain's Ever Ready was a sitting duck, having also failed to develop the long lasting alkaline battery range. It had failed on many other fronts as well. For example, it failed to realise the value of its brand name and replaced Ever Ready with BEREC (an acronym of British Ever

REady Company) to differentiate itself from its American competitor. British conglomerate Hanson Trust bought BEREC in 1981 and promptly relaunched the Ever Ready name, but it was unprepared to deal with the alkaline challenge and the company was wound down and then broken up.

The British Ever Ready company has actually made some comeback under its new owners, the American consumer goods company, Rawlston Purina, but Duracell is now established as the world's leading brand in the important and growing long-life sector of the market. Though 80 per cent of the world's battery market is still zinc carbon, in developed markets like the USA, alkaline batteries now predominate.

Duracell's success in batteries closely matches that of Michelin in tyres: both brands took on entrenched interests which, when faced with a superior, longer-life product, refused to take the threat seriously. As with tyres, the existing brands in time started to respond and their brand strength ensured that the newcomer did not just ride straight over them. But the battery market will never be the same again.

A leader in the long-life alkaline battery market, Duracell triumphed over established competitors such as Ever Ready.

DUREX

The most popular of all condoms sold in the UK are Durex brand condoms, produced by LRC Products. In recent years the AIDS crisis has led to a resurgence of interest in such products and considerable growth for the Durex brand.

The Durex name (from DUrability, REliability, EXcellence) has existed since the early 1930s and is used on many different types of condoms as well as spermicides. Until the early 1970s, public attitudes towards contraception meant that brand promotion was necessarily undertaken in a discreet, low-key fashion; opportunities for advertising and point of sale display were strictly limited. Now, however, the brand is highly visible and is promoted through advertising, public relations campaigns and sponsorship: motor cycling and hot air ballooning have both been used extensively in the past and Music TV has been used more recently. Durex retains a strong market position but, in the long term, it will have to face up to brighter and more dynamic rivals, such as Virgin's condom brand, Mates.

The Durex brand name, almost synonymous with condoms in the UK, returns to relevance with the AIDS crisis.

ELASTOPLAST

Elastoplast is Britain's leading first-aid dressing. Developed by Smith & Nephew, the brand is in the enviable position of maintaining leadership in all its markets worldwide. Invented in the 1920s, Elastoplast was widely promoted by Horatio Nelson Smith, the nephew in the corporate name Smith & Nephew.

The early success of the brand was due to its high-stretch fabric material coupled with an effective adhesive. The brand has a strong consumer and hospital heritage in the UK and has been responsible for pioneering the latest technology for treating wounds. Smith & Nephew has continually improved the brand's product range. It now encompasses a wide variety of innovative spin-offs, such as Waterproof Airstrip, Clear, Hypoallergenic and Cushioned. There are even Elastoplast plasters printed with children's favourite cartoon characters.

As a leading authority in the healthcare market, Smith & Nephew ensures that the product development of Elastoplast continues to bring the latest wound care developments into the consumer marketplace. In 1995 the company launched Elastoplast Ultra plasters. A breakthrough in the level of performance achieved by a plaster, Ultra has translated the latest medical ideas on moist wound healing from the hospital arena into an everyday convenience.

Elastoplast's owner, the socially committed but highly innovative Smith & Nephew, has been around slightly longer than the UK's National Health Service and probably retains more goodwill from the public.

ELIZABETH ARDEN

"Beauty should be a combination of nature and science." So said Florence Nightingdale Graham, who opened the first Elizabeth Arden store in 1910.

Located on New York's Fifth Avenue, it signalled the start of the modern cosmetics industry. It was also the launchpad for Graham's personal fiefdom, which she ran until her death some 56 years later.

Graham supervised every aspect of the business. The brand name, for example, was a combination of her favourite girl's name, Elizabeth, and the title of a favourite Tennyson's poem, "Enoch Arden". Graham was first and foremost a maker of cosmetics, and she passionately believed that cosmetics had to be innovative. With a team of chemists at her command, she experimented incessantly and eventually revolutionised the cosmetics world with her theory of "colour harmony", the notion of applying make-up to match your clothes rather than your skin colouring.

The colours in Graham's stores were as distinctive and co-ordinated as those in her rapidly expanding cosmetics range. They invariably featured red doors and damask pink interiors. The well-groomed society ladies who shopped there could be assured that the products would be of the same high quality the world over.

Graham's early products were some of her best and most enduring. They were also her favourites. Some found unexpected uses: the Eight Hour Cream, launched in 1935, was massaged into racehorses' legs and used to treat their bruises. The fragrance called Blue Grass was named after the Kentucky blue grass on which her racehorses grazed.

In more recent years, Elizabeth Arden lost its independence and was eagerly swallowed up by a number of multinationals, but its brand strength remains intact. Fragrance house Fabergé bought it in 1987 and launched a fragrance called Red Door. Two years later Elizabeth Arden was on the move again – this time into the hands of Unilever, who injected sophisticated chemistry to the Arden aesthetics.

A winning formula of nature and science, Elizabeth Arden has successfully broadened the appeal of its upmarket cosmetics.

ELLESSE

The word 'Ellesse' is a combination of Elerra, the Italian town where Ellesse headquarters are located, and the letter 'S' taken from the name of the founder, Leonard Servadio.

Ellesse was launched in 1959, when Servadio opened a shop named "Ellesse" specialising in men's slacks. Fit to bodyline, Ellesse's elastic jersey pants became a sensation of that time, enhancing the Ellesse philosophy that "clothes are the second outer skin of our body".

In 1975, Ellesse unveiled its tennis wear, pioneering the use of colours when all competitors restricted their tennis clothing to white. Ellesse adopted the halfball of a tennis ball for its logo; the colour of its logo was the red of passion and orange of a brilliantly shining sun. The Japanese Goldwin company started to produce Ellesse skiwear under licence in 1976; in 1990 Goldwin bought the Japanese trademark rights for Ellesse clothing and sporting goods. Goldwin handles skiwear and Goldwin Moda, a subsidiary of Goldwin, handles tenniswear, golfwear and swimwear under the Ellesse name. Ellesse currently has contracts with influential sports figures throughout the world.

Ellesse is the embodiment of stylish sports clothing, constantly challenging orthodoxies and universally recognisable through its bright orange and red logo.

ERICSSON

In the rapidly expanding and highly competitive telecommunications market, the Swedish company Ericsson is an international leader. In today's "information society", the brand is recognised for its advanced systems and products for wired and mobile telecommunications in public and private networks. A leading supplier of electronic defence systems, Ericsson has 75 000 employees and is active in more than 100 countries.

In a market that has experienced dynamic growth, Ericsson has been a leading supplier for more than a century, demonstrating its ability to keep ahead of technological change: in 1994 more than 60 per cent of Ericsson net sales came from products which did not exist on the market three years earlier. A particularly strong growth area is mobile telephony: Ericsson's mobile telephone systems serve 22 million subscribers in 74 countries.

Ericsson acts like a new kid on the block, despite its long heritage, ensuring a constant supply of new products and ideas that should see it prosper in today's increasingly deregulated telecommunications environment.

ESSO/EXXON

The ESSO name has its origins in the initials of the Standard Oil Company of New Jersey, the chief oil company of the Rockefeller Oil Trust. When the Rockefeller Oil Trust split up in 1911, the new Standard Oil Company of New Jersey did not retain complete rights over the ESSO name in all parts of the USA and the company was forced to trade under different names in some states. This was a clear impediment to the company's aim of coherent and global branding, and in 1973 it coined a new brand name, Exxon, for use throughout the USA and many other countries worldwide. The cost of the name change amounted to the incredible sum of $100 million, with most of the money spent on new signs and repainting the livery on its vehicle fleet.

'Exxon' was chosen mainly for its visual distinctiveness and legal availability (Maltese is the only language in the world with a double X). The fact that both ESSO and Exxon are approximately the same length and both have the same first letter simplified the cross-over between names. Care was also taken to use broadly the same colour combinations for the old and the new identities. Such was the sensitivity of the name change, and the legal and trade-mark procedures that it required, that the company surrounded its operation with a massive wall of secrecy. Today ESSO/Exxon is the biggest oil company in the world, with revenues of a massive $113 billion.

Esso/Exxon is the biggest oil company in the world, with revenues of a massive $113 billion.

Fairy Liquid has survived periods of faddishness and derision to become the world's favourite "gentle" washing-up product and a symbol of family harmony.

Founded over a century ago in Helsinki, Fazer is now a dominant player in the Scandinavian confectionery market and retains huge loyalty among Finnish consumers.

FAIRY LIQUID

Until the late 1950s, consumers expected to use the same bar of household soap for washing and cleaning. Washing powers also developed at the time, but washing liquids, of which the foremost brand was Procter & Gamble's Fairy Liquid, quickly supplanted all alternatives.

Fairy Liquid first reached the more progressive household sinks at the beginning of the 1960s, and it was quickly accepted as a status symbol for the young housewife who cared about her hands. From the start, the company emphasised Fairy Liquid's softness, indeed early advertising went: "Now hands that do dishes can be soft as your face with mild green Fairy Liquid."

The brand became the subject of jokes and cartoons in the 'Swinging Sixties', and even the empty bottles became a fad to be used for model rockets, windmill sails, pencil holders and feeders for little pigs. The success of the brand over the following 30 years has three main explanations. First, branding was very well managed, with continued and unfailing use of the mildness theme. Second, the company used the same advertising formula of a mother and daughter commercial. Third, Nanette Newman was hired to plug an economy message, namely that the brand lasted longer than rival brands.

Fairy Liquid reached a milestone in 1988 when it sold 100 million bottles in a year. In 1992, Fairy Liquid's branding formula was changed and the name modified to Fairy Excel. The famous bottle became dumpier and squatter, and added ingredients improved its performance against grease.

FAZER

Finland's foremost confectionery brand, Fazer had its origins in a Helsinki cafe in 1891. Karl Fazer quickly moved from simply catering to producing chocolates and sweets, putting a premium on quality. In 1908, his confidence and business had so grown that he moved to bigger premises and registered his marque.

In the 1920s, Fazer started making a broader range of foodstuffs, including biscuits, margarine, jellies and pastilles. Bread, hamburger buns and many new ranges of sweets and chocolates were to follow. In the last 10 years, Fazer has expanded rapidly over Scandinavia, buying businesses in Norway, Sweden and Demark. In 1991, when Fazer celebrated its centenary, it announced the sale of 49 per cent of the company to the British food company, United Biscuits.

Today Fazer is a hallmark for excellence and enjoys immense popularity. Two-thirds of Finnish customers have said in a survey that they buy Fazer products regularly.

FEDEX

Federal Express, the world's largest transportation company, was established just twenty-one years ago yet now delivers to over 200 countries each business day. The first company to introduce a time-sensitive package delivery system, FedEx employs 122,000 people, operates 500 aircraft and 37,000 vehicles across the globe.

Federal Express are the world's largest transportation company.

FIAT

FIAT, the abbreviation of Fabbrica Italiana Automobili di Torino, was founded in 1899 by the senator Giovanni Agnelli. The company quickly saw the export possibilities, and in 1909 the first FIAT arrived in the USA. FIATs arrived in Australia six years later.

The company not only exported the brand, but it began to license production of the vehicles to countries such as Austria, which turned out its first Fiat in 1907. By 1945 the FIAT was available in over 150 countries worldwide.

The group's strategy of innovation and internationalism continues to produce strong results. FIAT places great importance on applied research. From its origins in the motor industry, the company has also moved into industrial and agricultural vehicles, aeroplanes and public transport.

Fiat has seen a return to form in recent years and can now boast one of the youngest and most stylish car ranges around.

FIELMANN

Fielmann is Germany's premier spectacle brand. Founded in 1972 in Cuxhaven, the company today supplies every third pair of spectacles in the country and is the largest optician in Europe.

Fielmann has made its mark by insisting on the highest quality of craftsmanship. In both the technical and personal areas, the company ensures it has on hand motivated specialists who are wholly committed to the company's consumer-oriented philosophy. Fielmann's slogan is "You are the customer" and it stresses that its customer emphasis has been critical in reaching brand leadership status.

The company renounces short-term profit maximisation in favour of long-term success and also emphasises its price consciousness, promising to beat its rivals on cost, productivity and quality. Its slogan for its price consciousness declares: "Low prices for the many and not excessive prices for the few." Fielmann has over 7000 different frames and has launched designer lines in Paris, Milan and New York. It has 296 branches and sales of DM868 million (approx. £377 million). It sold 3·65 million pairs of spectacles in 1994.

Europe's largest optician, Fielmann claims its obsession with customer service and value for money has been the key to its success.

THE FINANCIAL TIMES

The pale pink paper of *The Financial Times*, adopted by a stroke of genius in 1893, is an immediate signal of brand identity. It has come to indicate worldwide a daily newspaper which provides first-rate objective and accurate coverage of international business information, analysis and comment.

An estimated million readers throughout the world read either the UK edition of the FT or its international edition, begun in 1979. The paper employs some 300 full-time journalists in London, 32 full-time foreign correspondents based in 19 major cities over the world and 70 stringers. Additional features explaining the brand's popularity are *The Financial Times on Saturday*, providing information and entertainment for its readers at leisure; its daily world share index first published in 1987; and the 200 or more surveys printed annually in the FT, giving analyses of developments in a wide variety of areas.

The Financial Times has extended its brand to make optimum use of its resources by establishing FT Information, FT Diaries, FT Television, FT Radio, and FT Electronic Publishing. Today's *Financial Times* was born of a merger in 1945 between two quite small-time City newspapers, the *Financial News*, founded in 1884, and the *Financial Times*, started in 1888, with a masthead claiming "Without Fear and Without Favour". In 1995 this masthead has disappeared but the reputation of the brand remains unchanged.

The FT's brilliant "No FT, no comment" ad campaign in the 1980s helped confirm the brand as the world's leading financial newspaper, and its vigorous brand extension activity is adding to this perception.

FINDUS

A brand which first built its strength on frozen peas and fish fingers, Findus now offers consumers the opportunity to capture the taste of the Orient in five minutes. Capitalising on the brand's reputation for high-quality convenient meal solutions and consumer desire for ever more adventurous products, Findus in 1994 launched new Lean Cuisine light meals (Mediterranean tuna pasta and Spanish paella), as well as a Taste of Asia range, including Chicken Chow Mein, Sweet and Sour Pork, Thai Prawn Rice and Szechuan Chicken. A new brand feature, these ranges come in pots which can be used in microwaves, eliminating the need to wash up.

Recognising the importance of continuous innovation and the need to expand the market, 1995 saw the French Pizza range boosted by the introduction of the Findus French Bread "Burger" pizza, with a choice of either cheese or bacon. Purple and yellow packaging, with "American diner" style illustrations, is designed to add impact and appeal to younger eaters. Findus is also using new packaging promoting the product's snack appeal to relaunch its French Bread Pizza range.

The Findus frozen food range, one of the UK's best-known grocery brands, has benefited enormously from continuous innovation and heavy marketing support.

FISHER-PRICE

In 1930, Herman G. Fisher, Irving L. Price, and Helen Schelle founded a toy business on the precept that each toy should have intrinsic play value, ingenuity, strong construction, value for money and action. "Children," they wrote, "love best the gay, cheerful, friendly toys with amusing action, toys that do something new and surprising and funny." These ideas were quickly translated into action. Granny Doodle and Doctor Doodle, two of their first toys, were wooden and gaily decorated and, when they were pulled, they moved their beaks and quacked merrily. Such lighthearted elements are now key distinguishing traits of the Fisher-Price line of toys.

Under its new owners, Mattel, Fisher-Price continues to enjoy a worldwide reputation for high-quality, durable toys with exceptional play value, as well as innovative (non-toy) children's products. The company also enjoys a reputation for customer care and service; its Consumer Affairs Department deals with 450 000 letters and phone calls a year. Eight in 10 of all infant and pre-school children in the developed world own a Fisher-Price toy.

A great believer in a toy's intrinsic play value, Fisher-Price is also committed to the concept of customer service.

FLORA

Flora is a good example of a brand which has capitalised and moved with ever-changing life-styles. Introduced into the market in 1964 as a sunflower margarine high in polyunsaturates, the brand did not gain any real prominence until the mid-1970s when consumers became inadvertently aware of the link between saturated fats and heart disease. From then on, in unison with advertising promoting the brand's health advantages, Flora's sales spiralled throughout the 1980s to position it as a leader in its field.

With the brand's future sponsorship of the London Marathon, the brand's profile is set to increase with its values of health and fun continuing into the next millennium.

Flora margarine is first choice for the cholesterol-conscious consumer.

FNAC

The Fédération Nationale d'Achat des Cadres (or FNAC, as it is more commonly known) was founded by two friends, Andre Esseland and Max Theret, in 1954. FNAC's superb relationship with its customers, its strong price controls, careful product selection and independence from suppliers have all contributed to its rapid and successful development as France's leading retail outlet. FNAC's culture, based on the core belief of consumer choice or 'customer liberty', has at times led to strained relations with manufacturers. Their original commercial policy has led them to be viewed by consumers as 'defenders of shoppers' rights.'

The leading French retail chain founded by two friends in 1954.

FORD

The Ford Motor Company is credited with making the motor car available to the masses. Founded in 1903 by the late Henry Ford and 11 associates, the company is now the world's second largest industrial corporation (based on sales – Fortune 500 list) and the second largest producer of automotive vehicles.

This is not to be scoffed at when the company's many problems during its existence are looked at. In court, Ford had to fight George Selden who held the patent on "road locomotives" powered by internal combustion engines. Selden had formed a powerful syndicate to protect his patent, licensing selected manufacturers, collecting royalties for every car bought or sold in America. After a lengthily fought-out battle, Ford won and, as a result, freed the entire motor industry from Selden's straitjacket.

Ford appeals to every generation, especially to the young, who prefer the sporty looks of the Escort model. It is also considered to be a good family car. This popularity of the brand stems from the foresight of Henry Ford, who insisted that the company's future lay in the production of inexpensive cars for a mass market.

In 1994, Ford's worldwide sales and revenues totalled $128·4 billion with the sale of 6·7 million cars and commercial vehicles. The brand is sold in over 200 nations and territories worldwide and has recently opened production in new trade markets such as Poland.

FUJI

A company with global ambitions has a head start when it sets up its headquarters beside Japan's Mount Fujiyama. Named after the mountain, Fuji's strategy is to make quality photographic products and sell them globally.

The company emphasises its good management practices, including an insistence on local hiring and local procurement, and a determination to form alliances with overseas partners. Fuji is also seeking to expand its worldwide networks for production, finance and marketing in accordance with evolving market conditions.

By establishing and developing its presence in the field of digital photography, Fuji is poised to enjoy an exciting future in the multi-media age. Recent developments include 'Utsurundesu' (Quicksnap, overseas), the Pictrostat 330 NExPO – Instant Colour Print System (Pictrostat 300 overseas) and products in the area of digital photography.

Fuji, already renowned for its high quality film, is poised to enjoy a new era of expansion as it develops its first generation of multi-media products.

Henry Ford's motor company has prospered over the years because of its commitment to mass-market principles and its enduring brand image as a manufacturer of affordable yet reliable cars.

GAULOISES

Apart from Maurice Chevalier, there is nothing quite as French as the Gauloise. The distinctive blue of the brand pack and rough-hewn product conveys the sense both of Parisian sophistication and of rustic simplicity. The feminine connotations of the brand name belie the brand's masculine character; Gauloise is considered a true fighter.

Seita, the brand's parent company, launched a sub-brand called Gauloises Blonde in 1984 to ward off competition. Seita appealed to its home markets by emphasising the brand's roots and origins to the native consumer. This high-risk advertising bore fruit, with massive returns of previous lost customer loyalty.

Today Gauloises is sold in over 100 countries.

The ultimate French accessory, the simultaneously sophisticated yet streetwise Gauloise has conquered over 100 countries as well as its own native land.

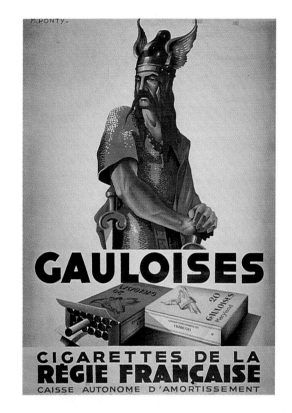

GAULOISES

CIGARETTES DE LA
RÉGIE FRANÇAISE
CAISSE AUTONOME D'AMORTISSEMENT

Gillette relaunched itself in the early 1990s and is now widely applauded for its hugely successful repositioning as a younger and more dynamic brand, in tune with New Man as well as Macho Man.

GILLETTE Ⓦ Ⓑ

Gillette has been at the cutting edge of marketing since it started promoting its razor in 1903. The company won an early lead by innovating, and then protected its position through patent and trademark registrations. Gillette expanded its international base to head off overseas competition and has undergone vigorous promotion ever since.

The company showed its flexibility and agility in the 1960s, when rival Wilkinson Sword launched a stainless steel razor blade. Gillette responded quickly to head off the challenge. Today the Gillette brand name serves as an umbrella under which the company markets its male blade and razor and toiletries products, including Gillette Sensor, Gillette Sensor Excell and the Gillette Series of high-performance male toiletries. The brand name was successfully aimed at women with the launch of the industry's first non-soap based shaving preparation for women, Gillette Satin Care for Women.

The brand continues to be the subject of massive support, with continuous development and an extensive and growing product range. Gillette was especially successful with its slogan, "The Best a Man Can Get", which was translated for export markets.

GITANES

Gitanes cigarettes are as synonymous with sophistication and class today as they were when they were launched in 1910.

Distinguished design has been a hallmark of the brand over the years, and top artists have been used for its poster designs. Between the wars, Gitanes hired world leading designers like Reno, Savignac, Guy Georget and Villemot. In the 1970s and 1980s, Ark Kane, David Bailey and Jacques-Henri Lartique worked for Gitanes.

Gitanes's packaging evokes the romanticism of Spain. The silhouette of a woman dancing holding her swirling skirt in one hand, and an open fan in the other, combines with the portrayal of swirling smoke to give a definite and appealing brand character. For a short time during World War II, the packaging carried an image of a smiling Sevilian face. A new package design by the Japanese graphic artist Mastunaga will be launched in 1996.

Gitanes has acted as a patron of the arts in its commitment to a pack design which conjures up the romanticism and style of Spain.

GOODYEAR

The Goodyear Tire and Rubber Company is one of the world's leading tyre manufacturers. It was established in 1898 by Frank A. Seiberling, but Goodyear takes its name from Charles Goodyear who discovered the rubber vulcanisation process in 1839.

When founded, Goodyear manufactured horseshoe pads, rubber bands, sundries for druggists and poker chips, but Seiberling was confident that the company's future lay in the production and development of carriage and automobile tyres. With its development and manufacture of the straight-sided tyre, Goodyear drove into the tyre market as a major player. Goodyear grew from strength to strength, first by pioneering and developing aircraft tyres, and then by introducing pneumatic truck tyres. By 1916, Goodyear had become the world's largest tyre company.

World War I enabled Goodyear to show its prowess in aircraft tyre manufacture and it set up a specialist division for that purpose. During World War II, the company made a hefty contribution to the war effort by manufacturing Corsair fighter planes, patrol airships and parts for fighting vehicles. Goodyear plants also made munitions, tank treads and military hardware.

In the 1980s, Goodyear ran into financial trouble and was the object of greenmail (the financial equivalent of blackmail) by companies seeking to take it over. By maintaining its tyre brand integrity, the company has pulled through as a profitable enterprise. It now has 87 plants in 25 countries and operates more than 2200 retail tyre centres around the globe.

Goodyear's pedigree as a tyre manufacturer catering to the needs of very different vehicles – military and aviation as well as automobiles – has helped it maintain independence in the face of attempted takeovers.

GORDON'S GIN

Gordon's is to gin what Johnnie Walker is to whisky, the brand name which commands greatest consumer awareness and respect. Both drinks are owned by United Distillers, probably the world's leading drinks brand-owners. Among United Distillers' other brands is Guinness.

Gordon's Gin was created in 1769 by Alexander Gordon and the juniper-based beverage is still made to the same original and highly secret recipe. Gordon's Master Distiller, Hugh Williams, is among the few who have access to the potent drink's constituents. Gordon's is of course famous for its green bottle and crisp, refreshing taste, but in Europe, Gordon's is sold with red and yellow packaging and this has led to some cheap imitations being sold to look like Gordon's.

The recent launch of Gordon's & Tonic in a can was designed to appeal to those who lead an outdoor, sociable life-style. The new tone was assisted with an advertising campaign catchlined "Innervigoration", designed to appeal to those seeking a kickstart to an active and exciting evening with friends, rather than those about to put on their slippers for a quiet tipple round the fire. Cinema advertising and clever, teasing posters have all tried to jazz up the Gordon's brand.

Gordon's Gin, with its top secret formula, is forging ahead with aggressive marketing plans designed to give the brand a much bigger slug of the young adult market.

GREEN GIANT

Green Giant is the leading American and Canadian vegetable brand. It is also the number one brand in frozen vegetables in Japan.

Created in 1907, Green Giant has developed a reputation for branding excellence. Its owners have treated the brand with care and conservatism, ensuring that it commands a premium price in a relatively undifferentiated, commodity-style market. The Jolly Green Giant values indicate a brand that is happy, almost childlike and healthy.

The brand has two interesting features. First, it is not the identical mark in each country. In France, for example, the Green Giant name on the tin is translated into French (Géant Vert), though the appearance and the positioning of the brand are consistent across all markets. Second, an unusual feature of the brand is that it has two registered marks. One is the highly distinctive Jolly Green Giant himself; the other, the brand name itself. The dichotomy arose purely by accident, but it illustrates that, however much care one takes in conducting due diligence on a brand name and a trademark, untoward events can still shatter the best laid plans. In this case, the manufacturers had wanted to follow the usual course and register the name, but local trademark law prohibited a company registering a mark

that was taken from a geographical location. Trademark authorities objected to the use of the Jolly Green Giant mark on the grounds that the Minnesota Valley was affectionately known as the Valley of the Jolly Green Giant. The company's failure to register the mark forced it to register the symbol itself to secure some form of statutory protection. With evidence of use, the name was later registered in its own right.

The Green Giant manufacturer, Pillsbury, is recognised as a leader in agricultural research and development. The company's sweet corn breeding programme is the most advanced in the world and it has refined an integrated pest management system, now the industry standard for responsible use of pesticides and other chemicals.

Green Giant has overcome branding difficulties to become the leading frozen vegetable supplier in North America and Japan.

GUINNESS

The famous stout has its origins in Dublin, where it was first brewed in 1789, but it has achieved the status of a world brand by dint of its exceptional colour and a series of advertising slogans and messages.

The famous thriller writer Dorothy L. Sayers was working for the Guinness advertising agency when she composed the memorable Guinness slogan to celebrate the Guinness toucan motif:

> If he can say as you can
> Guinness is good for you
> How good to be a toucan
> Just think what two can do

By dint of clever branding, Guinness had also become known as a healthy drink, rich in iron and a nutritious supplement for pregnant women. This reputation, rather than exceptional development of the product, ensured that the drink's branding remained secure.

In the 1960s, the Guinness family, who continued to run the company, diversified unwisely into a range of non-drink areas, and this threatened the future of the company. A new chief executive from Nestlé, Ernest Saunders, put the black drink's branding at the top of his priorities. He put Guinness into cans for the first time and spearheaded the "Guinless" advertising campaign, restoring the drink's popularity with a new, younger drinker. Saunders brought his company notoriety when it was involved in a scandal over the acquisition of the Distillers whisky group. However, the so-called 'Guinness Affair' gained such publicity that the drink benefited.

Guinness remains largely secure as the doyen of black stouts, a brand that is part Irish, part British and completely global for the informed and discriminating beer drinker.

The ice-cream of the connoisseur, Haagen-Dazs is an innovative blend of the exotic, the remote and the distinctly curious.

HAAGEN-DAZS

New York entrepreneur Reuben Mattus was making ice creams as early as the 1930s. He only hit on the Haagen-Dazs name in the 1960s and registered the brand as a trademark in 1961. The first three flavours manufactured were vanilla, chocolate and coffee.

The name's origins are rather less mysterious than they first appear. Mattus concocted the name with its curious spelling to give it a Danish ring, as the Danes were makers of particularly good ice creams at the time. The strange name has undoubtedly helped the company to promote an ice cream which was an innovative blend of the exotic, the remote and the distinctly curious. Haagen-Dazs has stayed the course, when many imitators have fallen by the wayside, by defending its brand name vigorously. The number of flavours has grown from the original three to 25 and the brand is particularly strong in the USA; in the early 1990s its made a strong pitch for the international market.

Haagen-Dazs has built on the excellence of its ice-cream brand by launching a retail chain. The USA has 250 Haagen-Dazs shops, and the rest of the world 85. Acquired by Pillsbury in 1983, Haagen-Dazs is now part of Grand Metropolitan, Pillsbury's acquirer in 1989.

HABITAT

The history of Habitat mirrors the vicissitudes of British style, society and corporate finance over the last 30 years. At its founding in 1964 Habitat stood at the forefront of the British fashion boom of the 1960s. Its new vision of modernity – functional, attractive, well-made and affordable – had a profound influence on British and international design, enhanced by its well laid-out shops which encouraged browsing rather than 'the hard sell'.

The early designs, mainly the work of Terence Conran, were eclectic in their influences: Scandinavian furniture, Italian colours, French cookware. Nevertheless the tableware, furnishings, textiles and other products remained distinctively 'Habitat' in their clean and practical lines. Habitat remains pre-eminently British although in recent years its star has dimmed as standards of domestic design, especially in the UK, have improved.

Although it no longer has a monopoly on aesthetically pleasing yet practical designs, Habitat's furniture and household items continue to exert a powerful hold over the middle-class imagination.

habitat

HALLMARK

Hallmark Cards Inc. owes its high profile to blanket coverage of a single, clearly-defined market. In the world of greetings cards it is the undisputed market leader, with sales of around 11 million a day in a hundred countries and 20 languages. Its creative staff of 700 design around 21 000 cards and 9000 related products a year. Special divisions cater for the Black American, Hispanic, Jewish and 'alternative' markets.

The company's lead is enhanced by its special shops, whose massive selections make them the natural first port of call for anyone with a card to buy. As a result, Hallmark's crown device logo and its slogan, "When you care enough to send the very best", are recognised by well over 90 per cent of all Americans.

Diversification extends little further than the traditional areas: gift wrappings, party goods, Christmas decorations, mugs, photo frames and the like. Recently, though, the company has also started moving into technology-based products such as electronic shopping.

Hallmark seems to be on the way to becoming a byword for greetings cards, such is its dominance – especially in the USA – of this dramatically expanding market.

THE FINEST TOYSHOP IN THE WORLD

Hamleys, which recently turned in a sparkling profits performance, has shown that becoming a British institution does not have to mean an end to forward-thinking marketing initiatives.

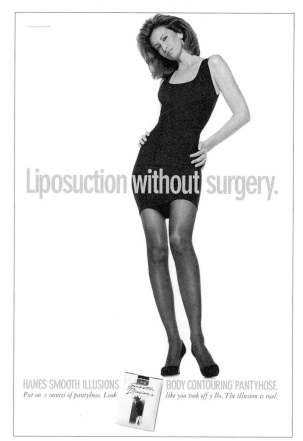

Constantly at the cutting-edge of fashion trends, Hanes Hosiery is a brand associated with customer-focused innovation.

HAMLEYS

Hamleys is a classic British brand. It runs the gamut from traditional to high-tech toys but weaves its marketing magic into all of them.

Christened "Noah's Ark" by founder William Hamley, the original, Holborn-based store was crammed with the best toys of his day. Weaned on this rich diet of innocent amusements, William Hamley's grandsons took over the business and in 1881 opened a new branch on Regent Street, where it remains to this day. In 1921, Hamleys opened on six floors of its Regent Street premises, thereby becoming the biggest toy shop in the world.

Hamleys today has become a major British attraction for adults as well as children, rivalling the changing of the guards at Buckingham Palace or the British Museum as a key stop on any tour of London. It is still one of the world's largest toy stores, stocking over 35,000 different toys, games and children's gifts. At Christmas this mecca of toy addicts is visited by some five million people.

HANES

Hanes Hosiery is one of America's leading hosiery companies, a byword for stockings and fashionable apparel for three generations. Hanes Corporation came into being when two hosiery companies bearing the same name merged in 1965. The resulting company instantly became a brand leader.

Since then, the company has won plaudits for pioneering many new hosiery developments. For example, Hanes was the first to replace silk with nylon in the production of stockings, and the first to recognise the changes in customer perception of colour and design in hosiery. Hanes was the first to introduce pastel shades in its products. Hanes was a marked beneficiary of the 1960s fashion for shorter skirts and more visible legs.

Hanes's leading products include seductively named items like Silk Reflections, Smooth Illusions and Resilience. Hanes's success with its L'eggs brand resulted in L'eggs going out on its own in 1972 as a separate company, called L'eggs Products Inc. Sara Lee Corporation acquired Hanes Hosiery in 1979 but continues to develop the brand as a separate and distinctive property.

HARIBO

Haribo, the world's biggest manufacturer of fruit and wine gums, started life as the humblest of cottage industries. In 1920, 27-year-old Hans Riegel from Bonn (hence the name HA-RI-BO) left his job with a sweet company to go it alone. The initial assets of the company amounted to just one bag of sugar, a copper kettle, a stool, a marble plate and an oven.

While Hans Riegel worked in a backyard washroom making bear-shaped fruit gums by hand, his wife Gertrud would deliver them to customers by bicycle. Soon the bicycle gave way to a car and the business grew. By the start of World War II, Haribo employed 4000 people making fruit gums and liquorice sweets. Hans Riegel died in 1945, and the following year his two sons Hans and Paul took over the business. In 1971 Haribo took over the bakery and sweet manufacturer Baren Schmidt. More recent acquisitions include Maoam (1986) and Vademecum (1993).

Haribo now sells enough of its trademark "Gold Bears" every year in Germany alone to circle the world three times, if laid end to end. The company has also become the world's largest manufacturer of liquorice products. Other Haribo products include "Weinland" wine gums, Happy Cola gums, cough sweets, chewing gum and cakes and pastries.

With five factories in Germany and seven abroad – in France, Austria, the UK, Denmark and Spain – Haribo's products are exported to 73 countries worldwide.

The world's largest manufacturer of wine gums and liquorice, Haribo is a textbook lesson in how to become a global player without losing the cottage industry qualities – personality, attention to detail – which are the foundations of success.

HARLEY-DAVIDSON

The Harley-Davidson Motor Company of Milwaukee owes its very survival to brand loyalty. At the start of the 1980s, after years of pressure from Japan, the company appeared to be in terminal decline: poor workmanship, antiquated manufacturing processes, indifferent management, and bad labour relations. From having a 77 per cent share of the US heavyweight bike market in 1973, sales slumped to 27 per cent.

Harley-Davidson is more than just a brand, it's a lifestyle.

But to a dedicated band of American bikers, the idea of Harley going under was unthinkable. Elvis Presley, Burt Reynolds, Sylvestor Stallone or the gum-chewing patrolman on a Japanese machine? The Harley, low-slung, grand and heavy, throbbed with adventure and the freedom of the open highway. There was nothing safe or anonymous about the Harley. So there was still life. Things turned around after a management buyout in 1983. The new management got rid of the weaknesses, building up a new reputation for quality and durability, and cashed in on the strengths through massive advertising. A new generation wanted to experience the classic American motorbike – the typical rider is in his thirties – and the market share is now back up to 50 per cent.

Exploiting an image like Harley-Davidson's is easy, demonstrated by the extension of the brand into male cosmetics and fashion clothing.

HARRODS

It is perhaps curious to list as an international brand a retail store which, in effect, has only one main outlet – in Knightsbridge in Central London. Harrods, however, is recognised worldwide and has a powerful reputation for quality and excellence, all in somewhat 'British'

context. Harrods is potentially one of the most licensable brands in the world because, being a luxury retail brand, it could be applied equally successfully to almost any up-market product. The introduction of Harrods satellite stores at major international airports is perhaps Harrods' first step towards becoming an international or even global retail brand.

HARVEY'S

The image of Harvey's Bristol Cream is almost identical to that of sherry itself – an old-world, patrician appeal, and very English. Its rather staid, old-fashioned bottle has its natural place beside the whisky decanter on the sideboard of a book-lined drawing room, with a fire burning in the grate.

The brand has a history to match. The Harvey family goes back to an eighteenth-century ship's master from Bristol. In the 1840s it started specialising in the Spanish wine trade, importing and blending its own sherries. Its mainstay was the dark sweet Bristol Milk. Then, in the 1860s, it came up with a new, smoother blend – cream compared to other people's milk.

Despite remaining what it has always been, an independent, single-product family company, Harvey's of Bristol now dominates the international sherry market. It accounts for 12 per cent of the 11 million cases sold annually, and Bristol Cream is by far the best-selling, and best-known, brand in the world.

While retaining its old-world, very English, patrician appeal, Harvey's Bristol Cream dominates the international sherry market.

HAVANA CLUB

As with tobacco leaves for cigars, Cuban sugar cane is considered internationally to be of ultimate quality. Unusual for a white spirit , the rum is aged for three years, making it the only matured spirit of its kind.

Havana Club is a market leader in the Cuban, old Soviet bloc and Eastern European countries and is set to advance in the West under the distribution of the Pernod–Ricard group.

Havana Club, aged for three years, is the only matured spirit of its kind.

HEINEKEN

At the core of every great brand is a great product – as demonstrated by Heineken. Company founder Paddy Heineken claimed for his company "one of the strictest quality control programmes I have ever encountered, ensuring that Heineken products meet the same high standard, throughout the world". This passion for product quality still characterises the Heineken brand and it is carried through into packaging, advertising and distribution. Great care has been taken to ensure that the distinctive Heineken label is updated periodically, but in a way which preserves all the existing brand equity and does not undermine long-term loyalties.

Heineken claims to be "Probably the best lager in the world". The world agrees.

HEINZ

The HJ Heinz Company of Pittsburgh, Pennsylvannia, is one of the twentieth century's best known, most vibrant and successful international companies. Founded by Henry John Heinz in 1869, the company not only markets the famous eponymous brand but also includes Weight Watchers, StarKist and Ore-Ida under the Heinz umbrella.

Although famous for its "57 varieties", Heinz now comes in over 3000 different permutations in more than 200 countries. This generates around $7 billion in annual revenues, with exports accounting for over 43 per cent of the total take. Heinz tomato ketchup is the company's flagship product and the number one ketchup worldwide.

Heinz has created some enduring advertising slogans, the most famous being, "Beanz Meanz Heinz". The baked beans product has also unwittingly benefited from its association with pop painter Andy Warhol. Heinz has prospered by not resting on its laurels. It has focused on brand renewal and innovation, paying careful attention to changing consumer needs.

Heinz is one of the few brands to have made the quantum leap to icon status and, despite repeated assertions that its heyday is over, the brand continues to produce handsome profits.

HERSHEY'S

Hershey's is the pre-eminent chocolate brand in the USA. Milton Hershey produced the first Hershey's milk chocolate bar over 100 years ago, priced at one nickel. His company pioneered the concept of mass availability, not just in every store but in specially selected, high visibility locations within every store.

Although many Americans perceive European chocolate as of higher quality than domestic brands, this has not prevented Hershey's from maintaining its dominance. This despite the scores of foreign chocolate brands that have gone to seek their fortune in the USA. Hershey's staying power lies in the high degree of consistency and consumer satisfaction delivered by the brand.

Although the company produces a wide range of strongly-branded chocolate products, including the famous Hershey's Kisses (introduced in 1907), Hershey's is careful to limit brand extensions. Indeed the brand could be considered a triumph of product over marketing, since for the first 60 years of its life it was not advertised at all.

Hershey's is to the USA what Cadbury's is to the UK, a brand that has become part of the national identity and which has prospered despite fierce competition.

HERTZ

Hertz makes the point that branding applies as much to services as to products. It also demonstrates that brand names do not have to be descriptive to be instantly recognisable.

Now a wholly-owned subsidiary of Ford, Hertz is the undisputed number one in the world of car rentals. It operates in 150 countries, with 5400 outlets controlling 450 000 vehicles. The company enjoys a very high profile. For instance, its name in yellow and black stands prominently near the information desk of most of the world's major airports.

Hertz's success rests on two central factors – a tradition of reliability and depth of infrastructure. The company grew out of the operations of the pioneer in the field, Walter Jacobs, who started renting out Model T Fords in Chicago in 1918. Its management practices have developed in line with its expansion. Long also a leader in the rental of heavy equipment for the building and construction industries, Hertz now offers a comprehensive range of back-up services such as computerised driving directions, cell phone services and insurance claims administration.

Undisputed leader in car rentals, Herts shows that branding can also apply to services.

HEWLETT-PACKARD

Few giants in the information technology market are bigger, more enduring, and more all-pervasive than Hewlett-Packard. Hewlett-Packard has been part of the IT revolution since its beginnings in the 1950s. In this time it has built up a formidable reputation for quality and technical innovation, often working in tandem with the other giants in the field: its computers, for instance, were among the first to exploit Intel's Pentium chip and its researchers helped develop parts of Microsoft's Windows operating system.

Hewlett-Packard's workforce of around 100 000 worldwide now handles orders of $25 billion a year, about half in the USA. Its products tend to be at the upper end of the scale, both in sophistication and in price. The fields covered are immense, ranging from fax machines and personal computers to specialist medical and scientific equipment and vast telecommunications systems, but it is always good for company profile to be the market leader in one area. In the case of Hewlett-Packard, this area is printers. Since 1984 over 30 million of its laser and inkjet printers have been sold. Perhaps more importantly, they are the industrial standard – all rival companies need to make their printers compatible with the methods developed by Hewlett-Packard, and in many cases pay licensing fees for their use.

Beyond the technological front, the company is very aware of its corporate image. It operates a stated policy of economic, intellectual and social responsibility, both through its educational and environmental projects and through philanthropic donations amounting to $67 million a year.

Part of the IT revolution since its beginnings in the 1950s, Hewlett-Packard means quality and technical innovation.

THE WORLD'S GREATEST BRANDS

HILTON

Hilton could have been a famous bank brand instead of the world's most recognisable hotel name. When founder Conrad Hilton set off to Cisco, Texas, in 1919, he had bank management on his mind and a deal waiting to be struck. Instead he bought a hotel and decided that brand management would be a lot more lucrative.

Three-quarters of a century later, Hilton owns, manages or franchises 225 hotels and resorts. The biggest hotel group in the world, it was the first genuinely international hotel chain, the first to put air conditioning in guest rooms and the first to offer a worldwide central reservations system. It also virtually invented the concept of the hotel franchise.

Hilton has built a formidable reputation as "America's Business Address", notably with its strong airport links, but it has been striving to match this success in the leisure market. Some of its most leisure-oriented resorts include the Hilton Aikoloa Village and the Hilton Hawaiian Village in Hawaii, the Pointe Hilton Resorts in Arizona and the Innisbrook Resort in Florida. The expansion of its resorts properties prompted a new corporate logo in January 1995. The Hilton Vacation Station concept, which offers an accommodation package tailored to families, is also a determined attempt to redress the business–leisure imbalance.

More classical properties include the Waldorf-Astoria and the Millenium in New York City, the Fontainebleau Hilton Resort and Towers in Miami Beach and the Palmer House Hilton in Chicago. Hilton also has sizeable gaming operations. Its Hilton and Flamingo brand casinos and riverboats now rank among the world's most profitable and popular.

With record breaking revenues of $1·5 billion in 1994 and a 40 per cent increase on this for the first half of 1995, the company shows no signs of weakening. True to Conrad's brand-conscious vision, the company plans to use aggressive marketing programmes to ensure that the Hilton name begins the new millennium with even greater recognition.

Somewhat confusingly, Hilton is now run as two distinct companies. The non-US hotels were hived off in 1949 under the name Hilton International. This company has been part of the UK-based Ladbroke Group since 1987. Hilton Hotel Corporation (the US-based Hilton) operates outside the USA under the name Conrad International; and Hilton International, which has a total of 160 hotels, also has some US properties, which it runs under the name Vista International. There is one point of contact, however, for the two Hiltons: they share a central reservations system.

Hilton Hotels, a name synoymous with comfortable but reasonably priced accommodation, looks set to enter the new millennium as a single entity, ending decades of division between the North American and European operations.

HITACHI

Hitachi was founded by Namihai Odaira in 1910 in an electrical repair shop in Tokyo to make five-horsepower electric motors. Over the following 85 years, Hitachi pursued state-of-the-art applied scientific research, moving into every area of electronic engineering and electronics. It approaches the twenty-first century making mainframes, supercomputers, workstations and leading edge microchips.

Hitachi is a massive Japanese conglomerate with four distinct divisions: Information systems and electronics; Power and Industrial systems; Consumer products; and Materials. Hitachi is a global corporation, with a wide range of joint ventures, alliance and co-operation agreements for research and development. Hitachi has net sales of almost $72 000 million, income of $634 million and more than 330 000 employees.

HITACHI

Hitachi's broad range of state-of-the-art products encapsulates the enormous advances in modern electronics engineering.

You know what you are getting when you book at a Holiday Inn, any one of the two thousand, anywhere in the world.

From generators to motorbikes to motorboat engines to cars, Honda shows no desire to restrict its horizons, although it is now accelerating its use of niche marketing techniques.

![Holiday Inn Worldwide logo]

HOLIDAY INN

Holiday Inn represents reliable, no-frills, value-for-money hotel accommodation throughout the world. The origins of the company go back to the growth in car ownership and the expansion of the American highway system in the early 1950s. As travel increased, people began to demand some sort of quality assurance in the motel business. The first Holiday Inn appeared in 1952 in Memphis, Tennessee and the chain grew rapidly. You knew what you were getting with Holiday Inn – swimming pool, restaurant, air conditioning, telephones in every room, children and parking free.

The secret of the chain's success lay in its franchising policy. This placed responsibility for quality and pricing on the individual operators, but within the budget/mid–end–of–market parameters laid down by central management. By 1964 there were 500 Holiday Inns in the USA. The group entered the European market in 1968 and by 1973 had spread into Asia. It is now the largest hotel chain in the world, three times the size of its nearest rival, with around 2,000 hotels worldwide, 94 per cent of them owned by franchise operators.

Holiday Inn was acquired in stages over the period 1987–1990 by the British brewing conglomerate, Bass. It is currently moving into new areas, notably casinos and more up-market hotels such as its four-star Holiday Inn Crowne Plaza brand and Holiday Inn Select, dedicated to the business traveller.

HONDA

More famous today for its cars and motorcycles, Honda has its roots in the manufacture of internal combustion engines and machine tools. Established as the Honda Technical Research Institute in 1946 by Soichiro Honda, it was two years before the first motorcycle rolled off the production line, and 17 years before the first four-wheeled vehicles appeared.

The Japanese company is still internationally recognised for its less glamorous products, such as small general purpose engines, ATVs (all-terrain vehicles), outboard motors and lawn mowers. But its biggest revenue generators today are the motor cars, of which it is one of the world's leading manufacturers, and the motorcycles, of which it is the biggest.

In 1962 Honda began a concerted effort to become a truly international player. It established Honda Belgium in that year. Honda motorcycle production in the USA started in 1979, and the first US-manufactured Accord followed shortly after in 1982. Honda cars made in the USA are now exported to 28 countries. There are European and US regional Honda centres, which ensure that the brand is tailored to these important local markets. Honda sales outlets and production sites can be found in some 36 countries and the company's long-term aim is to "mature into a global supply network which will flexibly respond to the diversification of demand and the unique circumstances of each country".

Taking all its various activities into account, the company produced almost nine million engines in 1995. With car marques such as the Civic, Acura, Legend, Concerto and Accord, Honda caters to a wide public. It has successfully moved from a mass-market proposition to one based on careful segmentation and niche selection. In 1995, with the launch of the Odyssey, the company announced its intention to develop a strong line in recreational vehicles. It is also a leading manufacturer of micro cars – an increasingly popular antidote to today's congested cities.

HOOVER

The Hoover vacuum cleaner "beats as it sweeps, as it cleans" and the success of Hoover's vacuum cleaners has made Hoover a household name around the world. Among the golden rules of proper trademark usage is one that states that the Hoover trademark should never be used as a verb, always as an adjective. So it is not correct to "Hoover your carpet", but it is acceptable to "clean your carpet with a Hoover vacuum cleaner". Such a rule risks appearing clumsy, as Hoover is so established as a verb without any obvious damage to the company's proprietary rights in the trademark.

Today the 87-year-old, US-originated brand is partly in Italian hands: the European arm was acquired in 1995 by Candy SpA, a privately owned, Brugherio-based manufacturer of electrical appliances. It remains the market leader in floorcare products, selling in excess of one million units a year. Hoover European Appliances Group (as the Candy subsidiary is called) employs 3000 people in 10 European countries and sells 400 000 white goods annually.

Hoover suffered severe embarrassment when an over-generous promotion offering Hoover purchasers air tickets to the USA was overwhelmed by demand, but the company has cleaned up the damage with little detrimental after-effect.

Having your brand name turned into a verb is quite an achievement, but just one of many for this much-trusted vacuum cleaning giant.

HORLICKS

Horlicks is often thought of as the bedtime drink, a result of its highly successful 1930s advertising campaign, "Night Starvation Story", which dramatised the benefits of sound, refreshing sleep, obtained from the regular bedtime consumption of Horlicks.

The original brand, malt and bran, was sold in the form of a dried powder as an infant food. With the addition of sterile milk before the drying process, Horlicks as we now know it was patented as a malted milk in 1883 by its founders, James and William Horlicks.

Horlicks remained a family concern until 1969, when the company was bought by the Beecham Group, under whose guidance the brand has kept abreast of new developments in the hot milk drinks market, whether it be the first "instant malted drink" or responding to trends towards convenience, health and variety with new pack sizes and flavours.

Recent advertising has seen Horlicks repositioned as a daytime, stress-relieving drink, aimed at women and, in particular, younger females.

Horlicks has subtly transformed itself from a bedtime drink for kids into a stress-reducing daytime drink for adults, particularly women.

HORNBY

Every father's favourite toy, Hornby is a household name and the UK brand leader in the field of model railways. Named after Frank Hornby (1863–1936) who invented Meccano, the brand has survived several changes of ownership since Meccano Ltd developed the first Hornby train in 1920.

The original strong brand image of solidity, authenticiity and attention to detail has remained unchanged by mass-production and technological change which added the electric train to the clockwork model in 1925 and introduced plastic to what had formerly been an all-metal system in 1949. In fact technological advance and increased volume throughput have allowed improvements: the locomotive driving wheel, for example, was a solid object with raised spoke detail in 1954; it now has plated nickel rims, rivet detail and see-through spokes.

New models of Hornby trains are constantly introduced to maintain interest in the brand and supply the needs of a changing market. Particular coups were the production in the 1980s of models of Thomas the Tank Engine and Friends and of British Rail's ill-fated Advanced Passenger Train, whose carriages tilted when cornering, as on the genuine article.

HORNBY® RAILWAYS

Hornby continues to supply up-to-date authentic model trains for fathers (and their children) to play with.

HOVIS

Asked to name a bread brand in the UK, most consumers will name Hovis. In a market which is typically fragmented, the brand has a wholesome, home-made, nutritious image which accords well with the current interest in healthy products.

The Hovis brand was created in 1886 by an innovative baker called Richard Smith who developed a flour containing vitamin-rich wheatgerm at a time when the usual practice was to remove the wheatgerm as it soured the flour. He took his discovery to a manufacturer, S. Fitton & Sons, and they marketed it as "Smith's patent germ flour". It did not sell well and with insight the makers assumed the name was at fault. So in 1890 a national competition was organised to find a better brand name. The £25 prize was awarded to a student for the name Hovis, derived from the Latin "Hominis vis" meaning the strength of man. A major new brand was born. The standard brown Hovis loaf with the name pressed into the side has changed little over the years, but Hovis has expanded its product range into more trendy whole-wheat and stone-ground loaves, capitalising on consumer interest in natural and healthy diets with plenty of roughage. Yet advertising in the 1980s concentrated on the bread's other great quality, its Britishness, and the ads conveyed a nostalgia for greatness. A recent development in the Hovis story is the development of the Hovis Half Loaf, "the half size loaf with full size slices".

For many years Hovis was a leading British brand of brown bread; today, under its "Raised the Hovis way" banner, it leads a multi-billion pound baked products market.

Hovis has recently capitalised on two great British concerns – healthy eating and nostalgia – and is using inventive brand extension techniques to broaden its already considerable appeal.

HUGO BOSS

Today's chic men's fashion brand has some real 'street cred' behind it. Founded in 1923 by Hugo Boss, the company was originally a manufacturer of working clothes, such as overalls and raincoats. Later on it moved into the production of uniforms. The marketing of Hugo Boss did not get seriously under way until the 1970s when it moved into profile-raising motorsports sponsorship activities. During that decade it also introduced fine Italian fabrics into the mainstream German fashion market.

Through a series of far-sighted marketing manoeuvres, Hugo Boss has come to represent all that is trendy in contemporary clothing.

The automation of the company's warehousing and shipping processes at the end of the 1970s allowed room for considerable expansion of the clothing range. Shirts were produced from 1981 (the year in which the company extended its sports sponsorship to include tennis); polo shirts, sweatshirts, knitwear and a cosmetics licence followed in 1984, and leatherware in 1986.

With turnover of DM1 billion (approx. £0·4 billion) the now publicly listed company fell under the control of Italian textile giant Gruppo Marzotto SpA, which thereby became the largest manufacturer of men's clothing in Europe. It is only relatively recently that the company has decided to exploit its brands. The concept of a new HUGO fashion brand was introduced in 1993. Along with the new BOSS and BALDESSARINI brands, this has helped the company extend its operations considerably.

It now has around 500 sales points in 29 countries, with a growing number of fully-owned "BOSS-shops". Taking its cue from the Far East and India, HUGO managed to win over the fashion police of the international catwalks in a very short space of time. The three brands generated a massive DM377 million – approx. £163·9 million – in the first half of 1995.

The company continues its long-standing commitment to sponsorship, albeit of a more cultural kind: it has just signed a deal with the Solomon R. Guggenheim Foundation in New York, which runs the city's famous modern art museum.

Hush Puppies, blazing the trail of branding in the shoe world.

HUSH PUPPIES

Hush Puppies blazed the trail of branding in the shoe world. Previously footwear manufacturers had been rather shadowy figures, producing goods under licence to the retail chains who sold them. To some extent this is still the case, with branding largely restricted to specialist areas, such as trainers and work boots as fashion garments.

But as well as providing 'image', branding offers a guarantee of quality. In the late 1950s, the casual footwear market was notorious for dubious workmanship. The reassurance that came with the name Hush Puppies, reinforced by the faithful, soft-eyed beagle, was instrumental in the brand's enormous and rapid popularity.

Hush Puppies is only one part of the footwear giant, Wolverine World Wide of Rockford, Michigan, the largest work and outdoor footwear company in the world. Launched in 1958, it is now by far the biggest-selling brand in the casual market, with annual worldwide sales of 26 million pairs (1994). From the outset Wolverine operated a policy of brand globalisation – it is the brand that is exported rather than the product – and now licenses and markets Hush Puppies in more than 60 countries. Much of the design work is now done in Italy.

The shoes are viewed as comfortable, well-made, good-value and slightly conservative. The one-time association with pigskin suede has been forgotten. Hush Puppies are heavily promoted worldwide, notably through flagship retail outlets in new licensee markets. In established markets, factory direct sales are becoming commoner. Advertising and, to some extent, designs are tailored to local life-styles. The name now also appears on a number of brand extensions, especially casual clothing, mostly for children.

The IBM brand promises technological leadership, reliability and quality.

IBM

International Business Machines – better known by its acronym IBM or by the friendly term "Big Blue" – is one of the best known and best respected brands in the world. The IBM brand quite simply promises technological leadership, reliability and quality.

A combination of computing inventiveness, management professionalism and marketing expertise won it the position in the 1950s of probably the world's leading brand. When Paul Rand created the now famous IBM logo in that decade, the IBM was the computer, as the Hoover was the vaccum cleaner. Such was consumer enthusiasm, customers even queued up outside the company's factories to pull them off the production line.

IBM led the way in computer technology for business and personal consumers through to the 1970s, when the company and the brand started to be victims of their own success. Clones and technologists undermined the IBM package, size made it harder for IBM to offer the former service excellence, and rivals offering less service but equally reliable products undercut its formerly premium prices. The brand was under threat.

Consumers rebelled against the former king of the computer, arguing that it had become arrogant, expensive and uncaring. The stock price fell, the management lost heart. IBM responded by creating smaller, semi-independent business units which carried their own messages. That did not work as the new smaller units failed to provide the continuity of the single IBM brand. IBM then sought to re-emphasise its brand name and rebuild a clear and unified identity. It backed this with a global advertising campaign conveying the image of a warmer, more flexible company, and a customer-driven organisation. Research now suggests the new messages are already paying dividends.

IBM has learned the hard way that branding is an evolutionary process. It must respond to customer needs and expectations, and it requires constant updating and monitoring. One false step, and the work of generations can be threatened.

IKEA's distinctive blue and yellow logo symbolises good value, pleasant and functional furnishings, light and comfortable in the Swedish mould.

IKEA

IKEA is the leader in home furnishing stores, and can claim large credit for creating a market which has mushroomed in the last decade. In fact IKEA traces its history back to 1943, when a Swede called Ingvar Kamprad started a mail order firm.

Kamprad was a remarkable man. He was only 17 years old at the time and his sole experience was selling fish from his bicycle, but the mail order business boomed. The name he gave the firm, IKEA, was composed of his initials together with those of the farm and parish where he grew up. IKEA published the first of its catalogues in 1950 and opened its first store in Almhult eight years later. From these small beginnings grew a world-leading store chain whose distinctive blue and yellow logo symbolises good value and pleasant if functional design. The IKEA product is invariably light and comfortable in the Swedish mould, and its stores are located out of town, where there are parking and restaurants for the adults and facilities for the children.

In 1994 some 116 million people visited IKEA stores, which are all run under franchise from the company.

INTEL

'Intel inside' is one of the best known and simplest catchlines in the computing industry. It makes sense for those who know nothing, and it speaks volumes about the sophistication of the technology for those that think they know everything.

Intel is the world's leading supplier of microprocessors and other semiconductor products to the computing industry. Approximately 75 per cent of computers are based on Intel-architecture technology. Launched in 1971, Intel grew by at least 22 per cent every year in the 1980s, and it topped 30 per cent annual growth in the 1990s. Unusually for a high-technology company, Intel has invested heavily and successfully in advertising. Intel's message is that

business success starts with the Pentium processor, and it has been rammed home as far afield as Peking and Tokyo, London and the Americas.

Intel has offered a steady stream of high-performance microprocessors at affordable prices and it has worked with industry leaders to develop the hardware and software technologies that will make PCs increasingly useful and productive.

'Intel Inside' is one of the best known and simplest catchlines in the computing industry.

The Interflora brand name and the winged messenger allow independent florists to work together in the provision of a highly sophisticated international service.

INTERFLORA

Commercial floristry is a business where, as in catering, the product has to be prepared on the premises. It is a business which, therefore, lends itself to small proprietor-managed businesses. Interflora is a member-owned Association of independent florists – 60,000 world-wide – who co-operate in the provision of a high speed, personal, international delivery service. A private currency, called by members the Fleurin, and based on the Swiss franc, is used to settle internal accounts and the Association also assists with training and the maintenance of trading standards.

The core *raison-d'être* of Interflora is, however, the provision of a world-wide flower delivery service under a single brand name. In this it has been remarkably successful – Interflora's annual business is currently well in excess of £60 million, the brand name inspires confidence and reassurance and is synonymous with the service offered.

IVORY

When Ivory was launched by Procter & Gamble in 1879, it claimed three firsts: it was the first inexpensive white soap to improve on the purity of the premium soap of the day, called Castile Soaps, it was distributed nationally, and it floated. This last was a particularly valuable quality as many bathers at the time drew their bath water directly from cloudy rivers.

Ivory also has an interesting design feature: it comes with a patented notch which allows the bar to be easily broken into two to lengthen its lifespan. The brand is also very versatile, suitable for washing babies as much as washing clothes. When 50,000 users were questioned in 1911 to discover how they used the soap, answers ranged from poisoning flies, to cleaning brass and copper, to shaving.

Procter & Gamble has paid great attention, not merely to Ivory's product development, but also to its price. The company has twice cut the price, but Ivory has managed to stand out from the crowded soap market by dint of its history and careful brand positioning.

The soap with a notch and an interesting history, Ivory is suitable for washing babies and clothes alike.

JACK DANIEL'S

Jack Daniel's is officially a "Tennessee Whiskey", categorically named because of its final distilling process of being seeped through vats of finely ground hard maple charcoal. After gaining whiskey-making knowledge from his preacher mentor, Dan Call Jasper (Jack) Newton Daniel was in full-time liquor production at the tender age of 13. With the Federal Government's regulation of all whiskey making operations in the early 1860s, Jack Daniel's Distillery was to become the first registered in America.

An image of honesty and believability is consistent in Jack Daniel's advertising – all adverts use real employees and the copy is in a conversational manner, creating an emotional involvement between the brand and the consumer. The parent company, Brown-Foreman, claim Jack Daniel's is the leading liquor brand in the USA in terms of brand awareness. The whiskey continues to be a major contributor to the company's profit, with great demand in over 100 countries.

Jack Daniel's is an image in men's minds ... an emotional response to a soft-spoken, restrained personality that attracts simply because it never seems to try too hard ... (*The Jack Daniel's Character*, 1955).

JACOBS

From small beginnings do great empires arise. In 1895, Johann Jacobs opened his "speciality shop" selling coffee to German burghers with good taste. More than one hundred years later, Jacobs is an important part of one of the world's greatest food conglomerates, Philip Morris.

Jacobs Café has almost a third of the coffee beans market and a quarter of the instant coffee market. With more than 15 varieties of coffee brand under the Jacobs umbrella, every taste and need in the coffee-drinking community is catered for. The Jacobs leading brand is Jacob's Café Krönung which was launched in 1966, with the famous slogan, "Jacobs Café-Wunderbar", and never looked back.

A merger with Suchard/Tobler in 1982 created Jacobs Suchard, one of Europe's most important food producers, whose operations covered coffee, confectionery and drink products. The merger of Jacobs Suchard with Kraft General Foods Europe in 1993 created Kraft Jacobs Suchard, now a subsidiary of the world's most powerful and largest packaged consumer goods company, Philip Morris Companies Inc. In 1994, Kraft Jacobs Suchard alone achieved operating revenues of US $8·9 billion.

Jacobs Café has more than 15 varieties of coffee brand catering for every taste and need in the coffee drinking community.

Jag clothing is fun, fresh, confident and energetic in accord with the Australian life-style and spirit.

JAG

The JAG fashion brand is Australia's answer to Levi's. The name first appeared on the back of a pair of washed indigo denim jeans in 1972, and ever since has been at the forefront of Australian fashion.

The brand personality, which is in complete accord with the Australian life-style and spirit, may be summed up as being fun, fresh, confident and energetic. The brand has been greatly extended beyond its original denims to include womenswear, menswear and chidrenswear. There are also two sub brands, Jag Intimates and Jag Timewear.

Jag is heavily promoted via leading fashion magazines, outdoor and other media in Australia and New Zealand and has wide consumer recognition. The company is a major Australian and New Zealand retailer, owning a total of 21 retail stores.

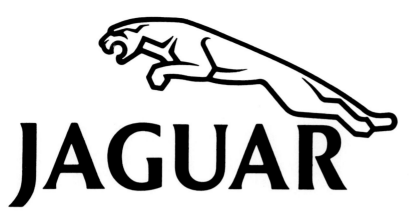

JAGUAR

The epitome of the stylish saloon-style sports car, Jaguar remains a viable and respected brand.

JAGUAR

The doyen of stylish saloon-style sports cars, the Jaguar embodies the longevity of the brand, even when all else is falling down around it. In the 1970s, when British Leyland (the marque's original maker) was embroiled in industrial relations problems, Jaguar also suffered. The car was contaminated by the parent company's notorious unreliability.

And yet the Jaguar, like the Mini, pulled through as a viable brand and vehicle. The value of the brand was well demonstrated when Ford bought the company for an enormous premium over the net tangible assets of the company. The American company has brought a disciplined management to the business and lined the car up against its Mercedes-Benz counterparts to enable it to renew their old rivalry.

JAS

Japan Airline System started life in 1971 as a domestic airline devoted to comprehensive regional coverage. Since then it has achieved remarkable growth, carrying 17 million passengers annually on 85 domestic routes.

In recent years, the company set itself the goal of becoming a global airline, and has pursued a programme of building up its portfolio of international routes. JAS's first international route, between Narita and Seoul in South Korea, was launched in 1988; its latest, between Japan and Guagzhan, began in October 1995.

JAS has followed international airline standards and placed great emphasis on excellent service and safety. The airline will enter the twenty-first century as a very reliable and competitive airline with high credentials in efficiency, personalised service and safety.

JAS enters the new millennium as a very reliable and competitive airline.

Jeep Grand Cherokee 1996

JEEP

The Jeep brand of go-anywhere, do-anything vehicle started life as a military truck. Today it has gone full-circle (on its excellent lock) and has become a popular and handy get-around for country types and the upwardly mobile. In the latter role it is, of course, facing hot competition from slicker Japanese models, but the Jeep is all about roughness and military-style toughness.

The Jeep was designed in 1940 by Karl K. Pabst in response to an invitation from the US Army for a military general-purpose vehicle. Known by many nicknames, ranging from 'Peep' and 'Blitzbuggy' to 'Beetlebug' and 'Panzer Killer', the vehicle was trademarked by its then owners, the Willys Corporation, as 'Jeep' in November 1940. Quite where the name came from, no one is sure. Like many things in World War II, it was probably thought up on the spot to fit a need, and it just happened to last. Some say it was chosen to sound like 'GP' (standing for general purpose), others that it was taken from a popular cartoon character of the 1930s that could do almost anything and was famous for making the sound 'jeep'.

Jeep Corporation, today owned by Chrysler, makes many models of Jeep, but the Grand Cherokee is particularly favoured. This is seen as a cheeky vehicle which excels in its sports utility vehicle ride and handling.

JELL-O

Not many brands in the USA can claim to be a real American institution, but when the gelatin dessert JELL-O celebrates its hundredth anniversary in 1997, it will justly claim to be one of them. Developed by Peter Cooper (of Tom Thumb Locomotive fame) in 1845, it was only manufactured commercially when a cough medicine manufacturer named Pearl B. Wait took Cooper's idea 50 years later and adapted it for the market with the help of Cooper's wife, who coined the name JELL-O.

The brand experienced chequered fortunes until 1925, when the JELL-O Company and the Postum Cereal Company joined forces to form the nucleus of General Foods corporation. Today JELL-O has evolved into a massively successful brand with a 99 per cent name recognition among all Americans.

Like many of the world's leading brands, JELL-O has succeeded by being a truly differentiated product and by denying its competitors any opportunity to catch it up. Even with an easily copied recipe, JELL-O still has no real challenger in the gelatin market and is truly a heavyweight among American brands.

JELL-O is a very important brand in the portfolio of Kraft Foods Inc. being by far the market leader in its field.

Whether "Red", "Black" or "Gold", Johnnie Walker is the world's leading brand of Scotch whisky.

JOHNNIE WALKER

Johnnie Walker is the world's leading brand of Scotch whisky. The brand's fame is truly global; from Nigeria to Cambodia to Iceland, Johnnie Walker is so established and trusted that it is used as currency and frequently smuggled across state lines for bartering purposes.

Johnnie Walker comes in three "colours". The Red is the standard product, the Black the premium and the Gold the superlative product primarily aimed at wealthy Japanese buyers. Owned and marketed by United Distillers, Johnnie Walker is presented in many different guises across the world. For example, the brand is treated as a romantic accompaniment in South America, but as a hard-nosed outgoing man's drink in the USA.

Such has been the prestige of Johnnie Walker that it has become the frequent object of attention from counterfeiters. The copies range from the outright fake (often a locally produced spirit with added colouring) to products which use the distinctive square bottle, the diagonal label and other brand "cues". Such attempts at copying may carry another brand name – Johnnie Hawker from Indonesia is an example – in the mistaken belief that, as long as the counterfeiter does not copy the name, he is safe from attack. In fact, Johnnie Walker is renowned for the toughness with which it pursues counterfeiters, wherever they lurk.

JOHNSON & JOHNSON

One of the world's leading and most diversified health care corporations, Johnson & Johnson is dedicated to developing and marketing improved products.

A talk by the English surgeon Joseph Lister in 1876 inspired American Robert Wood Johnson to found what is today a worldwide family of more than 168 companies marketing health care products in about 150 countries. Johnson's first attempts to manufacture antiseptic dressings were medicinal plasters, the forerunners of its present well-known Band-Aid brand. Johnson & Johnson now serves a broad segment of medical needs, ranging from baby care, first aid and hospital requirements to prescription pharmaceuticals, diagnostics and products serving family planning, dermatology and feminine hygiene.

Claiming to be the world's leading and most diversified health care corporation, Johnson & Johnson perpetuates its founder's dedication to developing and marketing improved products. Recent innovations have been Tylenol Extended Relief, one of a range of Tylenol brands sold from Tylenol stores in 15,000 retail outlets in the USA, and Johnson's Health Flow Feeding System, a baby bottle and nipple, designed to facilitate bottle-feeding.

The company operates according to the terms of a "credo" which lists its responsibilities in order of importance. The first is to the people who use its products and services; the second to its employees; the third to the community and environment; the fourth to the stockholders.

Johnson & Johnson

Customers aged from 8 to 48 buy from Just Jeans, one of Australia's leading jeans retailers.

JUST JEANS

Just Jeans has built its position as one of Australia's leading jeans retailers by promoting itself as an added-value "fit specialist".

The name Just Jeans, while appearing to limit the product, has not stopped the company marketing successfully to a wide age range – from eight to 48. Its core consumers, however, fall into the 18 to 28 bracket.

KEEBLER

Keebler today is one of America's best known biscuit and snack companies, but its origins were humble. Cookies baked by a Philadelphia shopkeeper and baker, Godfrey Keebler, won renown in the mid-nineteenth century for their quality and freshness. Accordingly, a company was formed. Keebler and his heirs thrived on the east coast of the USA, and in 1927 they linked up with other bakeries to form the United Biscuit Company. In 1966, the company was renamed Keebler, which also became the single brand name for all its products.

Keebler produces cookies, crackers and salty snack products under many well-known brand names, including Zesta Saltines, Town House Crackers, Wheatables and Chips Deluxe. Keebler has taken up the challenge of consumer resistance to fat with the launch of no less than five new crackers and four new cookies. The company claims its reduced-fat chocolate chip cookie not only minimises the fat but also maximises chocolate taste.

As its brand mascot, Keebler has the amiable Ernie Keebler and his friendly Keebler Elves who work at the Hollow Tree Bakery. The Elves create "uncommonly good" products in a magic oven and are among the best recognised advertising characters in America.

Minimum fat and maximum chocolate taste characterise Keebler's reduced-fat chocolate chip cookies.

KELLOGG'S

Kellogg's is a world leading food brand. Its food products have an enviable position of quality, taste and consumer acceptance, rarely matched by "own-label brands". The brand portfolio leader is Kellogg's Corn Flakes, which has maintained its position for generations. It is still the preferred cereal for millions of children and adults alike.

The Kellogg's brand is massively and successfully supported with a high percentage of total sales being ploughed back into advertising and brand promotion. From the early days of TV advertising, Kellogg's has used high-profile celebrities and catchy jingles to highlight the brand to the public. In the UK, celebrities such as Bob Monkhouse, Sooty and Harry Corbett, and Arthur Askey have all lent their talents to the campaign, the latter coining the jingle "Oh what a glorious thing to be, a golden crunchy rice crispie..."

But undoubtedly the main reason for the brand's success is its meticulous management, in a company whose corporate culture is intensely "brand-centric".

Kellogg's Corn Flakes, Kellogg's brand portfolio leader, is the favourite cereal of millions of children and their parents.

KFC

In the early 1990s Kentucky Fried Chicken faced an enormous challenge – enhancing the image of the brand at a time when consumers were increasingly aware of the benefits of healthy eating.

One of the manifestations of the need to redefine Kentucky's corporate and brand strategy was the abbreviation of the name from Kentucky Fried Chicken to KFC. The abbreviation of the name but the retention of the familiar Colonel Sanders character has been an outstanding success and has played a significant contribution to increased sales. No other chicken restaurant has reached the same level of sales across the world. With the market growing at a rate of 13 per cent per year the potential for expansion, especially within Europe, is great.

The familiar Colonel Sanders has been an outstanding success.

KIT KAT

Kit Kat is one of
the world's best
known and oldest
confectionery
brands. The
Rowntree's Chocolate
Crisp was launched in
1935, but in 1937 an
imaginative naming decision
dubbed it the Kit Kat, probably after the
notorious London gaming club of the eighteenth century.

Best-selling UK
confectionery brand, Kit
Kat was probably named
after the notorious
eighteenth-century
London gaming club and is
packaged in red and white,
the colours of St George.

Kleenex tissues offer the
fashion-conscious
consumer a range of
pastel shades to
coordinate with bedrooms
and bathrooms.

Within two years, Kit Kat was the best selling Rowntree
product. It became a classic British brand, with wrapping in red
and white, the colours of St George, the English patron saint.
During World War II, Kit Kat was advertised as a wartime food.
Later it was sold on the richness of its full-cream milk and the
star of its advertisements was Kitty the Kat.

Kit Kat embraced the leisure snack market in 1957, its
advertisements going on television with the slogan, "Have a
break, have a Kit Kat". The slogan was an instant success and its
sales leapt 22 per cent. Rowntree has undertaken subtle
modifications since then to keep it up to date, but, to its credit,
the emphasis has been on continuity rather than drastic change.
For example, the red and cream colours on the wrapper were
replaced by red and white for greater brightness and a new
typeface has been introduced. The continuity has been sustained
by Nestlé, who acquired the brand in 1988.

The price paid for its acquisition demonstrated for the first
time the importance of brand valuation for brand owners. Nestlé
paid £2·5 billion for Rowntree, a massive premium over
Rowntree's tangible net asset value and two and a half times
Rowntree's capitalisation before the takeover. The single Kit Kat
brand accounted for a large part of that premium, and for much
of Rowntree's intangible asset value.

Kit Kat is the best selling confectionery brand in the UK with
sales of over £210 million. Its dual role as a confectionery bar on
the sweet counter and biscuit in the supermarket assures it of
continued supremacy. The managing of Kit Kat offers two lessons
for brand managers: first, not to be afraid of branding continuity
where the message is clear and proven; second, the winning
product sets its own rules and has a niche on its own above the
throng.

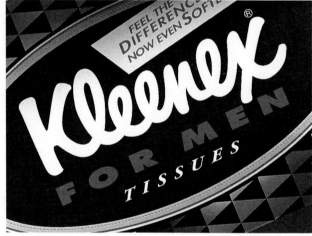

KLEENEX

Kleenex started life in 1924 as a "Sanitary Cold Cream
remover" and it was not until 1930 that its use as a
handkerchief was promoted. This, combined with the special
"Serv-a-Tissue" pop-up box, introduced in 1929, established
the brand.

The brand retained a remarkable consistency of packaging –
largely blue and white – until 1970, when Kimberly-Clark, the
brand's founder and owner, was forced to rethink. The result was
an influx of pastel shades to suit the more fashion-conscious
consumer and to co-ordinate with bedrooms and bathrooms.

Kimberly-Clark has always taken considerable care to maintain
unequivocal rights over the trademark, both through registration
and through common law. The brand-owner has built on the
Kleenex brand with great skill, so Kleenex Softique was
developed with a light scent, and Kleenex Ultra tissue has an oil-
free lotion with three-ply thickness.

KODAK

W B

Kodak for more than a hundred years has meant photography. The brand owes as much to the well-known yellow packaging of its films and photographic materials, its familiar logo and heavy advertising campaigns as to the fact that, throughout that period, it has led the photographic and cinematic world.

Company founder George Eastman is quoted as saying his achievement was "to make the camera as convenient as the pencil". In 1880 when Eastman, as junior clerk in a savings bank, fascinated by photography, registered the patent on his plate-coating machine, interest in photography was keen but its practice was limited to professionals. Eastman's development of the roll film and the inexpensive box camera were the keys to his success in making photography a leisure activity for the masses.

The name Kodak was first registered on 4 September, 1888 and Eastman later related how he came to create it.

"I knew a trade name must be short, vigorous, incapable of being misspelled to an extent that will destroy its identity and, in order to satisfy trademark laws, it must mean nothing. The letter K had been a favorite with me – it seemed a strong incisive sort of letter. Therefore, the word I wanted had to start with K. Then it became a question of trying out a great number of combinations of letters that made words starting and ending with K. The word Kodak is the result."

How little has changed! From the first Kodak camera advertised with the slogan, "You push the button, we do the rest", in 1888, and the much-loved Brownie introduced in 1900, Kodak has progressed to become a world leader in imaging technology. With manufacturing operations in Canada, Mexico, Brazil, the UK, France, Germany, Australia and the USA, the company aims to be the world's best in both chemical-based and electronic or digital imaging, with a continual flow of new products incorporating breakthrough technology, for example its development of Photo CD, in conjunction with N.V. Philips of the Netherlands, or the Kodak Creation Station.

Kodak abundantly succeeds in making "the camera as convenient as the pencil".

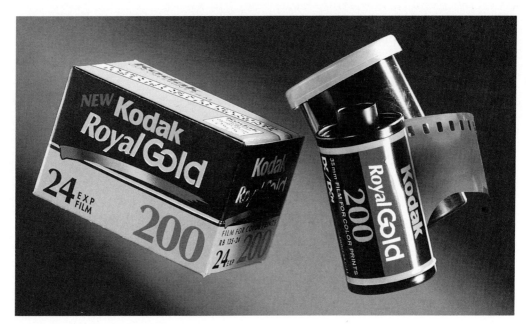

Philadelphia was launched in Germany in 1962, since becoming a favourite with German families.

KRAFT

Kraft Foods Inc, part of America's largest food company, Philip Morris, practises world-leading branding skills. Its products are of high quality, they have well managed brand identities and the company conveys a sense of dependability and trust, as well as the ability to adapt to changing consumer needs.

Kraft made its name as a manufacturer of processed cheese, which its founder J.L. Kraft pioneered and patented in 1916. One of Kraft's famous soft cheese brands is the world-leading Philadelphia brand. Kraft is now the market leader in the cream cheese segment and Philadelphia is the most intensively marketed brand. Kraft continues to expand its soft cheese product line with different flavours including herbs, tzatziki, pears, pepper and mousse.

Kraft is a master of advertising, marketing, innovative sales and ingenious packaging developments, and continues to reap the rewards of its efforts.

THE KRUGERRAND

There are few items of pure physical investment that have been branded with any success. Gems of all sorts have never been treated as products and their value has derived from their rarity. However South African gold miners have found that gold can be packaged to appeal both to gold-bugs (that is, professional investors in the metal who treat it as a commodity) and to the general public who like the idea of owning a solid piece of precious metal with an exclusive branding.

The proof that gold can have such an appeal is the Krugerrand, which is a coin with legal tender containing exactly one troy ounce (31·1035 grams) of pure gold. Launched in 1967, the coin became a financial investment and achieved international recognition and tradability. The Krugerrand was first mass-produced in 1970 and from 1973 it was actively marketed as a consumer product. The results surpassed anything its originators could have imagined. By 1995, more than 1440 tons of gold had been sold in the form of 54·4 million Krugerrands. The coin is minted in four denominations: one ounce, half ounce, quarter-ounce and tenth of an ounce.

KRUGERRAND

The Krugerrand makes the idea of owning a solid piece of precious metal with an exclusive branding a reality for the general public.

LAND ROVER

Postwar austerity inspired the launch of the Land Rover, but conspicuous consumption in the 1980s ensured its continuing success. Launched in 1948, the multi-purpose, all-terrain, four-wheel drive Land Rover was conceived as a short-term solution to the government's need to produce cars in volume, especially for export. Simple to build, strong and easy to operate, it was an immediate success.

Orders poured in from all over the world, particularly Africa and the developing countries. Land Rover could go where no vehicle had gone before. Purchasers crossed all demarcations of society and income group – farmers, foresters, police and armed forces all wanted it. George VI tested one at Sandringham and Balmoral and ordered the first of many to be used on royal estates.

Almost half a century on, the brand still stands for ruggedness, longevity and fitness for purpose. Considerable improvements and embellishments have been added to successive models and Land Rover has launched sub-brands, such as the luxury station wagon, the Range Rover, and Defender and Discovery models to capitalise on this symbol of upward mobility.

Able to go where no vehicle had gone before, the Land Rover brand still stands for ruggedness, longevity and fitness for purpose.

LAURA ASHLEY

Laura Ashley stands for a certain kind of refined, nostalgic Englishness. By highlighting the familiarity and ordinariness of the company's name as well as the pastoral look and feel of its products, Laura Ashley expresses what its chairman describes as the English values of the countryside, the family and tradition. Based on these core brand values, Laura Ashley, which was founded in 1957 by husband and wife Bernard and Laura Ashley, has built an international brand of considerable value, spanning dresses, furnishings and even perfumes.

The Laura Ashley shops have grown powerfully in the face of tough economic conditions at the premium end of the retail market. When the company went through a particularly tough period in 1991, it resolved to redouble its focus on the brand, recognising this as its greatest source of

long-term growth. Despite the early death of its founder and a number of management problems, the Laura Ashley brand has survived unscathed as a unique commercial blend of charm, homeliness and sophistication.

Based on the English virtues of the countryside, the family and tradition, the Laura Ashley brand is a unique commercial blend of charm, homeliness and sophistication.

A massive name in Italy, Lavazza coffee is rich in meaning and values.

LAVAZZA

Lavazza has succeeded in transforming a classic commodity – coffee – into a product rich in meaning and values; today Luigi Lavazza SpA is the uncontested leader in the Italian coffee market as well as the world authority on expresso.

Lavazza is a massive name in Italy with almost half the domestic retail market. It is present in over 11 million Italian households, and over 70 per cent of coffee drinkers drink its brands. Lavazza also heads the public catering and the vending machine sectors. Lavazza began to sell abroad in 1982 when it launched its first subsidiary in Paris. Since then, subsidiaries have opened in Germany, Britain, Austria and the USA.

LEA & PERRINS

Lea & Perrins is the original Worcestershire sauce. A court order proves it and forbids any competitor from making the same claim.

This versatile brand was first produced in 1835 by Messrs Lea & Perrins of Worcester, using a recipe imported from India by Lord Sandys, the then Governor of Bengal. As with so many great recipes, this one was arrived at by chance. Left in a storeroom for the governor to collect, some jars of a local sauce were forgotten about and only rediscovered two years later. They were found to have matured into an extremely good flavour.

Lea & Perrins today is enjoyed around the world in over 100 countries. The biggest Lea & Perrins fans are New Zealanders, who consume the equivalent of one bottle per person each year. Uses for Lea & Perrins vary according to cultural taste: Americans throw it on their steaks, Australians never barbecue without it, Malaysians apply it to their satay, Caribbeans creole with it and bartenders everywhere know that no Bloody Mary is complete without it.

Americans throw Lea & Perrins on their steaks, Australians never barbecue without it, Malaysians apply it to their satay, Caribbeans creole with it and bartenders everywhere know no Bloody Mary is complete without it.

L'EGGS

L'eggs started off in 1969 as a project within the Hanes Company to test the market appeal of branded hosiery. The tests proved conclusively that customers were willing to pay for a well-marketed brand, and L'eggs became a leading name within five years.

The L'eggs branding was carefully implemented. For example, the name is extremely ingenious. L'eggs came to the fore when skirts were getting shorter and legs were becoming sexier and more visible. The brand name implicitly acknowledges this but tempers it with an eye-catchingly humorous spelling. L'eggs has attained the powerful position of being regarded as the customer's friend. The company seeks to satisfy all shapes and sizes, with advanced production techniques giving it an extremely wide product range. The makers say that L'eggs aims to give women confidence and security as well as an attractive look, whether they are at work or play.

To ensure the constant availability of the product in customer outlets, the company provides sales representatives and direct distribution from local warehouses. Point-of-sale presentation, distinctive egg-shaped packaging and intense advertising and promotion have brought widespread attention to the L'eggs brand. L'eggs Products, now a division of Sara Lee Corporation, continues to innovate and cater for the needs of the modern woman by introducing new brand lines; the newest products for 1995 are L'eggs Silken Mist and L'eggs Smooth Silhouettes – the latter the most successful product launch in the history of the company.

L'eggs hosiery aims to give women confidence and security as well as an attractive appearance at work and play.

LG

The Korean Chaebols, or conglomerates, are steadily driving a wedge into virtually every Pacific Rim market, and even further afield. Foremost among these tough, diversified and technologically sophisticated combines is LG, which was formerly known as Lucky Goldstar. LG now states its aim as "creating value for customers through management based on esteem for human dignity". But competitors should not be lured into a belief that they will be treated with anything but fair-minded toughness.

Lucky Goldstar was founded in 1947 as Rakhee Chemical Industry Ltd. The company got its major break by making Korea's first radio, and it has never looked back. It is now active in such areas as chemicals, energy, electrical goods, electronics, machinery, metals, trade finance, construction, public services and sport. Well, they don't call these Korean companies conglomerates for nothing!

LG started exporting in the 1950s with plastic products and it is now a global company with 39 subsidiaries, 39 joint ventures and over 130 branch offices stretching from Asia to the USA, from Japan to the European Community.

LG, formerly known as Lucky Goldstar, is a leader amongst the tough, diversified and technologically sophisticated Korean Chaebols, or conglomerates.

Since the introduction of LEGO in 1934, over 300 million children in 120 countries have played with LEGO bricks.

LEGO

Introduced in 1934, LEGO is one of the basic creative materials used by children around the world. It is recognised as an educational aid as well as a toy. The brand's owner, the LEGO group, works closely with educationalists, research institutes and other professional advisers to ensure that the LEGO brand surpasses all product and ethical standards.

As market leader, and the leading European toy brand, LEGO distinguishes itself by constantly developing its product range and diversifying into new areas. Through the subsidiary company, LEGO Licensing, an ambitious brand extension programme has encompassed a wide variety of

initiatives. Recent ones include a range of clothing developed by the Danish company Kabooki and interactive playbooks published by Reed Books Limited.

The core brand has also seen a rash of new developments to enhance its appeal and keep it firmly up to date. Primo, part of the Duplo system, is aimed at babies aged six to 18 months, and Aquazone is a new underwater-themed product. Meanwhile, LEGOLAND, famous for its LEGO towns and villages, has opened one new theme park, at Windsor, UK, and another is set to open at Carlsbad, USA, in 1999. These new developments will no doubt increase the five billion hours a year already spent by children playing with LEGO bricks.

LEVI'S

Jeans today are general wear for both sexes of any age from all sectors of society for practically any occasion. And Levi Strauss is the prestige brand of jeans.

It was also the original brand, launched at the height of the gold rush in 1850 when Levi Strauss, a Jewish immigrant from Bavaria, went to California to make his fortune selling tents and awnings for the miners' wagons. He bought a consignment of tough brown canvas specifically for this purpose, but soon found that the miners wanted more useful products – like trousers. Levi therefore had waist-high overalls made, roomy, practical and virtually indestructible. The miners bought them and called them Levi's. Later, a stronger fabric was introduced, a durable cotton woven in the south of France called *serge de Nîmes* and dyed indigo. Its name was shortened to denim and the trousers were known as blue denims, then as blue jeans after the Genoese sailors who wore them.

Levi's jeans have been associated in turn with gold mining, cowboys and the US Army, but the character of the brand has not changed. They are designed and made to be worn hard by people who live the way they want to live. Today they have become acceptable fashion wear and there are more than 20 styles of Levi's jeans, as well as the classic 501 jeans, which were successfully relaunched in 1985.

The brand is strengthened by distinctive features added to Levi's 501 jeans over the years: embossed buttons; copper rivets to strengthen trouser pockets; a double line of orange stitching on the back pockets, on which there appears an American eagle; a leather patch which depicts a tug-of-war between two horses and a pair of jeans; finally, a red tab on the back pocket for easy identification of the brand.

Acceptable fashion wear today, Levi's jeans are designed and made to be worn hard by people who live the way they want to live.

95

Life Savers' distinctive shape differentiates them in a very crowded candy market.

LIFE SAVERS

Life Savers candies were introduced in 1921 by Clarence Crane, a chocolate manufacturer from Cleveland, Ohio, as an alternative confectionery which would not melt in the summer months in the mid-West.

The new mints that Crane devised were also given an original shape to differentiate them in a very crowded market. The mints would be circular, and Crane hired a pill-maker to mould his new mint products with a hole in the centre. The sweet was named and trademarked as Life Savers because of the similarity it bore to a lifesaving ring.

Life Savers has maintained its strong position in the US confectionery market by extending its range of flavours to include fruit and peppermint.

LION

Shokobutsu Monogatari is a leading Japanese brand of soap and soap-related products. It is made by Lion, who make a wide range of consumer products, including detergents, health, beauty and pharmaceutical products and foods.

'Shokobutsu Monogatari' is Japanese for "Vegetable Story", but it appears on the product in Chinese characters. Western brand names usually appear on the product in Katakana characters, so the use of Chinese characters gives the brand the exotic appeal of Chinese medicine. This impression is developed through the use of white packaging to convey purity and freshness.

Shokobutsu Monogatari pioneered the use of natural raw materials in strong commercial soap brands in Japan, creating a trend in the market and a powerful brand property. Lion has extended its use of Shokobutsu Monogatari to include a shampoo, a conditioner, a hand soap and a number of creams.

The use of Chinese characters on packaging gives exotic appeal to Shokobutsu Monogatari soap and soap-related products made by Lion.

LIQUID PAPER

In the mid-1950s, a secretary in Dallas, Texas, went in search of a correction fluid that could correct her typewriter errors. After a lengthly process of trial and error with white opaque solutions, she developed Liquid Paper correction fluid.

The product found a yawning gap in the market, and office supply stores across the USA snapped it up. In due course, Liquid Paper Corporation was founded, and was bought by Gillette in 1979. Gillette has expanded the Liquid Paper brand with a range of typing products including dry correction products and adhesives.

Liquid Paper correction fluid, discovered by a secretary, is today the secretary's best friend.

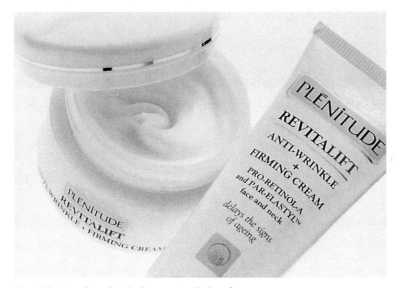

From hairdressing trade supplier to leading cosmetic and bodycare firm.

L'OREAL

L'Oreal, founded by chemist Eugene Schueller in 1907, has been transformed from a hairdressing trade supplier into the world's largest cosmetic and bodycare firm, manufacturing more than 500 brands sold across 150 countries.

One of L'Oreal's greatest assets is its sheer size and the spread of its business. l'Oreal has invested massive sums of money (just how much has never been disclosed) in developing and marketing global, or potentially global, mass market brands such as Ambre Solaire, Plenitude and Studio Line. L'Oreal has also been successful in the cosmetics and fragrances sectors with brands such as Lancôme, Helena Rubinstein and Cacharel.

LOUIS VUITTON

A family brand that has for more than a century carefully sustained a reputation for top-of-the-market luxury travel goods, Louis Vuitton today is an industry leader. Its success, the company claims, comes from a consistent strategy which focuses on impeccable quality, direct management of a network of stores and control over production, building the value of the brand name and developing a multicultural organisation able to react quickly to new opportunities.

Since Louis Vuitton, a carpenter's son from the Jura region in eastern France, sold innovative flat-topped trunks from his first shop in Paris in 1854, the firm has nurtured the crafts of trunk-making, saddlery and fine leather work. Present-day Louis Vuitton luggage, small leather goods and handbags made of leather or canvas combine this craftsmanship with the capabilities of computer-aided design. The product range includes items conceived and made using centuries-old designs and methods and contemporary creations from the design department.

The brand symbol, the Louis Vuitton monogram, was first introduced on a canvas bag by Louis's son George in 1896. Originally intended to combat counterfeiting, it also made luggage immediately recognisable by the traveller and, above all, it created a distinctive brand. The monogram canvas is still one of the company's most important lines.

Louis Vuitton's distribution network comprises a limited number of sales outlets, all managed directly by the company and strengthening the brand's international reputation for quality and luxury through their interior design and elegant presentation of products. From Paris to Tokyo and London (where the first store opened in 1885) they all feature the same design concept, using only quality materials: light oak, natural leather and brass.

Louis Vuitton, top of the market luxury travel goods.

LUCKY STRIKE

This famous cigarette brand celebrates its 125th birthday in 1996. Introduced to the United Kingdom by wartime GIs, the brand, with its distinctive 'toasted' tobacco flavour, has become one of a gallery of US classics, a potent symbol of the 'American way'. With their instantly recognisable 'target logo' and clean white packaging 'Luckies' are a powerful international brand to the benefit of their owners British American Tobacco.

LUCOZADE

In a textbook example of advantageous brand repositioning, Lucozade today is marketed as a nourishing drink for healthy people of all ages. Originally a drink for sick children, it developed with a degree of logic into a drink for convalescents, a household name, with a royal warrant. Repositioning began in 1983, when Daley Thompson, British Olympic decathlon gold medallist, was used to promote Lucozade as a sports drink, marking its transition to a healthy everyday energy replacement drink. The launch in 1990 of Lucozade Sport, the isotonic sports drink, and serious sports sponsorship confirmed Lucozade's relevance for sport. Today it is the official sport drink of British athletics.

Lucozade was first developed in 1927 by a Newcastle pharmacist, W.W. Hunter, who intended it for children recovering from flu. Early batches used in hospitals were marketed as Glucozade. Today the repositioned brand has been extended to include new flavours such as Orange Barley,

Lemon Barley, Tropical Barley, Lucozade Light and NRG, aimed at the youth sector, as well as Lucozade glucose tablets. Packaging changes mirror the change in brand image. A bottle with a resealable top introduced in 1982 was matched three years later by Lucozade sold in cans.

A textbook example of advantageous brand repositioning, Lucozade, once a drink for sick children, is now sold as a nourishing drink for healthy people of all ages.

LUFTHANSA

The global airtraffic market is forecast to grow by an average of four to five percent for the foreseeable future. Lufthansa, the German airline with a stronghold in Europe and operations in North America and the Asia-Pacific is aiming to maximise its share in this projected growth.

Lufthansa has a history of buying stakes in niche carriers within markets to which it seeks greater access. In 1994 they bought a 38 per cent stake in a Scottish regional business air carrier. It is this investment in smaller airlines that will enable Lufthansa to extend its penetration within Europe and maximise its share of the global airtraffic market.

The German airline with a stronghold in Europe and operations in North America and Asia Pacific.

LUXOTTICA

Men no longer fail to make passes at girls who wear glasses. On the contrary, they pursue them through superstores, specialist opticians and anywhere else these fashion-seekers can be persuaded to part with their money. No wonder, then, that branding companies have moved into the market with a vengeance. And least surprising of all is the fact that the fashion-conscious Italians have seen the market growth with longsighted vision and are now pushing for all they are worth to absorb it.

Foremost among the brands in this business is Luxottica, a company which goes the whole way from designing the fashion to making the frames. They have an incredible 1700 styles of frame available, in virtually every colour and material one could imagine. Luxottica sold no less than 13 million sets of frames to some 140,000 customers in 1994.

In pursuit of the peaks of high fashion, Luxottica tied up a licensing agreement with Giorgio Armani in 1988. Since then it has formed relationships with ten top fashion houses, such as Yves Saint Laurent and Brooks Brothers. Luxottica has broken through into sunglasses by acquiring Persol Spa and its investment in Brico Srl has given it a break in the sports sector.

Luxottica goes the whole way from designing the fashion to making the frames of its glasses.

LYCRA

The Lycra® brand is one of the world's best known brands in textiles. Dupont, the owner of the Lycra® brand, recognised from the outset that the success of its elastane business stream would depend on Dupont's ability to create a powerful brand at the consumer level. From the very beginning therefore Dupont determined to build a distinctive consumer brand with a differentiated set of brand values and a relevant and attractive brand personality. Lycra® was the result.

Lycra® fibres were first used in 1960 in corsetry to improve comfort. It then introduced elastane into Swimwear which proved to be an outstanding move. Lycra® quickly became the 'fashion statement' of the intimate apparel and swimwear segment. The brand became so well known at a consumer level that consumers started to demand that intimate apparel and swimwear garments bear the Lycra® brand. One of the cornerstones of the success of Lycra® has been its unerring commitment to innovation. Lycra® invests significant resource every year in ensuring that it stays ahead of fashion.

Owned by Dupont, Lycra is one of the world's best known brands in textiles.

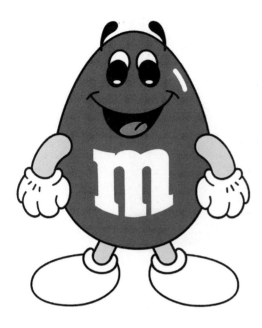

The creation of characters aimed at the children's market helps convey M&M's image of a 'fun' and friendly brand.

M&M'S

Mars, the owner of M&M's, passionately believes in promoting its brands with skill and aggression. A key plank in the promotion strategy for M&M's has been the creation of characters aimed at the children's market. This has helped convey the image of a 'fun' and friendly brand.

M&M's has benefited from Mars' policy of globalisation in recent years, and the brand is no longer so heavily skewed towards the USA. In the UK, for example, it has replaced Treats and, in a relatively short space of time, become firmly established in an important new market.

MADIT

Madit is a range of branded high-grade motor oils made in Slovakia and sold across Eastern Europe. Madit products are branded with personality suggesting they are modern, of good quality and good value. The brand's key slogan, "Madit holds more" has received many plaudits, including the 1994 Worldfest Charleston Golden Award.

Introduced in 1964, the Madit name derives from "Motorovy ADITivovany Olej" which translates as Additivated Motor Oil. Madit's parent company, Slovnaft, is one of the first former Eastern bloc companies to be given a credit rating by western financial institutions which will enable it to borrow from western banks without first obtaining a state guarantee.

Originally designed by Bedrich Udrzal in 1953, the logo still represents two distillation towers (black) and crude oil as seen in a test-tube (yellow).

MAGGI

The Maggi brand name, linked to the red and yellow Maggi colours, stands for affordable and nutritious food that is easy to prepare. Today the brand covers a multitude of products, ranging from spices and sauces to pasta and potato-based dishes – and, of course, the powdered soups which first earned the company its reputation.

The first instant soup product, a dried pea-and-bean-flavoured mixture, was developed by a Swiss, Julius Maggi, in 1886. The same year, he produced a spicy sauce, Maggi Würze, and designed its distinctive four-sided brown bottle. In 1887 Maggi moved to Germany and later acquired factories in Paris, Milan, Prague and Amsterdam. Bought up by Nestlé in 1947, Maggi is a respected and established international brand with a reputation based on ability to adapt to a changing market and investment in new product development and food technology.

The Marks & Spencer house brand, St Michael, has been brilliantly extended to encompass a vast range of products, from food to fashion, endorsing them all with its guarantee of good taste and good value.

The red and yellow Maggi colours stand for affordable and nutritious food that is easy to prepare.

MARKS & SPENCER AND ST MICHAEL

The green and gold Marks & Spencer colours and their brand name, St Michael, are immediately recognised by the British public at large, while the words "M & S" have almost entered the language, indicating one of the foremost names in British retailing.

Today St Michael presides over all products manufactured to Marks & Spencer orders, from shoes to home furnishings, from gourmet prepared foods to stylish lingerie, a guarantee of their standards of quality and value.

The company, begun in 1884 when a Russian Jew, Michael Marks, hired an open stall in a Leeds market, introduced St Michael in 1928 to cover a limited range of textiles. Around that time Marks and Spencer initiated its then revolutionary policy of buying direct from the manufacturer. The saint was adopted partly to match St. Margaret, brand symbol of its first textile supplier, partly to honour Marks and Spencer's founder.

Marks & Spencer zealously guards the reputation St Michael has earned over the years. Customers buying items bearing the St Michael brand label – whether they be flowers or knickers – know that the products were made to the company's specifications and conform to the high standards it prescribes for materials and manufacturing methods.

The public responds by regarding Marks and Spencer with pride as almost a national asset, while a buying trip to one of Marks & Spencer's 285 stores in the UK is considered a must by large numbers of visitors to the country. This is despite the fact that there are some 327 Marks and Spencer stores outside the UK, from the first established in Paris in 1975 to the latest in Hong Kong.

MARLBORO

To most people Marlboro is synonymous with the image of the "Marlboro Man" and Marlboro country. But it was in fact aimed originally at women. Launched in 1924, the cigarette had a red filter tip which was made much of in the early advertising line: "A cherry tip for your red ruby lips".

This strategy did not, however, produce the expected results and in 1955 the brand was radically relaunched as an indispensable companion for the rugged, independent sort of guy who spent his time in the great outdoors. Or, at least, for the kind of guys who fantasised about such things. The move proved a hit. By the 1970s, Marlboro had unseated Camel as the top-selling cigarette brand in the USA.

Marlboro today is also the world's leading international cigarette brand, instantly recognisable by its red and white packaging livery. But there are challenges ahead. US cigarette companies are being hounded by anti-smoking groups who actively campaign to ban tobacco advertising and smoking in communal and working environments. The brand has also suffered from its association with "Marlboro Friday" – a day in 1993 which saw blue-chip US companies battered on Wall Street following a warning that the seemingly invincible Marlboro was being forced to cut prices. However, this scare proved short-lived. Marlboro and other famous brands have bounced back from the global recession of the early 1990s and reports of the demise of the brand now appear to be greatly exaggerated.

Indispensable companion for the rugged, independent, outdoor guy, Marlboro is the world's leading international cigarette brand, instantly recognisable by its red and white packaging.

The "My Mate Marmite" advertising campaign aims to win over the younger generation to their parents' favourite spread.

MARMITE

Marmite is an archetypal British brand. Widely known as a sticky savoury mess, Marmite is a yeast extract and promoted as a good source of vitamin B.

Marmite had its heyday during the two world wars, when the government distributed it to boost nutrition during the times of food rationing. Many people born during World War II and in the postwar baby boom are still loyal consumers of the brand.

The brand's association with a bygone age is not an unalloyed benefit for Marmite. The extent of brand loyalty shown by the older generation is matched by lack of interest shown by a younger generation who have steadfastly resisted its blandishments. The task of repositioning the brand, which today is owned by CPC, is not easy, but the recent "My Mate Marmite" ad campaign has seen a resurgence in popularity and some growth for one of yesterday's best brands.

Coming in all sizes and even as an ice-cream, Mars bars revolutionised the UK chocolate market in 1932.

Martini Dry.
Gusto secco da scoprire.

Martini is the the drink of the "beautiful people". Its advertising stresses the brand's cosmopolitan outlook.

MARS

It seems an all too common sight today, but the Mars bar revolutionised the chocolate market when it was launched. Its soft nougat and caramel centre was a thing of strange beauty in the exclusively block chocolate market of the time.

Launched in the UK in 1932, it remains a market leader and continues to show its innovative roots. Product size, for example, has been a key to the brand's dominant distribution: Mars bars come in single, king-size, four-pack, fun-size and snack-size forms, among others. Then there is the trend-setting Mars ice-cream, which opened up an important new market for Mars and its competitors.

Mars has been a big fan of sponsorship over the years. Its name has been attached to a host of sporting events, notably the London Marathon in 1985–87, the 1992 Olympics and the 1994 World Cup.

MARTINI

Until the 1970s the many worldwide outposts of Martini & Rossi all had their own independent capital and a marked local character, but with the growing internationalisation of the spirits market and the creation of the EU, the holding company decided it was time to concentrate its energies within a single management unit – the General Beverage Corporation.

Martini has been heavily promoted over the years with the now legendary "Anytime, Anyplace, Anywhere" slogan. The advertising – upbeat, up-market and aimed at a younger audience – has emphasised the brand's flexibility, its social as well as literal mobility. The brand retains its old but distinctive visual image. The label's intricate rococo motifs and gold medals (awards received in the nineteenth century) remain a powerful portrayal of refinement.

Now part of the portfolio owned by the Bacardi–Martini group, Martini is available in four vermouths. The brand accounts for a large slug of the company's annual $3·5 billion turnover.

MARUHA

Maruha, the former Taiyo Fishery Company, is one of the world's largest fishing and food processing companies. Founded in 1880 by a Japanese fish trader, Maruha lost all its assets at the end of World War II. In 1945, it hurriedly rebuilt a fishing fleet to save the business. From then it went from strength to strength.

The word 'Maruha' is the phonetic rendering in English of the Japanese word describing the company's new trademark, which has particular significance for the company. The circle of the trademark symbolises both the earth and the sun. Within it is a pattern that represents both wave and fish, creating seven parts ocean to three parts land – the proportions of the earth.

The new image expresses the company's global commitment to maintaining co-existence between corporate activities and the natural environment. Maruha has been a pioneer in Japan of megabrand marketing. Each brand carries its own image, identity and role within a systematic framework to create a unified and dynamic corporate image.

Maruha is also a long-standing and highly regarded corporate brand name. It provides the highest quality canned foods, frozen foods, and much processed fish. Other well-known Maruha brands are Marivest and Bay Stars.

The diversified business encompasses fish trading, food processing, acquaculture, fish feed, pet food, sugar refineries, refrigerated carrier and cold storage services, food processing plant management and engineering, and restaurants. Maruha aspires both to make the best use of the world's food resources and to serve customer needs.

Maruha, one of the world's largest fishing and food processing companies, aspires both to make the best use of the world's food resources and to serve customer needs.

MASTERCARD

Accepted at over 13 million locations in 230 countries, with more than 22,000 member financial institutions and the world's largest electronic banking and ATM network, MasterCard™ International is using the power of its brands to shape the future of money.

Through its family of payments brands, MasterCard™ offers consumers the flexibility of all ways to pay with its flagship credit brand, its Cirrus™ ATM brand, its Maestro™ on-line debit brand and its newly-introduced stored-value brand called MasterCard™ Cash.

While each of these brands is among the global leaders in its category, the MasterCard strategy is to create a powerhouse superbrand by leveraging and uniting the equity of its individual brands. The MasterCard superbrand will be built on the distinctive brand promise of unparalleled security, unmatched access and – most importantly – unrivalled acceptance.

MasterCard, accepted at over 13 million locations in 230 countries.

MATTEL

Fifty years old in 1995, Mattel is a worldwide leader in the design, manufacture and marketing of children's toys. The name is derived from the names of the company's founders, Harold MATson and Elliott Handler. The two men initially manufactured dolls' furniture in a garage workshop.

Mattel is a worldwide leader in the design, manufacture and marketing of children's toys.

Named after the Nashville hotel where its formula was tested, Maxwell House was the original of today's instant coffee.

MAXWELL HOUSE

The sources of brand names are many and various, but few (in the foods area) owe their origins to a hotel. The appropriately named travelling salesman Joel Cheek did just that when, as a show of gratitude for giving him the thumbs up, he named his coffee after the posh Nashville hotel where he tested its formula.

The Cheek & Neal Coffee and Manufacturing Company – for that was the name Joel gave to his company – was formed in 1901 to build innovative coffee brands. He succeeded beyond all expectations, inventing instant coffee in 1942 and developing the first coffee percolators in 1966.

To expand Maxwell House worldwide, Kraft Foods (owners of Maxwell House) joined up with Pepsi-Cola International to form the "Maxwell House Beverage Company" as a global marketing vehicle for the Maxwell House products. The new concern will produce two ready-to-drink canned coffees: Maxwell House Black (coffee with sugar) and Maxwell House Rich (coffee with milk and sugar).

The alliance will bring Pepsi's long-term objective of becoming a total beverage company with a ready-to-drink portfolio ranging from carbonated soft drinks to bottled water, juices, tea and coffee nearer fruition. Kraft Foods will benefit from Pepsi's state-of-the-art manufacturing facilities and extensive distribution channels in China and throughout Asia.

McDonald's simple logo, the homogeneous interiors, the
concentration on families and children, the classless decor
and appeal comprise a branding formula that knows no
national borders and invades no personal space.

McDONALD'S

Nothing compares with McDonald's for the power of a
branding idea, the skill of its execution, and the longevity and
width of its appeal. McDonald's is the quintessential American
brand which has travelled the world on the strength of two
quite distinct phenomena – one cultural, the other
commercial.

McDonald's has ridden on the back of cultural changes in the
postwar world. As the Berlin Wall fell, McDonald's was the
archetype of American value and it was among the first products
to be eagerly imported into the former communist world. There

is barely a country without a Golden Arch indicating that
McDonald's has arrived to wave the flag of foreign, specifically
American, investment and cultural values. McDonald's says that it
operates nearly 16,000 restaurants in 83 countries.

If that is the larger context of the McDonald's explosion, the
narrower one is that McDonald's has perfected the practice of
product and design consistency. The simple but effective logo,
the homogeneous interiors, the concentration on families and
children, the classless decor and appeal add up to a branding
formula that knows no national borders and invades no personal
space. The company sums up the McDonald's effect thus: it is not
just a product, it is an experience.

McVITIE'S

McVitie's is the quintessentially British biscuit. More than five million McVitie's digestive biscuits are eaten in Britain every day – about seventy are crunched every second. McVitie's Digestive is the company's flagship brand, worth over £40 million and accounting for nearly half of all sales of digestive biscuits in Britain in 1995.

The brand was started by Robert McVitie, a Scottish baker who began baking biscuits in Edinburgh as long ago as 1830. The first digestive biscuit was made in 1892, by Alexander Grant, originally as a product to aid digestion. McVitie's uses only the best quality ingredients for all its biscuit baking and is the only biscuit baker to have its own chocolate refinery.

McVitie's has a constant programme for introducing innovation into the biscuit market by launching top quality biscuit recipes with high consumer appeal. In 1995 alone, the company launched 36 products, both sweet and savoury.

McVitie's are the master-bakers: from digestive aids to absolute indulgence.

MERCEDES-BENZ

Mercedes-Benz offers a triple promise of excellent engineering, comfort and style. Mercedes says the car provides "engineering by engineers". The brand exudes powerful expressive values, embodying safety, heritage and longevity, for the status-conscious and prosperous motorist. The Mercedes "S" Class is widely acclaimed as the best car model in the world.

This doyen of German automotive makers took its name from the daughter of one of its biggest customers. When Emil Jellinek, a motor enthusiast and businessman, bought up a quarter of the output of Gottlieb Daimler and Wilhelm Maybach, the proprietors of Daimler-Motoren-Gesellschaft, he insisted as part of the deal that they name the car after his daughter. He also drove Daimler and Maybach to distraction with his demands for increased engine power, reduced fuel consumption, lower traffic noise and greater reliablity from his vehicles. But Jellinek should be

given the credit for building one of the world's finest car brands.

In 1926 Daimler combined with their competitors Benz to form Daimler-Benz A.G; the three-pointed star adopted by Daimler in 1909 continues to grace the bonnet or boot of the leading motor marque.

The Mercedes brand exudes powerful values, embodying safety, heritage and longevity, for the status-conscious and prosperous motorist.

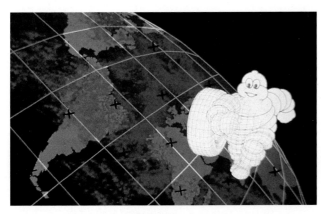

The Michelin brand name and the famous Bibendum character constitute an outstandingly powerful brand in respect to all types of tyres.

MICHELIN

For most of the last thirty years Michelin have dominated the world tyre market and have displayed an obsession with product quality, a passion for production efficiency and an attachment to brand values which have left competitors reeling. The Michelin name and the distinctive device mark of Bibendum (the little man made out of tyres) have assumed a position of enormous authority in relation to tyres world-wide.

Michelin was founded in 1890 but its success in recent decades can be directly related to its pioneering work in steel-braced radial tyres from the 1930s onwards. It was recognised by tyre technologists as early as the last century that a steel-braced radial tyre represented the 'ultimate' tyre – a radial construction would ensure that a solid slab of rubber was presented to the road to maximise grip, supple sidewalls would ensure a good ride and steel bracing would stop the tyre squirming and deforming and would therefore minimise wear.

Most tyre manufacturers, however, chose to give only faint recognition to the steel-braced radial tyre and this attitude persisted well into the 1960s. After all, they argued, steel bracing might result in a harsher ride and it was known that manufacturing tolerances on radial tyres were far higher than on cross-ply tyres. They were none too keen either, to promote tyres which lasted three to four times as long as existing tyres.

Michelin cared nothing for such arguments – they knew how the best tyres should be made and they focused all their efforts in one direction. By the mid-1960s both consumers and car manufacturers recognised that Michelin had got it right and competitors found themselves with the daunting task of catching up with a highly efficient competitor who was setting high performance, price and quality standards.

In recent years as tyre technology has become more ubiquitous Michelin's product lead has been closed but the brand's reputation for performance, quality and value remains.

Microsoft®

Microsoft software products make personal computers more user-friendly.

MICROSOFT

It is not every company that has a road named after it, but Microsoft, based at 1 Microsoft Way, Redmond, Washington, USA, is a bit out of the ordinary. Its profits, for example, are unusually high ($1·45 billion in 1994–5 on a turnover of $5·94 billion), and have grown for each of the past 20 years.

Founded in 1975 by William H. Gates and Paul Allen, the company soared to success on the coat tails of IBM, for whose PCs it became a key software supplier. Its original product, the MS-DOS operating system, now runs on over 120 million PCs. But rather than resting on its laurels, Microsoft branched out in the mid-1980s into an array of software products designed to make personal computers more easily manipulated by the lay person. The company now has around 50 subsidiaries and is a truly global player, stretching from Argentina to Australia, and from the United Arab Emirates to the United Kingdom.

Its most popular applications today include Microsoft Windows and Microsoft Office. It has also moved into CD-ROMs, with products like Encarta, the multi-media encyclopaedia and, most recently, multi-media games. The latest version of Windows, launched in August 1995, broke with tradition: instead of using a generational number in the title, the company opted for the year of launch (hence, Windows 95). This reflects a more general drive to transform Microsoft from a predominantly business-oriented brand into a mass-market consumer brand. After all, Gates's much-quoted vision is for "A computer on every desk and in every home".

Marketing spending has shot up dramatically over the past couple of years. In the run-up to the launch of Windows 95, the company began a global advertising campaign which introduced the slogan, "Where do you want to go today?" This doubled the previous year's $50 million budget. The actual launch of Windows 95, arguably the most hyped event in the history of the PC, was supported by spending rumoured to be in the region of $1 billion (although a large proportion of this came from the 3700 Windows service providers and retailers).

Another key area for brand extension is interactive television (ITV) which, says Microsoft, "promises to revolutionise the technological landscape and have a significant impact on social behaviour".

MIELE

The washing machine that made Miele a leading household product company was developed after years working on products for farmers. Carl Miele and his partner Reinhart Zinkann had already created less memorable products such as a milk separator and a butter churn before they invented their heavy-duty coal fired tub washing machine in 1901.

That was the year they formulated their first slogan. The words "Forever better" characterised their approach to their product then, and it remains the company motto. Miele has seen the importance from day one of communicating with customers, as well as understanding their needs for reliable and up-to-date household equipment.

The founders, Miele and Zinkann, went on to develop one of the best known slogans in German advertising history, "Nur Miele, sagte Tante, die alle Waschmaschinen kannte" (Auntie says only Miele understands washing machines) and Auntie Sheila became a well-known and friendly figure in Miele's advertising. Set against this skill at communication was a belief in technology and brand building. "We must strive to cherish and respect the principle of quality. We will not therefore let ourselves be forced into the position of trading quality against price," said the founders.

Highly inventive in technical terms – Miele invented the mechanical washing machine, made the first electrically powered dishwasher in Europe, and now uses computers to simplify washing machines, dryers and dishwashers – Miele has a defined brand policy and stresses issues such as dealer training, customer and staff communication and product aesthetics.

Míele

"Only Miele understands washing machines," says Auntie Sheila, a well-known and friendly figure in Miele advertising.

MILKA

A good example of a brand that has kept its character from the days of its conception is Milka. Launched by the Swiss confectionery producer Philippe Suchard in 1901, the brand still uses the image of a small cow in front of an Alpine panorama set on lilac paper that appeared on its original packaging. Today Milka's brand embodies high quality chocolate enjoyment and the brand strength of competence, authenticity and tradition.

In 1986 the brand began to expand from its home bases in Switzerland and Germany into the wider European area. Now in the portfolio of Kraft Jacobs Suchard, Milka remains one of the top brands in its market. In 1994 it won the German Marketing Award for its brand strategy.

Another component of the Kraft confectionery portfolio is the Toblerone brand, whose greatest mark of distinction is its most unusual pyramid-shaped package. The Swiss ring of the name, the nutty confection and the premium price enhance this valuable if specialist brand.

A small cow grazing on a Swiss mountainside and set on lilac paper still means Milka's top-quality chocolate.

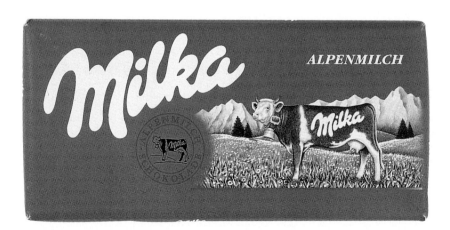

MITSUKOSHI

Mitsukoshi Ltd was established in 1673 and incorporated in 1904, making it one of Japan's oldest and most prestigious retailers. The company has a domestic network of 14 major department stores, including major locations in Tokyo and Osaka, 94 satellite shops and overseas activities in 19 major metropolitan centres world-wide.

Mitsukoshi's activities include department store operation, wholesaling, importing and exporting, real estate agency activities, construction, travel agency operation, life and non-life insurance, consumer finance, promotion and others.

All of the company's department stores rank among the leading retailers in their respective areas, with the Nihonbashi Main store in Tokyo being particularly noteworthy.

Mitsukoshi is Japan's leading retailing and department store group and the support of Mitsukoshi is frequently central to new brand success in Japan.

MOBIL

The Mobil Corporation is a major international oil, gas and petrochemical company. It owns 20,000 service stations around the world which sell Mobil products. In North America alone, two out of every three cars produced there use Mobil Motor oils.

Mobil believe that their customers' loyalty is their most important asset and aim to cater to them in the best possible way from product development to customer service. The company has also achieved outstanding recognition for its environmental policies and awareness from numerous worldwide governments and companies.

Mobil has developed strategies to encourage consumer awareness and sales in relatively new markets. For example, it has signed an agreement with Mercedes-Benz, agreeing to co-operate in the car after-care market in Russia. Mercedes-Benz will

exclusively recommend Mobil products to its dealers in the country and list recommended Mobil products in its owners' manuals.

For its future, Mobil is investing in high-growth markets such as those in the Pacific Rim, where over 30 per cent of its worldwide refinery capacity originates. In addition, the brand is seeing increasing sales in the new markets in the region, including China, Malaysia, Singapore and Thailand. Mobil, with its strong resources in the field of natural gas production, will benefit from the increasing market demand for this clean-burning fuel as it becomes the fuel of choice in many applications, including electrical generation.

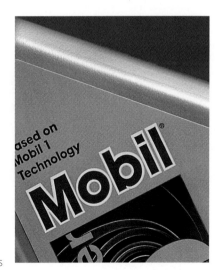

In North America, two out of every three cars produced use Mobil Motor oils.

MOËT & CHANDON

Moët & Chandon champagne, founded by Claude Moët in 1743, is a brand leader in its native France and across the world. It is consumed in over 150 countries and has a distinguished presence everywhere from royal marriages and coronations to state and great sporting events.

Moët & Chandon is the locomotive of change in champagne. Moët sees its responsibility as improving every element of the product as the years go by. Its research programmes are forever striving to improve the quality of sparkling wine. The results of this research are shared with the rest of the industry, thus ensuring that champagne's reputation remains paramount. Some projects benefit the beer industry too; for example, the Bufom/Eureka programme aims to analyse and control the bubbles produced in foaming beverages. This project, followed in conjunction with Heineken, should lead to a better understanding of bubbles in sparkling wines and foam in beer.

With over 250 years of success and the continuing quest for perfection, Moët & Chandon remains and should remain a leader of its industry.

Moët & Chandon champagne is an indispensable ingredient of every occasion from royal marriages and coronations to state banquets and great sporting events in over 150 countries.

MONOPOLY

Monopoly is the most famous board game in the world with an appeal that seems never to weary or to become outdated. The concept of trading in real estate has never failed to excite the public, and the concept that the real thing can be replicated on a board by the least advantaged to give the illusion of ownership and wealth must surely always entertain and be relevant.

Monopoly was created during the American Depression by one Charles Darrow. Out of work and with more than a few moments to kill, he and friends experimented with games to amuse themselves. Monopoly became so popular within the local community that Darrow had to subcontract the production to outside sources. An initial approach to the games manufacturers Parker Brothers was declined on the grounds that the game had no final goal, took too long to play and had 52 fundamental playing errors. Darrow was undeterred and continued production on his own. A year after the rejection, following reports of its phenomenal success, Parker Brothers reconsidered his proposal and bought the rights. This was a move it never regretted.

Today Monopoly is licensed in 32 countries and translated into 24 languages including Braille. In each country, the property locations are based on areas relevant to the locality. The Soviets originally banned the game believing – reasonably enough— that it countered socialist values, but in 1989, in an early example of *glasnost*, the first Russian Monopoly set was produced. Such was its popularity and scarcity that during the American National Exhibition in Moscow, the six Monopoly sets on display were stolen.

Monopoly appears in many categories in the *Guinness Book of Records*; one entry reveals that the longest underwater game of Monopoly lasted 1080 hours. The game has also been played by American astronauts in space. During World War II, the British War Office specially commissioned Monopoly games to be sent to prisoners of war in enemy-occupied territory; the 'boards' contained silk scarves printed with escape routes from their particular prison, local currency, thin files and a tiny compass, giving a whole new meaning to 'get out of jail free'.

Monopoly celebrated its sixtieth anniversary in 1995, but this is a brand name that will be recognised well into the twenty-first century.

Monopoly, the most famous board game in the world, is played in 24 languages on appropriate boards.

MOTOROLA

Motorola, the company that transmitted Neil Armstrong's 'one small step' message from the moon in 1969, is frequently cited as one of the best run and most innovative companies in the world. When Motorola's founders began building car radios in the back streets of Chicago it is hard to imagine they envisaged one day they would be one of the world's largest suppliers of wireless communications equipment. Motorola's success has resulted from its commitment to constant reinvention of its products combined with its ability to spot and develop future technologies. Whilst Motorola has traditionally been associated with the business to business market, more recently they have focused their attention upon developing the consumer market. The power of the Motorola brand has enabled them to make this transition with relative ease.

Mustang caused a sensation when it was launched by Ford in 1964. Though the current Mustang is, arguably, a little more prosaic, the brand's appeal is still strong.

MUSTANG

The Ford Mustang, affectionately known to Americans as the ponycar, was introduced in April 1964 and since then more than six million have been sold.

In the mid-60s the Mustang was a phenomenon – the original Mustang cost a very reasonable $2,368, had a 170 cubic inch (2.8 litre) six cylinder engine, floor-mounted three speed manual transmission, bucket seats and an attractive sports car styling. Buyers could order Mustangs in three models – convertible, hardtop or fastback..

The car proved to be enormously appealing to Second World War baby boomers who wanted a different car from that of their parents.

The first year sales estimates were exceeded in just four months and more than 417,000 Mustangs were sold in the first year. Surprisingly, 16 per cent of these were sold to people in the 44-55 age bracket, 50 per cent of buyers already owned another car and most buyers specified optional high performance V8 engines, power steering and automatic transmission.

In the 1960s Mustang captured the mood of the moment; it was young, exciting and optimistic and, for many Americans, is still inextricably linked with the Beatles era, college days and early adulthood.

Today, although the Mustang is quite different from its predecessor of thirty years before, the Mustang brand name still has a special spot in the hearts of American motorists.

NEC aims to meet the challenge of the twenty-first century by advancing societies worldwide towards deepened mutual understanding and the fulfilment of human potential.

A brand almost synonymous with instant coffee, Nescafé continues to add to its range.

NEC

NEC is a prominent Japanese-owned brand name of our modern multi-media society. Founded in 1899, it was successfully nurtured from its C&C (computers and communications) concept of the late 1970s. Based on the supposition that a new global society would arise from the integration of computer and communications technologies, the brand found a fitting and welcome place within the information highway of the 1980s.

NEC, long associated with the values of technological ability and reliability, has expanded from its initial manufacturing of telephones and switchboards to become a global enterprise producing a vast range of products from computers and semiconductors to electronic goods for the home. The company takes its philosophy and values very seriously. With widespread excitement and uncertainty about what the next millennium may hold, the company has set itself the further goal of establishing its brand name as connotative of internationality, youth and warmth. It has adapted its philosophy to meet the challenge of the 21st century: "NEC strives through C&C to help advance societies worldwide towards deepened mutual understanding and the fulfilment of human potential."

Furthermore, as the new century approaches, the company's operations will expand, giving NEC a broader range of values, including service, software and business, that play important roles in the lives of the individual. This expanded realm will be defined and symbolised by the phrase, "C&C for Human Potential". NEC aims to become a truly global corporation and is now working through every aspect of its business operations to reinforce its brand image.

NESCAFÉ

W B

Nescafé is a textbook example of the modern business maxim: think global, act local. Over the course of half a century the brand has been carefully adapted to suit local needs, traditions and cultures. This enlightened stewardship has helped it to conquer a large part of the planet.

Nescafé instant coffee made its first appearance in 1938, although Nestlé had been working on the project since 1930. Anxious to off-load a major coffee mountain, the Brazilian government had asked Nestlé to step in – a fortuitous start, perhaps, but there is nothing undeserved about the brand's subsequent success. Nestlé has invested continuously in both product development and brand support. Milestones in its history have included the introduction of freeze drying, agglomeration techniques to produce granules and aromatisation processes to enhance the taste of pure coffee.

The company has also profited from its launch of special blends based on high-quality arabica beans and other coffee varieties, such as Colombian. More recently, Nestlé has been at the forefront of the coffee revival, launching a range of added-value speciality coffees such as Cappuccino.

Nestlé's brand support has included eye-catching packaging innovations and substantial investment in advertising and sales promotions. Consistent brand management has been a key factor in Nestlé's success: advertising themes have been carefully researched and retained over a long period of time, with subtle modifications and updating. A good example of the brand's constant advertising is the "couple" ads in the UK, which have continued for decades. The brand's appearance has also been remarkably consistent. This level of professionalism has produced an unusually high degree of customer loyalty and brand recognition.

NEWCASTLE BROWN

Newcastle Brown started life in 1927 as a regional beer in the north-east of England. Today it is the top selling British bottled beer and one of the biggest beer brands in Europe. It is both a cultural phenomenon and a case study in first-rate branding. Its original image was identified with industrial life in the north-east, when workers in shipbuilding, mines and steelworks used it to quench their thirst. It was promoted as "The One and Only" and its advertising was peppered with local Geordie phrases.

"Newky Brown" is a modern, young person's beer, bought in a bottle and served cold.

The brand gained substantial backing in 1960, when it was bought by Scottish Breweries, owner of a large pub chain. In the 1980s, Newcastle Brown was hit by the fashion for chilled lagers. It was rebranded as a modern, young person's beer, bought in a bottle and served cold. Its slogan – "Keep a cool head", got it into some trouble with the British advertising authorities who thought that it might suggest that it was non-alcoholic, but, despite this hiccup, the rejuvenated brand has continued to prosper. It is now sold in 40 countries. Beer drinkers worldwide appear to like the bitter taste and the new image of "Newky Brown".

NEWSWEEK

"I think there's room for another news magazine ... that does a more thorough job of reporting, that can dig out the facts behind the news and give the news more meaning." So said Thomas J. C. Martyn, founder of *Newsweek*, to a prospective employee in 1933. On 17 February of that year, *Newsweek* went on sale, with a cover price of 10 cents ($4 annual subscription).

Today the news weekly has a claimed 24 million readers worldwide. Over the past 60-odd years, it has passed some major milestones: in 1937 it became the first news magazine to use signed columns in its commentaries; in 1945 it went international by setting up publishing operations in Canada, Tokyo and Paris; in 1972 it became the first news magazine to feature a woman columnist; and in 1986 it became the first US magazine of any kind to publish a foreign language edition (Japanese). *Newsweek* is also the proud owner of seven National Magazine Awards, more than any of its rivals.

More recent developments have included the launch of a CD-ROM edition, published quarterly, and an on-line product called Newsweek InterActive. This is available on the Prodigy network. Both brand extensions have benefited from *Newsweek*'s image overhaul in 1985. This resulted in a new, more immediately identifiable logo and look combined with the division of the magazine into six main sections.

Owned by The Washington Post Company, *Newsweek* had revenues of $337·6 million in 1994, which although slightly up on 1993 was not enough to prevent a 21 per cent slide in profits ($14·2 million). "Fashion," said *Newsweek*'s annual report, "has steered some advertisers away from national magazines." Nevertheless the company is confident that its long-term strategy and increasingly upmarket readership will overcome these immediate obstacles.

24 million readers worldwide now read *Newsweek*.

NIKE

The Nike brand, adopted in 1971 and named after the Greek goddess of victory, today is the paradigm of sports and fitness innovation, with total revenues approaching $4 billion in 1993. A series of sports shoes with innovative soles, running from the "Waffle Trainer" in 1974, to the "Tailwind" in 1979, from the "Air Trainer High" in 1987 and the "Air Stab" in 1988, were linked from the start with apparel. A Nike T-shirt in 1971 began the enterprise which today incorporates Nike International Apparel and Nike F.I.T. Fabrics, built for comfort and protection during high intensity outdoor workouts.

The championship successes of athletes wearing Nike gear have made Nike an international force; international markets make up 33 per cent of revenues. But the company began in America's running centre, Eugene, Oregon, where a top US track coach, Bill Bowerman, met Phil Knight, a member of his track team at the university. Their aim in founding Nike then, as now, was to help athletes run faster.

A feature of the brand's rapid ascent is endorsement contracts with international figures, starting with tennis star John McEnroe in 1978 and including André Agassi in 1989.

Paradigm of sports and fitness innovation, Nike sporting gear helps athletes run faster.

NIKON

Nikon has been synonymous with fine optics since the company was founded in 1917. They have developed outstanding know-how in optics, precision manufacturing and electronics, placing its products at the leading edge.

Cameras and lenses, which have given the Nikon brand a powerful reputation, are just one area where the Company's technology has been brought to bear in serving customer needs. Steppers and mask wafer inspection equipment used in the manufacture of highly reliable integrated circuits, surveying instruments, colour printers, microscopes and binoculars are also important parts of the company's product portfolio.

Nikon's activities are guided by a passion for optical and precision excellence.

NINTENDO

Game Boy, in the portfolio of Nintendo, the world's largest manufacturer and marketer of video games, is one of the newest brand names to have entered the English language dictionary. This is a result of its strength and familiarity with the public. Spanning a broad section of society, the brand can be seen in use either on public transport or in the offices of businessmen and by high society.

The world's biggest name in portable electronic games, Nintendo is determined to steal the limelight back from newcomer Sony as it launches its long-awaited 64-bit games consoles.

Game Boy is one of the best selling portable games systems in the world, with approximately 40 million owners worldwide. It is popular with both sexes, with over 40 per cent of its owners being women. The brand's most popular games, "Super Mario Brothers" and "Donkey Kong", have become well-known names in their own right, an unusual feat in the games market. The video game, "Donkey Kong Country" has been voted Video Game of the Year (UK, 1994) and has become the fastest selling video game ever, with 17·5 million copies sold worldwide.

With support from over 500 game developers and third party publishers worldwide, and its financial commitment to development and publicity, Nintendo should see itself and Game Boy reach new goals in the future of the home entertainment market.

Nintendo GAME BOY™

NISSAN

Nissan is the world's fifth largest car manufacturer. It was founded in 1911 by Masujiro Hashimoto and its earliest car was named 'Dat' from the first letters of the names of the three financial backers, Den, Aoyama and Takeuchi. In 1931, after a merger, the company was named Datson (literally 'son of Dat') and this was changed to Datsun in 1932 after a tidal wave destroyed the Ayokawa factory: 'sun' was considered to have more favourable associations in Japanese than 'son'.

Datsun was merged into the Nissan Jidosha Kogyo in 1934 and the Datsun and Nissan names were both used until 1982 when it was decided to phase out the Datsun name in favour of Nissan. Today Nissan manufactures cars, trucks, aerospace equipment, textile machinery, and industrial and marine equipment.

PRIMERA

Thirty years ago the Nissan and Datsun brand names were little known outside Japan. Now, Nissan is one of the world's leading automotive brands.

NIVEA

A small brand philosophy handbook produced by Nivea's German owner, Beiersdorf AG, states: "Nivea is the brand of the nineties ... a generous brand with a fair offer ... an unpretentious brand ... a brand for everybody ... an 'ageless' brand." Taking its name from the Latin for snow-white (nivis), Nivea is a 1990s brand that has also adapted well to other decades. Nivea Cream was invented in 1911 and made available in 1912. Its popularity rested on the fact that it was the world's first stable water-in-oil emulsion.

The brand of the 1990s, Nivea takes its name from the Latin for snow-white.

The brand's owner, Beiersdorf, takes its name from Paul Carl Beiersdorf, a Hamburg pharmacist who in 1882 began producing a range of medical plasters, ointment-impregnated gauze pads and paste sticks. However he soon sold out to a local businessman, Oscar Troplowitz, who extended the product range to include dental care products and cosmetics. Troplowitz was also a very forward-thinking employer, introducing to Hamburg the eight-hour working day, holiday pay, maternity protection, free lunches and pension schemes.

Beiersdorf became a limited company in 1920 and a public company two years later. Today it operates in 36 countries and has over 50 global affiliates and 17,500 employees. Nivea is the world's biggest toiletry brand, enjoying revenues of DM1·8 billion (approx. £0·8 billion) in 1994, an increase of 16 per cent over the previous year. Brand extensions have played a large part in Nivea's continued success. Recent launches include a new range for mature skin, a face cleansing cream called Nivea Visage which has already become Europe's number one, and Nivea Vital, a five-strong product range unveiled in 1995 after more than six years in R&D.

Nivea's biggest branded competition comes from Oil of Ulay and Plénitude, but it also faces the growing threat of private label copycats. Beiersdorf, however, is confident that continued brand extensions and swift international launches will help it stay one step ahead of the game.

NOKIA

Incongruously Nokia began in 1865 when a mining engineer, Fredrik Idestam, established a forest industry enterprise in south-western Finland. Today's company takes its name from a groundwood mill it ran on the Nokia River.

Cashing in on the opportunities offered by the increasing popularity of mobile communications and the continuing liberalisation of the telecommunications market, the Nokia international telecommunications and electronics group concentrates on enhancing its image as a globally oriented company. With the corporate head office in Helsinki, the group has operations in over 40 countries, including 13 with manufacturing facilities; its shares are traded on stockmarkets in Helsinki, London, New York, Frankfurt, Paris and Stockholm; and in 1994 the domestic market accounted for only 11 per cent of net sales. Vigorous brand advertising campaigns emphasise the brand name and slogan, 'Nokia: Connecting People', with its well-known logo, in overseas markets.

Telecommunications accounts for 70 per cent of Nokia operations and it has achieved an important position in strong growth segments, such as cellular phone networks and cellular phones. It is a pioneer in digital telecommunications and the world's second largest supplier of GSM/DCS cellular networks. Equally Nokia Mobile Phones, sold in some 100 countries, is Europe's largest and the world's second largest manufacturer of mobile phones, with products for all the major digital and analog systems. Nokia also develops advanced cable products and is a significant European manufacturer of consumer and industrial electronics.

Nokia international telecommunications and electronics group is named after a groundwood mill on the Nokia river.

OIL OF ULAY

Now owned by Procter & Gamble, Oil of Ulay has its origins in World War II. It was developed by South African chemist Graham Gordon Wulff as a skin treatment to prevent the burn wounds of British Royal Air Force pilots from dehydrating.

During the early 1950s, Wulff teamed up with marketer Shaun Adams Lowe and founded the Adams Group. They sold the product door-to-door in South Africa. Later, expansion took the product to Australia, the UK, USA, Netherlands, Canada, Germany and Mexico. By the 1970s the brand had extended into several product lines and was worth approximately US$5 million. Today Oil of Ulay is one of the leading cosmetic brands in the world and is known as Oil of Olez in continental Europe.

Dating back to World War II, Oil of Ulay is one of the world's leading cosmetic brands.

The concept of co-operation and dialogue between Olivetti products and their users makes Olivetti equipment invariably aesthetically pleasing and stylishly designed.

OLIVETTI

Design and consumer orientation, the two facets of the best Italian branding, are nowhere better exemplified than in Olivetti products. The Olivetti company was founded in 1908 by the engineer Camillo Olivetti and is today one of Europe's leading office automation equipment and information technology companies.

The company has supplied systems to the public sector and is responsible for the automatic teller machine network in Italy and the system that controls Italian traffic lights. Olivetti is also a major supplier of software and hardware for the education sector.

Olivetti equipment is invariably aesthetically pleasing and stylishly designed, with the assurance of the best possible interface between humans and machines. The concept of co-operation and dialogue between Olivetti products and their users lies at the heart of the brand's positioning. This is utilised to its maximum value in the slogan,' La nostra forza e la vostra energia' ('Our strength is your power').

OLYMPUS

The Olympus Optical Company is a classic example of Japanese branding ingenuity. Founded in 1919 under the name Takachiho Seisakusho, it drew its inspiration from Japanese mythology: Mount Takachiho was the site of the fictional Takamagahara (the name meant "Plains in the high heavens"), which was said to be home to a number of Japanese gods. But, aware that the name might not travel well, its owners changed it in 1921 to Olympus – a reference to Mount Olympus, the divine dwelling place of the greater gods of Greek mythology.

The process of internationalization did not begin in earnest until the late 1950s, but the company soon made up for lost time. Today it has more than 20 foreign subsidiaries and has recently begun an "organic globalisation programme" that should see this number increase. Exports already account for 60 per cent of turnover.

The first Olympus products were microscopes, and the company has continued its strong involvement with the world of optoelectronics and optomechatronics. Spurred on by Japan's high incidence of stomach cancer, It pioneered the endoscope market with the creation of the world's first gastrocamera. Its product range today also includes camcorders, cameras, microcassette recorders, tape recorders, printers, measuring equipment, reagents and clinical analysers. The Olympus branding philosophy boils down to "uncompromising quality and reliability".

The Olympus Optical Company is a classic example of Japanese branding ingenuity – even its name is adapted to the English-speaking market.

OPEL

From its beginnings as a European orientated car manufacturer Opel has been utilised by its owners General Motors to spearhead expansion into markets outside the USA and Western Europe. Aided by General Motors' strategic decision to develop 'world cars', Opel has become an international operation with global export sales and local assembly and manufacturing capabilities. The Opel model range represents highly effective segmentation of the market place with brands such as the Vectra, Corsa, Omega, Senator, Calibra and Frontera effectively servicing different market requirements. From the new supermini, the Corsa, to the rugged four wheel recreational drive Frontera and the stately Senator, Opel looks set to deliver world-class cars for a parent company which demands no less than world-class standards.

The spearhead of General Motor's campaign to expand into Europe.

ORAL-B

Oral-B enlist dental professionals to keep their innovative oral care products up-to-date.

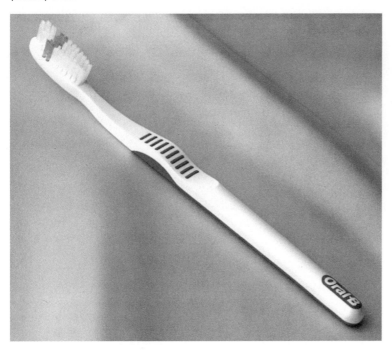

Unlike many brand names, Oral-B has a straighforward derivation. "Oral" signifies that it is a product which relates to the mouth; "B" stands for brush – an oral brush. In fact, the initial in the name has an implication of medical authority, which creates consumer confidence.

Oral-B Laboratories, now a multinational division of the Gillette Company, began business in 1950 when a Californian periodontist developed a successful toothbrush. Oral-B explains its success as the fruits of a continuing partnership with dental professionals, to refresh its product and scientific thinking, and keep the products up-to-date.

Oral-B develops, markets and distributes world-wide a broad array of innovative oral care products, including interdental products, speciality toothpastes, mouth rinses, professional dental products and, of course, toothbrushes. The company's latest innovation is the Oral-B Indicator toothbrush, the first toothbrush with a built-in replacement alert and an Advantage Control Grip with dual-material handle.

ORANJEBOOM

The penetration of the UK market by the Dutch pure premium lager, Oranjeboom, graphically illustrates scientific brand promotion aimed at creating a classic brand and differentiating it in an overcrowded market. Cashing in on growing demand for premium lager and the success of brands with perceived authenticity, strenuous advertising campaigns followed research, identifying customers as discerning individuals who knew what they liked and were confident anough to choose accordingly.

Proclaimed "Crown Prince of Lagers" and with the slogan, "Oranjeboom talks in my language and is the best-tasting Dutch premium lager", advertising aims at an audience for whom intellectual effort counts. They employ a more cerebral approach to create distinction for the brand. Stressing the brand benefits of Oranjeboom's strong premium quality, smooth

continental taste and the fact that it was imported, advertising also emphasised as a plus factor the lager's stylish bottle, introduced in 1991.

Today Oranjeboom's brand standing is clearly thought to be on the up, competing successfully with Beck's and Budweiser and coming to equal Grolsch.

Discerning customers, who know what they like and are confident enough to choose accordingly, drink Oranjeboom, "Crown Prince of Lagers".

Oreo cookies – two biscuits sandwiching a rich cream – are a cult product in the USA.

OREO

Nabisco-owned Oreo cookies is a leading cookie and cracker brand in the USA. It also has a strong showing in the global markets.

A rich cream sandwiched between two biscuits – either plain or chocolate – Oreo has acquired the status of a cult product in the USA. Even the intricate patterning on the product is greatly admired.

The five star passenger
train service.

ORIENT EXPRESS

Quality, comfort and exoticism are some of the
terms synonymous with the Orient Express, the
five star passenger train service. With an original
passenger list ranging from Edward VIII and Mrs
Simpson to Mata Hari, the Venice–Simplon Orient
Express enables travellers to recapture the luxury
and essence of the 1920s.

OROTON

Founded in 1938, Oroton is Australia's leader in
high-quality fashion accessories and
leathergoods for men and women. It has
achieved this position by building a reputation
for classic styling and top-notch quality.

The brand is licensed to a carefully selected
number of manufacturers and importers. It is now
a global competitor with offices and showrooms in
major markets such as New York and Hong Kong.
Oroton has a far-reaching distribution network
throughout Europe and South-East Asia. With its
continuing commitment to aggressive advertising,
promotion and licensing, Oroton's winning streak
looks set to continue.

The classic styling and top quality of Oroton fashion accessories have taken
them far beyond Australia into the wider world.

The source of Refreshment

OUTSPAN

Outspan conjures up an image of healthy living and the Great Outdoors and is the byword for citrus quality and consistency.

OUTSPAN

Outspan is the trademark for the produce of the South African Co-operative Citrus Exchange (SACCE), and is today one of the leading names for citrus fruits. The name Outspan – a Dutch word meaning the welcome halt during a long wagon trek – suggests healthy living and the Great Outdoors. It was first used in 1934 and still remains the byword for citrus quality and consistency.

Branding and name recognition are paramount at Outspan, so every Clementine, Satsuma, Delta Seedless Valencia and Star Ruby grapefruit bears the familiar Outspan name sticker.

While Outspan started as a South African brand, today Zimbabwe, Swaziland and Mozambique participate in the SACCE, and the four countries send more than 33 million cartons to 40 countries, largely from the port of Durban. Ambitious plans include a bid to raise that figure to 60 million by the year 2000.

OXO

The brand name Oxo first appeared on a jar of liquid beef extract in 1900, when it was sold as a health supplement. At the 1908 London Olympics, the company was the official caterer and supplied the marathon runners with Oxo drinks. The company also managed to persuade the entire British team of athletes to recommend Oxo in a special souvenir brochure for the Olympics. Great explorers of the time also took supplies of Oxo on their expeditions, notably Shackleton in 1907 and Scott (to the South Pole) in 1911.

Liquid Oxo was a great success, but a two-ounce bottle was still quite expensive and the company searched for something that would retail for a penny. So the Oxo cube was born in 1910. By the mid-1950s, the brand was facing a crisis as it came to be associated with wartime austerity and not with postwar Britain, with its new aspirations to prosperity.

The brilliant and highly successful "Katie" TV campaign, which started in 1958 and ran for 18 years, changed all that. Katie, a recognisably good cook, demonstrated the product's versatility and she also showed that it fitted into contemporary life-styles. Similar campaigns still run today and the brand, now owned by Van den Berg, is seen as a young, up-to-date product, closely associated with good cooking and family values.

A young, up-to-date product – despite a long history – Oxo is closely associated with good cooking and family values.

PALMOLIVE

In a market dominated by giants, Palmolive holds its place as one of the best-known names in soap. With a clear brand message that this is a washing agent that is gentle to the skin, the US company Colgate-Palmolive-Peet has extended the brand to include shaving cream, shampoo, a whole range of beauty products and the dish-washing liquid claimed to "Soften hands while you do the dishes". Branding has been strengthened by strong advertising campaigns – in some markets based on a fictitious manicurist, Madge – and distinctive packaging echoing the green of the soap.

One of the best known names in soap.

PAMPERS

Vic Mills, a Procter & Gamble researcher, spent some time in 1956 looking after his newborn grandchild and developed an understandable distaste for changing diapers. So he set his P&G team the task of creating one that would be effective, disposable and, most importantly, marketable. Although such things already existed, they were rarely used. Consumers considered them a poor substitute for the real thing and for emergency use only – when travelling, for example. They were also relatively expensive.

P&G's initial tests brought mixed results. When a group of Dallas babies tried the product, the 93°F heat made it too uncomfortable. And when Pampers was given its first full market test, in December 1961, the mothers trying it in Peoria, Illinois, were happy enough with the results but offended by the proposed price of 10 cents. The launch price in 1962 was reduced to six cents.

Pampers – other brand names considered were Tads, Solos and Larks – proved an immediate success, and a good example of the importance of market research. The brand has been continuously modified since its introduction, notably with the introduction of a premium quality range called Luvs, and the addition in 1984 of refastenable tapes, double elastic leg gatherers and improved absorbency. 1985 saw a complete brand overhaul with the launch of New Pampers, backed by a $500 million investment in new technology. This was swiftly followed in 1986 by the arrival of Ultra Pampers, a thinner but more absorbent diaper. This was improved yet again in 1994.

Pampers is one of P&G's most widely distributed brands, selling in more than 80 countries.

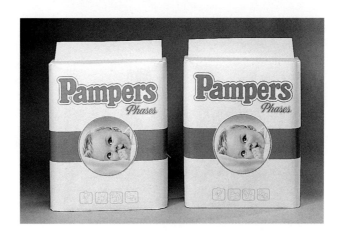

Babies in more than 80 countries keep dry in Pampers.

PAPER MATE

The ballpoint pen was invented in the early 1930s and first sold commercially in 1945. However, virtually all of these early pens had problems. The ink would clog, leak, smear and rub off on clothing. The emerging ball pen industry had its first major technological breakthrough in 1949 with the introduction of a pen using a revolutionary new ink, which dried instantly and was non-transferable; the pen was called Paper Mate.

The Gillette Company acquired Paper Mate in 1955 and has been introducing new and better popularly priced writing instruments since then. Paper Mate offers refillable and non-refillable pens under the Dynagrip, Flexigrip, Write Bros, Rubberstick, flair! and Eraser Mate brands.

A revolution in its day, the Paper Mate pen comes in a variety of forms.

PARKER

Founded in 1892 by George Safford Parker, the Parker Pen Company pioneered the leak-proof fountain pen. Over the years Parker has developed a reputation for the durability and craftsmanship of its products.

Parker pens have traditionally been used for historic signings around the world, and the company holds a royal warrant as the sole supplier of pens and inks to the British Royal Household. Among the most famous of Parker's line of writing instruments is the Parker Duofold, which was introduced shortly after the turn of the century and is still popular today. In 1933, Parker became a part of the Gillette Company, which is today the worldwide leader in writing instruments with its Parker, Paper Mate and Waterman brands.

Parker, the aristocrat of pens, is used for historic signings as well as in Buckingham Palace.

PEDIGREE CHUM

Pedigree Chum is a worldwide brand renowned for its quality and consistency. Recognised by its yellow packaging and red rosette (blue in North America), it has become trusted by dog owners as a brand offering the best nutrition for their pets.

Brand-owner Mars continues to support the prestigious dog show, Crufts, and has proved, time after time, that top breeders feed their dogs Pedigree Chum – thus strengthening its famous slogan: "Top breeders recommend it". Pedigree

Chum was the first brand to introduce the concept of "varieties", launching chicken, liver and rabbit & heart in 1973. A further development was the launch of Pedigree Chum Puppy Food in 1978 – the first canned dog food developed to cater to the specific nutritional requirements of a puppy. The product also acts as an important introduction to the brand at the earliest stage for a dog and its owner.

Continuing product development, launches of new varieties and range extensions should ensure this brand keeps clear of the competition in the years to come.

PENGUIN

Sixty years old in 1995, Penguin has become a household name in book publishing, signifying good books at affordable prices in paperback form.

The first ten paperbacks bearing the Penguin brand symbol on the cover included works by top authors such as Agatha Christie, Ernest Hemingway and Compton Mackenzie. They cost sixpence each, the price of a packet of cigarettes at the time. The revolutionary product met no competition until Pan Books was launched in 1946, but strong branding and skilful editorial policy have enabled Penguin to retain its image and reputation for low-priced excellence in today's highly competitive market.

The introduction of new lists helps keep the brand vigorous: for example, topical Penguin Specials, King Penguins, Penguin Classics and the Twentieth Century Classics series; as well as Puffin, the children's list. The company has also achieved celebrated coups, such as the publication of *Lady Chatterley's Lover*, *Spycatcher* and *The Satanic Verses*.

Penguin, a household name in publishing, signifies good books at affordable prices in paperback form.

Pentel supplies the world
with writing instruments.

PENTEL

Pentel was founded in 1945 in the belief that education would play an important role in postwar Japan. Initially a small business venture manufacturing and distributing art materials, the company now operates worldwide and is credited with developing two-thirds of all writing instruments since its conception.

The brand recently launched a new pen – the Clean Pentel – with the ability to destroy bacteria. It is made out of an inorganic, siver-based antibacterial material called Amenitop, which sterilises bacteria and viruses attached to its surface. Other products within Pentel's vast product line include the Sign Pen, Ball Pentel, Automatic Pencil, Correction Pen and Stylo.

PEPSI-COLA

Launched in 1898 by pharmacist Caleb D. Bradham, Pepsi is one of the world's oldest and most successful soft drinks with sales in 1995 of over $19 billion. It is by far the largest brand in the Pepsico portfolio, which also includes the products 7-Up, Mountain Dew, Mirina Orange, Ocean Spray and Lipton Original.

Pepsi has shown a talent for brand extension rarely achieved by its rivals. Its famous cola range today includes Diet Pepsi, Caffeine Free Pepsi, Caffeine Free Diet Pepsi, Pepsi and Pepsi Max – the world's first no-sugar, maximum cola taste brand. Pepsi Max alone had a sales figure of over $500 million in 1995 and is now distributed in 50 of the 190 plus countries in which Pepsi is available.

The traditional feuding between Pepsi and Coca-cola over market share continues with them vying for consumer loyalty in the new markets of China, India and Eastern Europe. Pepsi, striving to differentiate its brand further from the many cola brands in the market, launched its revolutionary 'Blue' look in April 1996 in various key markets. The new royal blue graphics are designed to transform the image of the brand. Partnering it is the new tag-line, 'change the script', aimed at strengthening Pepsi's strategy of attracting a more youthful consumer than Coca-Cola. Larry McIntosh, the vice president of International Advertising explains, "It [the tag-line] speaks to teenagers' universal desire to shake up the status quo and encourages them to look and think about Pepsi in a whole new way." Previous successful consumer trials in Bahrain lauded the 'new look' as being "modern" and "trendy".

To publicise the redesign, many high profile events occurred; for example, Air France's Concorde was painted blue and flew to 10 cities where launch events were imminent. The masthead of the British tabloid *The Daily Mirror* was printed in blue rather than its usual red on the launch day. Pepsi aims to feature its new packaging in all of its international markets by the end of 1997.

Pepsi's new 'Blue' look transforms the image of the brand and makes teenagers think about Pepsi in a whole new way.

PERNOD

Pernod is distributed in more than 140 countries but has its strongest following in Northern Europe.

The origins of Pernod are to be found in an "Absinthe Elixir" created by a French doctor during the late eighteenth century. In the early 1800s Henri-Louis Pernod, who valued absinthe more as an apéritif than for its medicinal properties, began producing it as a drink and thus created the brand that is known today.

Pernod merged with Ricard in 1975 to form the Pernod-Ricard Group, a strong bond that ensures top quality and high brand awareness. Today Pernod is associated with the French way of life, its composition and taste making it an original and unique product.

The dominant force in the bottled water sector.

Pernod symbolises the cosmopolitan, sophisticated French way of life.

PERRIER

The French penchant for mineral water owes its origins to the poor quality of the domestic supply. Perrier is the dominant force in the bottled water sector.

In early 1990 the Perrier brand suffered the kind of product quality problem which gives brand owners nightmares – independent testing in the United States detected minute traces of benzene, further tests in other countries confirmed the US findings and the company was forced to remove all supplies from the market for a period of several weeks. The cost to the company of withdrawing the product, of lost sales in the interim and of additional advertising and brand support has been estimated at over one billion French Francs (c£100 million).

Yet Perrier has bounced back – the sheer power of its brand has enabled it to reclaim market share and dispel negative connotations . This can be attributed to Perrier's clear-cut brand values which, over the years have been enforced through a powerful and cohesive marketing strategy. Perrier is stylish, fashionable and timeless… a brand whose personality is as effervescent as its content.

The "white lady", the famous advertising image of Persil, owned by Henkel of Germany.

Henkel's Persil as it was, 1907–91.

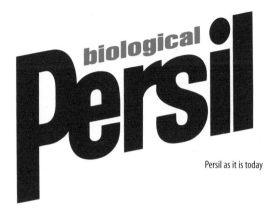

Persil as it is today

PERSIL

The detergents market is one of the most competitive and product innovative areas of the retail grocery trade, with many brands coming and going during its long history. One brand which has enormous strength in the industry is Persil, its name deriving from two of its ingredients: PERcarbonate and SILicate.

Persil has an interesting history. Originally developed in Germany, the brand is now owned by two separate groups: Unilever in the UK, Ireland, France and the Commonwealth; and Henkel in most other West European and six Eastern European countries. The two Persil trade marks are of common origin. However, in France, the trade mark was owned by a third party before its absorption by Unilever. The brand was registered in France as "Le Persil", its trademark also comprising an illustration of parsley. This expired in the late 1920s.

Throughout its history, Persil has prided itself on its understanding of the changing needs of its customers and its ability to supply products that meet those needs. Unilever introduced a "low-suds" detergent in the 1970s to suit front-loading washing machines, liquid products in the 1980s and bleach-free colour detergents in the early 1990s. Likewise Henkel introduced the first biological detergent (with enzymes) in 1970, a phosphate-free brand in the 1980s and its latest product, "Persil Megapearls".

The brand advertising of both companies continues to be very powerful, with the white lady (Henkel) being as famous as the Michelin man and Dulux dogs in their respective markets. Unilever continues to focus on the combination of cleaning and care in its 1995 campaign, "Persil performs brilliantly and it shows", based on the situation in which everyone is relying on Mum and Mum is relying on Persil, told with typical British humour.

Persil is a market leader in most of its markets, in particular those of Austria, Germany, Switzerland and the UK.

Perspex acrylic sheets have a versatile usage ranging from signage to aircraft canopies.

PHILEAS FOGG

Where once we nibbled crisps and peanuts with our sherry, we now eat Phileas Fogg New York Bagel Chips (Pastrami Flavour) and Chicettas.

Phileas Fogg Snacks is a brand which has not only achieved success in a highly competitive market but has actually transformed that market. Named after the character in the Jules Verne classic, *Around the World in Eighty Days*, the brand, launched by Derwent Valley Foods in 1982, specialises in premium quality snack foods with flavours from around the world. To a market almost entirely dominated by major, well-established companies purveying potato crisps and peanuts, Phileas Fogg's Tortilla Chips, Californian Corn Chips, Punjab Puri and Mignons Morceaux encouraged other aspirant brands and provided an incentive for manufacturers to become bolder and more innovative. In the process, consumer interest increased significantly and the overall market expanded to encompass a vast range of snack foods.

The brand, strengthened by distinctive and colourful packaging, bearing the image of the eponymous hero, is produced in Consett, County Durham and has helped to rescue a community devastated when its local steel mill closed in 1979.

PERSPEX

Perspex is a brand of acrylic sheet manufactured by Britain's Imperial Chemical Industries (ICI). Though the name is frequently and wrongly used generically, it is in fact a registered trade mark and has been so since 1934.

It was originally produced for use in the canopies of wartime fighter aircraft and is still used for that purpose in today's modern jets. The major current applications for Perspex sheet include the manufacture of baths – owing to its glossy surface and ease of cleaning – and its use in international signs, where its high quality and excellent colour range make it a natural choice. Perspex recently celebrated 60 years as a worldwide leading acrylic material.

Phileas Fogg has transformed the snacks we nibble with our sherry, introducing new, exotic varieties.

PHILIPS

Europe's largest electronics group began life as a light-bulb business. Headquartered in Eindhoven, Holland, it was founded in 1891 by Gerard Philips.

Light bulbs still feature in the Philips product portfolio, but they have been joined by a huge array of electronic products, such as semiconductor chips, computers, defence electronics, domestic appliances, hi-fi and audio equipment.

The Philips shield was adopted in 1938 and, together with the Philips trade mark, constitutes one of the most widely recognised corporate identities in Europe.

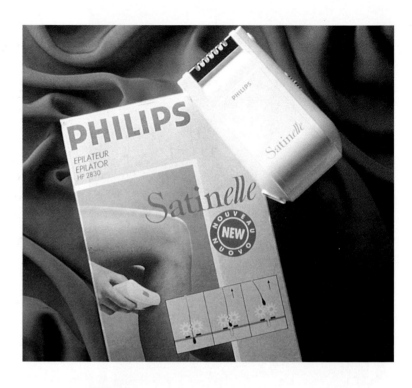

From a beginning as a light-bulb company a century ago, Philips is now one of the most widely recognised corporate identities in Europe.

Piaggio, leading western manufacturer of light urban transport, produces winner after winner, from the Vespa scooter to the Zip & Zip "bimodel" scooter.

PIAGGIO

Piaggio is the leading western manufacturer of light urban transport and the third largest in the world. In 1994 it manufactured and marketed 850,000 two-, three- and four-wheeled vehicles and over 500,000 bicycles, as well as automotive and motorcycle components.

In 1996 the Vespa scooter, one of the most successful products of the Piaggio Group, celebrates its fiftieth anniversary. It is just one of the series of winners the company has produced since the Piaggio family's connection with the group began in 1884. They include the plastic-bodied scooter, the Sfera, which won the Compasso d'Oro award in 1991, and its latest technological achievement, the Zip & Zip, the world's first "bimodel" scooter.

Operating with the tag-line, "Piaggio – The Movers", the brand intends to convey its aim of offering "Freedom through Mobility" through its stylish, top-quality products.

PILLSBURY

The Pillsbury company produces a range of refrigerated dough products, frozen foods and other grocery products for international consumption. Its leading brands include Haagen-Dazs ice-cream and Green Giant vegetables, although most people associate Pillsbury with the lovable Pillsbury Dough Boy. Such is the strength of this icon that Grand Metropolitan are re-introducing the brand into the UK market after its withdrawal in 1993.

The Pillsbury Dough Boy is the epitome of the Pillsbury brand.

PIMM'S

Pimm's is the quintessential English summertime drink, whose natural home is Henley, Royal Ascot and Wimbledon.

Although not registered as a trade mark until 1913, Pimm's' origins go back to around 1823, when James Pimm opened an oyster bar in the City of London. Pimm invented a gin sling – "No.1 cup" – a blend of gin, herbs and fruit liqueurs, which proved so popular that, when he sold his business in 1865, the new owner branded the drink "Pimm's" as a mark of quality. Pimm's was originally sold by the pint over the bar, the first bottle appearing in 1859.

Today Pimm's is sold worldwide (over half of its sales are abroad). Its market is also predominantly middle- to upper-class, perhaps a reflection on its early consumers and the fact that it was sent to British Army officers abroad, thus building up a reputation and following.

During the summer months Pimm's has a 33 per cent share of the speciality drinks market. Recent advertising campaigns have aimed at a broader, more youthful audience in an attempt to expand on its appeal.

The summer drink *par excellence*, Pimm's is associated with garden parties on rolling lawns.

ESTD. 1840

PIMM'S ®

POWER IS NOTHING WITHOUT CONTROL.

Carl Lewis, 'the fastest man for the fastest tyres', photographed by Annie Leibovitz. The 1994–95 campaign highlighted the prowess of the brand.

One of the world's largest Pizza restaurant chains, with a presence in over 88 countries.

PIRELLI

Pirelli has succeeded in making the highly unglamorous and humble tyre an object of fashionable interest and a powerful brand. It has effected this transformation through two routes. First, it has used design and style to reach the general public. Second, it has won the motor aficionado's plaudits by devoting considerable resources to research and development.

Here Pirelli is able to draw on synergies with another part of its business – cables and systems. Pirelli is the world's number two manufacturer in this sector. It also manufactures integrated components for telecommunications and power transmission.

From its conception, Pirelli has used top artists and designers for its poster advertising campaigns. During the 1950s and 1960s, Pirelli used famous designers such as Pavel M. Engelmann, Max Huber, Bruno Munari, Raymonde Savignac and Armando Testa. More recently, Pirelli has used performing artists and sports stars such as Hollywood's Sharon Stone. She featured in 'Driving Instinct', the first Pirelli advertisement to be broadcast all over Europe. In another ad, famous photographer Annie Leibovitz photographed top US sportsman Carl Lewis wearing red high-heeled shoes.

Like the majority of long-established brands, Pirelli has adapted its logo to suit the evolution of styles and fashion, but the elongated P has remained consistent throughout, an instantly recognisable hallmark of quality and familiarity. The Pirelli calendar adds an Italianate naughtiness to the brand which enhances its appeal among the red-blooded members of the motor sports fraternity. Today the calendar is a collector's item.

PIZZA HUT

From its humble beginnings as a Pizza restaurant in Wichita, Kansas, Pizza Hut is today one of the world's largest pizza restaurant chains, employing over 220,000 people in 88 countries. Through its ability to adapt products and identify new opportunities in the face of stiff competition Pizza Hut has firmly established itself as market leader. Not only was it the first company to introduce home delivery in the States, but it can also be credited with inventing pan pizzas, and more recently stuffed crust pizzas. This stuffed crust 'sub-brand', which was only introduced in 1995, represents 36% of total sales and has exceeded volume forecasts by 500%.

It is Pizza Hut's emphasis on market research and new product development, combined with high standards of product quality and customer service, that are accountable for sales of over 1.2 million pizzas every day. Who else can say with confidence that their annual sales of pepperoni slices would stretch twice around the world and to the moon?

PLANTERS

Planters nuts are today a prominent part of the American branding landscape, and they are an important component of the PlantersLifesavers Company, a subsidiary of RJR Nabisco, which is now owned by KKR Industries. But back in 1906, Planters was the sole brand owned by two Italian immigrants, who chose the name because they felt it sounded "important and dignified". Little did they know that 90 years later it would be worth hundreds of millions of dollars on a vast conglomerate's balance sheet.

The two men were innovators and reaped the rewards of their daring. At a time when peanuts were bought in bulk for only 10 cents a pound, the idea of selling branded salted nuts in penny and nickel bags was unheard of. The Planters offering of two-ounce bags for the equivalent of 40 cents a pound showed incredible chutzpah, not to say a sound nose for a profit. The partners believed, however, that customers would pay extra for a

branded product, and it would be easily identifiable when they wanted to buy another bag.

Since that time, Planters has gone on to become the largest peanut producer in America and the brand has succeeded by offering a quality product, combined with steady brand support.

Planters give a new, sophisticated look to monkey nuts.

POLAROID

Polaroid is the world leader in high-quality, hard copy imaging, producing cameras and film for instant photography as well as for more sophisticated business and technical markets.

Polaroid's successful branding combines customer friendliness with technological expertise. The first Polaroid camera was known as the Model 95. It produced sepia-toned monochromatic images in 60 seconds. The launch of Polacolor Land Film in 1963 ignited the instant colour photography market. The SX-70, which arrived in 1972, was a folding camera which ejected the picture through rollers at the front. Subsequent innovations have been based on this principle, and the current 636 CloseUp is a best seller.

Today a $2 billion concern, Polaroid was founded in Cambridge, Massachusetts and it continues to be headquartered there.

The 636 CloseUp is the latest in Polaroid's long line of innovative cameras.

PORSCHE

The strength of the Porsche brand was severely tested in the last global recession. The famous German sportscar brand suddenly found itself, like many luxury goods manufacturers, out of favour. Sales dropped from a record of just over 30,000 in 1989–90 to just under 15,000 in 1992–3. But the relaunch of the Carrera 911, updating one of the most distinctive and enduring car designs ever, gave Porsche a turbo-charged exit from the doldrums. It is now back in the black and sales have begun to climb. The company has even dared to talk about repeating its record output.

It has plans to launch a cheaper car in 1996. The Boxster, expected to be priced around DM75,000 (approx. £32,609), will be the first two-seater Porsche since the Spider. The company, founded by Ferdinand Porsche in 1931, has also recently undertaken its first-ever TV advertising, running campaigns in the USA and Germany. This has, it claims, "resulted in a noticeable improvement of the Porsche image and goodwill for the brand amongst the general public".

Porsche is less well known as an engineering and design consultant, but projects for other manufacturers account for up to 40 per cent of its work. The world's best-selling car, the Volkswagen Beetle, was created by Porsche, and the first Porsche-branded car, the 356, was initially made from Beetle components.

Since the launch of the 356 in 1949 – the first 46 of which were made entirely by hand – Porsche has stamped its name on the racing world more than any other manufacturer, with 22 000 competition victories. But perhaps Porsche's greatest victory is in the fact that 75 per cent of all the cars it has ever produced are still in use in some form – either on the roads, at classic car events or in museums.

POST-IT

3M's Post-it Notes have evolved in two decades from a laboratory curiosity into one of the world's best-selling office and consumer products.

3M's Post-it Notes are aide-mémoire for everyone everywhere.

In 1974, 3M scientist Art Fry used his church choir for an experiment. Fed up with hymn markers that kept falling out of the prayer book, he decided to put his laboratory research into adhesives to good effect. The result was a marker that remained attached to the page but which could be removed without causing damage. Realising the potential of this product, 3M began test-marketing. Surprisingly initial reaction was unfavourable, with consumers unappreciative of the product's value. The idea was almost killed off. However, a final attempt by the company to gain acceptance for the product via samples and demonstrations in banks, stores and offices was received with rapturous approval.

Post-it today comes in many formats, shapes and sizes, and has a sub-line of products including tape flags and glue sticks. A new development is easel-size Post-it pads designed for brainstorming sessions and formal meetings.

Relaunching the Carrera 911, one of the most distinctive and enduring car designs ever, pulled Porsche out of the recession.

PRO-SPECS

PRO-SPECS has done the equivalent of the 100 metre dash by becoming Korea's leading sports footwear brand in a relatively short space of time. Launched in 1981, it might not have had such a successful start if its owner, the Kukje Corporation, had stuck to the full-length title from which the brand is derived: Professional Specifications.

Clearly recognisable by its red and white logo – a stylised version of a crane in flight, symbolising the sporting drive for ever higher achievements – PRO-SPECS was given a huge boost when it was designated the official shoe supplier to the 1986 Seoul Asian Games and the 1988 Seoul Olympics.

The brand has been vigorously extended so that it now covers over 70 different kinds of sports shoes, clothing and equipment and 60 types of mountain-climbing and leisure equipment.

With over 30 per cent of its domestic production exported to more than 100 countries since 1986, PRO-SPECS generates revenues well in excess of 120 billion. The brand is poised for further international growth: in 1992 it signed licensing contracts with partners in Brazil and Hong Kong, offering access to Latin America and China.

Kukje has also recently developed an advanced technology sub-brand called TECH-MAX. Combined with a very eye-catching design, this product has proved extremely popular in the company's overseas markets.

The red and white crane in flight symbolises PRO-SPECS' rapid rise to become Korea's leading sports footwear brand.

PRUDENTIAL

The Prudential Insurance Company of America (not to be confused with the major British company of the same name) is a massive financial services brand. Under the flagship of The Prudential, the company markets a host of insurance, financial and real-estate services both in North America and, increasingly, the rest of the world.

The Prudential logo is the well-known 'rock' symbol, originally derived from the Rock of Gibraltar. This symbol has undergone a number of evolutionary changes, yet today is still one of the most identifiable corporate symbols in America.

Like other financial institutions, the Prudential has responded to the uncertainties of financial markets in recent years by diversifying the brand into other, less volatile areas and by stressing personal service.

THE WORLD'S GREATEST BRANDS

QANTAS

Qantas Airways celebrated its 75th anniversary in 1995 by becoming a public company. It was founded in 1920 as Queensland and Northern Territory Aerial Services but has expanded dramatically since then. The airline now serves over 90 destinations in 26 countries and employs over 25,000 people worldwide. It has also acquired an awesome reputation: for the past five consecutive years, an annual survey of business leaders has voted Qantas the best corporate image in Australia. It was ranked ahead of companies such as Mercedes-Benz, Microsoft and Cannon.

Qantas merged with Australian Airlines in 1992, giving it a much larger slice of the Australian domestic market. The merger meant that passengers could now fly on the one airline from virtually anywhere in Australia to 25 countries.

In 1994, Qantas undertook the largest corporate revamp in its history. The aircraft interiors, airport lounges and staff uniforms were all redesigned. As a result, Qantas Airways now showcases, across its vast domestic and international network, the very best corporate craftsmanship that Australia has to offer. Qantas has also launched an extremely successful advertising campaign featuring contemporary Australian performers and their version of the Peter Allen song, "I Still Call Australia Home". The advertisements filmed the performers against a backdrop of international destinations and colourful Australian landscapes, clearly positioning Qantas as an Australian airline covering a large international and domestic network. All these changes combine to build strength in a brand that is already regarded as a national icon.

Business leaders vote Qantas the best corporate image in Australia.

QUAKER

The Quaker Oats Company has become a broadly based food and drinks producer, yet the original product, Quaker Oatmeal, is still the flagship brand. This seems appropriate for a company which prides itself on its roots and plants its famous trade mark clearly on most of its products.

Quaker believes that brand strength correlates with high profitability. Indeed it refers to the Quaker brands as its "Value Portfolio" and sees these as the engine of growth and success. A high percentage of annual sales is ploughed back into this "portfolio".

Quaker's main beverages sold on a global basis are Gatorade, a "thirst quencher", and Snapple, a range of juices and iced teas.

Quaker Oats almost unfailingly mean porridge, but today the company's range has expanded far beyond this.

German margarine brand Rama is using brand extension to stay ahead of the competition and capitalise on the trend towards healthier eating.

RAMA

With 26·6 per cent of the German margarine market, Rama is the jewel in the crown of the panoply of leading brands owned by the Union Deutsche Lebensmittelwerke GmbH. A firm supporter of strong and consistent branding, the Union markets Rama as the vegetable alternative to butter and the ideal breakfast spread. Brand positioning emphasises that Rama is made of 100 per cent high-quality, pure vegetable oils, contains the essential, energy-giving vitamins A, D and E, tastes good on bread and is equally suitable for kitchen use.

Brand extension cashes in on current health concerns, with Rama Balance containing 25 per cent less fat than standard Rama but retaining all its best qualities. Unlike other half-fat margarines, it is recommended as ideal for cooking.

RAY-BAN

Tom Cruise wore them in the film *Risky Business*. They were Don Johnson's sunglasses in the television series *Miami Vice*. From the start, the American optics company Bausch and Lomb conceived Ray-Ban as their premium quality brand sunglasses. Anti-Glare Goggles, their first commercial sunglasses, introduced in 1936, were priced at 3·75 dollars when ordinary sunglasses cost around 25 cents. Would consumers pay so much extra for a quality product? They would – and still do for Ray-Ban sunglasses, the name adopted the following year.

Since World War II, when Ray-Ban were standard government issue, the brand has expanded in line with growing consumer perception of sunglasses as a fashion accessory. By 1956 many new styles were being introduced yearly, no longer mirroring prescription frame styling but more advanced in shape, decoration and colour treatment. Some 20 years later, the brand appeared with lens types to satisfy the demand of the fashion market for colour-coordinated combinations and of the sports market for special performance lenses. The technical excellence of the brand, combined with its attention to innovation, has earned Ray-Ban a reputation in fashion for quality-based designs and the brand loyalty of a large sector of the market.

Ray-Ban, the perennially fashionable and expensive sunglasses brand, is a classic example of the importance of pricing in the marketing equation.

READER'S DIGEST

Who reads *Reader's Digest*? The seeming invisibility of RD's many millions of readers remains one of the world's greatest mysteries – and a cause of much amusement to the owners of the world's most successful publication. While its readers may not be as high-profile as those of some other titles (it is sold mainly through subscription) there is no questioning their loyalty.

Published in 18 languages and in 47 different editions, RD has a monthly circulation of 27 million and a claimed 100 million readers worldwide. Its carefully constructed mix of humour, homily and condensed versions of previously published articles has ensured a very solid core for what is an increasingly diversified operation.

RD also publishes an ever-lengthening list of hardback books ('how-to', reference, travel, cooking, history, religion, geography and children's) and condensed books (abridged versions of well-known titles), as well as series books such as the Reader's Digest/American Medical Association Home Medical Library. Then there are the music collections – from classical to country and jazz, to rock – and the videos. All of the above sell in the multi-millions.

Reader's Digest dates back to 1922. Issue number one, subtitled "The Little Magazine", was dated February of that year and published in Greenwich Village, New York, by DeWitt Wallace and his wife, Lila Acheson Wallace. The wayward son of an academic, "Wally" had a background in advertising and selling and was convinced his personal brand of self-improvement would make good copy. The first print-run was 5000 copies. Unable to sell his idea to a publisher, Wally had decided to mail it direct to his readers.

After four years the circulation had exceeded his target of 15,000 by 5,000. But in the next three years it skyrocketed to 216,000, and by 1936 it had reached 1·8 million. Worldwide revenues in 1994 were $2·8 billion, with profits of almost $400 million. The company employs 6,700 people in more than 50 locations worldwide.

Sports shoe giant Reebok has used authenticity, excitement and innovation to fuel its breathtaking growth over the past decade.

REEBOK

Joseph William Foster was an athlete who put a spike in his shoes to help him run faster. That was back in the 1890s. The device was so successful that he started to sell running shoes of this kind for leading athletes. The founder's grandsons took up his trade and set up a company called Reebok, the name taken from an African gazelle, which in time swallowed Foster's company.

In 1979, an American took Reeboks to the US market and, although they were more expensive than any other running shoes, they proved a big hit. The Reebok range expanded quickly to include items such as women's athletic shoes and shoes for aerobics. The Reebok Freestyle became the best-selling athletics shoe of all time. Reebok's sales soared from $13 million in 1983 to $3·3 billion in 1994. The company describes its corporate strategy as 'creating innovative products that generate excitement in the marketplace'.

Reebok has two broad goals: to build businesses in specific sports categories and to create authenticity for the entire brand. The company developed its ground-breaking 'pump' technology in the late 1980s.

Created by a fervent believer in self-improvement, *Reader's Digest* has become a phenomenally successful publication and a prime example of how a great brand is more than the sum of its parts.

REESE'S

Like baseball and apple pie, Reese's is quintessential Americana and its Peanut Butter Cup remains one of the best-loved confectionery brands in the USA. But it should be remembered that the familiar orange, yellow and brown wrapped peanut butter cups, produced by the HB Reese Candy Company, had a slow start. Initially distributed through wholesale jobbers, vending machine operators and syndicated stores, the brand had only modest success during the 1940s and 1950s. However this eventually grew into nationwide popularity, which in turn led to increased manufacturing capacity.

The company was subsequently acquired by the Hershey Chocolate Company. In 1976 the first variation was made to Reese's Peanut Butter Cups – in the form of Reese's Crunchy, offering the flavour and texture of chopped peanuts. Following this successful launch, Reese's became available in a jar format. Today the brand comes in a variety of seasonal extensions, including peanut butter eggs and peanut butter pumpkins. Reese's remains one of America's best-selling chocolate and confectionery brands.

One of the best-selling confectionery brands in the USA, Reese's is considered as American as apple pie – well, almost.

RENAULT

Renault is the twelfth largest company, and the fourth largest vehicle manufacturer in Europe, producing almost two million vehicles a year. Like many European and American car companies it can trace its lineage back to the turn of the century: indeed, the marque's reputation was such that in 1905 King Edward VII ordered a 14/20 hp Landaulette.

Renault produces almost 2 million vehicles a year.

REUTERS

Reuters is the largest provider of news and information to the international financial and business communities and the world's media.

Since the founder, Paul Julius Reuter, used pigeon post to bridge the gap in European telegraph lines in 1850, Reuters has proved adept at developing and exploiting new modes of communication. The pigeons have long since been replaced by satellite and cable. Investment in information technology and networks and the breadth of its coverage have enabled Reuters to stay one step ahead of the competition. With news and market data being updated over 1,000 times per second and transmitted to more than 340,000 terminals in 158 countries, Reuters is a true information revolutionary.

Reuters, the world's largest provider of electronic information.

The Business of Information

Revlon, the manufacturer of cosmetics, skin care, fragrance and personal care products has established itself as a producer of technologically innovative products.

REVLON

Revlon, the manufacturer of cosmetics, skin care, fragrance and personal care products has established itself as the producer of technologically innovative products through brands including ColorStay, Age Defying, and Charlie. It is this technological edge combined with an extensive distribution network that has enabled it to aggressively launch its new products and realise its ambition of developing global brands. This is epitomised by ColorStay, a cosmetics brand, which has exceeded sales forecasts in all of the 100 markets within which it has been launched.

The liquorice-flavoured Ricard, a brand closely associated with glamorous sports like yachting and motor racing, is a favourite of French and Mediterranean pastis drinkers.

RICARD

The pastis, Ricard, was discovered and named by the Frenchman Paul Ricard in 1932. Ricard is the best known pastis in France and a leading spirit globally.

Pastis are aniseed-flavoured spirits but Ricard differs importantly from its French cousin, Pernod, in that it contains liquorice, which gives it a distinctive colour, smell and taste. The use of aniseed in drinks goes back centuries and traditional elixirs from all round the Mediterranean have laid claim to its restorative powers.

Ricard is mostly sold in France and neighbouring European countries, where it has universal recognition. The brand is also active in sports sponsorship, particularly yachting and motor racing. Ricard is now part of the Pernod Ricard Group.

It could have remained a small-time manufacturer of surfboards, but Australian brand Rip Curl used ambitious marketing to become an internationally recognised maker of fashion clothes and mountain wear as well.

RIP CURL

A home-grown product of Australian surfing, Rip Curl is now an international brand, supplying everything the surfer may require. Today, ten corporate licensees make and sell its products in the USA, France, New Zealand, South Africa, Brazil, Argentina, the Middle East and Japan, while it has distributors in Britain, Germany, Spain, Switzerland, Guadeloupe and Martinique, Tahiti and French Polynesia.

Rip Curl was founded in 1969 by two local surfing enthusiasts in a garage in Torquay, Victoria, close to the surfer's paradise of Bells Beach. The brand retains their personal imprint and their claim that the people who run the company are the test pilots and surfers themselves. Aiming to integrate the adventurous lifestyle and ethos of surfing with a new approach to business, they first concentrated on producing improved designs of surfboards. As surfing boomed in the 1970s, the brand was quickly extended to wet suits, and then to suits for windsurfers, sailors and water skiers, and more recently to mountain wear.

The brand's focus remains surfing and the production of functional items that meet the specific demands of surfers and the surfing environment, to give surfers not only the product they want but the product they need. Today another extension – Rip Curl Surfwear – is the company's largest product division and a major force in the Australian clothing market, setting fashion trends by its creativity and quality. It is complemented by Rip Curl surfing accessories, including bags and watches.

The brand's status has been enhanced by sponsorship of professional surfing contests as well as of top surfers. In addition, a campaign called 'The Search' has been initiated for the 1990s, taking participants on surf trips to exotic locations in pursuit of the essence of "The Surfer's Life – Adventure, Friendship and the Perfect Wave".

THE RITZ HOTEL

The Ritz, one of the most prestigious hotels in the world, situated overlooking Green Park in the heart of London, is associated with glamour, luxury and exclusivity. Owned by the Barclay brothers and opened in 1906, it boasts 130 bedrooms, three private function rooms and the Palm Court Room, made famous for its afternoon teas. With a guest list ranging from Charlie Chaplin to Andy Warhol, Jackie Onassis and Patrick Swayze, this well-respected venue has established itself as being at the forefront of hospitable yet unobtrusive service.

The Ritz, one of the world's most prestigious hotels, overlooking Green Park in London.

RITZ CRACKERS

Ritz Crackers, the savoury biscuit, was one of the major brands acquired by Danone from RJR Nabisco in 1988. This allowed the world record takeover of RJR Nabisco by leveraged buyout specialists Kohlberg Kravis Roberts, who paid $24.5 billion! The French multinational Danone (formerly BSN) is the French biscuit market leader trading mainly under the name "Jacob's Bakery."

The savoury snack that cost £24·5 billion.

RIZLA

Rizla is a leading brand name of cigarette rolling paper. Founded in 1876, when Napoleon's Registrar granted a licence to Citizen Lacroix to manufacture fine papers, this rice paper has a worldwide sales figure of $110 million, with production facilities in Belgium, France and Wales.

Rizla, its name created from the French word for rice (riz) and the family name Lacroix, has a share of nearly 80 per cent of the UK market, and supplies over one thousand million booklets a year to customers in nearly 100 countries. Rizla's different lines are known by the colours of the packaging, namely red, blue and green, but there are also sub-brands, including Liquorice and Vetaire Supercool. On its visual material, Rizla uses a distinctive plus sign.

Rizla was acquired by a consortium led by Union Bank of Switzerland in 1994.

It may be a humble cigarette rolling paper brand, but Rizla's global reach is formidable and its name recognition enough to make many more prestigious products turn green with envy.

ROBINSONS

Robinsons is as much a part of Wimbledon, the famous London tennis tournament, as are strawberries and cream and bad weather.

Since its launch in 1903, the brand has gone from strength to strength and now accounts for 35 per cent of the UK dilutables market. Robinsons Barley Water, well known for its nutritious attributes, came onto the market in 1935, and in 1948 was extended into a range of fruit-flavoured squashes. Eager to meet the needs of an increasingly health-conscious and fast-paced society, Robinson recently introduced a sugar-free product line and a more portable "Light" version.

Robinsons was bought by Britvic in 1995 and is currently the eleventh biggest grocery brand in the UK.

Shrewd and sustained sponsorship and advertising have made the Robinsons soft drink brand seem the essence of Britain's Wimbledon tennis tournament.

ROLEX

A Rolex watch, more than almost any other item of jewellery, is a "must" for many people around the world.

It was not until the early part of this century that it became normal to wear one's watch on one's wrist – until then the fob or pocket watch was the normal type of personal timepiece, worn on a chain to discourage thieves and prevent breakage.

The Rolex Watch Company, originally founded in London by Hans Wilsdorf, produced in 1910 a miniaturised watch to be worn on the wrist. It was embedded in a solid metal case to guard against shock and moisture and in 1914 a Rolex watch was awarded a Class A certificate by Britain's Kew Observatory – it was sufficiently accurate to be used as a marine chronometer.

The famous Oyster waterproof watch was introduced in 1926 but otherwise the appearance, qualities and performance of Rolex watches have remained largely unaltered for three-quarters of a century. Rolex is a classic watch and the pleasures of owning such a beautiful piece of engineering appeal as strongly today as ever before, despite the advent of the quartz watch.

ROLLS-ROYCE

The epitome of expensive, luxurious, super-comfortable motoring, the Rolls-Royce brand has survived every vicissitude, including world recession, to emerge unscathed as the ultimate in stately elegance and technical perfection. This is a brand so well-established that the price, quality and history of the product differentiate it and distance it from any rival. By appealing to a tiny, but extremely committed, consumer niche with pure expressive values of status and ownership, Rolls-Royce epitomises the quality of brand depth.

Motor-enthusiast and aristocrat the honourable Charles Stewart Rolls met north of England engineering genius Henry Royce for lunch at the Midland Hotel, Manchester (now the Holiday Inn Crowne Plaza) in 1904. From their collaboration aimed at producing the best car in the world, the first Rolls-Royce emerged. From then on, Phantom has followed Silver Ghost, Silver Cloud followed Silver Wraith, and Silver Spirit succeeded Silver Spur in an almost unbroken cavalcade.

Royal patronage is a plus in brand promotion. The first British owner of a Rolls-Royce motor car was the Duke of Windsor. Today the Queen has five official state Rolls-Royce cars at her disposal, one of which, in 1994, became the first vehicle through the Channel Tunnel. Nor was this prestige limited to the UK. Tsar Nicholas II imported two Silver Ghosts; Lenin had nine Rolls-Royces. Some state heads adapted their cars to fit exotic needs and tastes, so the Maharajah of Bharatpur had searchlights fitted for tiger shooting and solid gold, silver and mother of pearl interior accessories.

In 1985 Rolls-Royce Motors celebrated the production of a total of 100,000 Rolls-Royces and Rolls-Royce-built Bentleys since 1904, the relatively low figure reflecting the exclusive nature of the brand. Today the company places increasing emphasis on the limited-edition niche and bespoke models.

The embodiment of quality, luxury and exclusivity, the Rolls-Royce brand has survived world wars and global recessions and continues to inspire brand managers around the world.

ROTHMANS

From its founding in a rented room in 1890 Rothmans has developed into a world class manufacturer of blended fine tobaccos. Whilst the production of cigarettes has been aided by the introduction of new technology Rothmans maintain a traditional service (they still deliver their cigarettes to clubs and embassies by coach and footmen). Assured and confident, the Rothmans brand has maintained the integrity with which Louis Rothman established the company over 100 years ago.

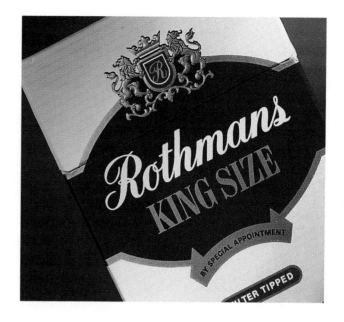

Rothmans still hand-deliver their cigarettes to clubs and embassies.

ROYAL DOULTON

Royal Doulton is the benchmark for premium china and other ceramic products. Its name is associated with British royalty and is internationally synonymous with excellence and style. Brands like Royal Crown Derby, Minton and Royal Albert sell in 80 countries and still have the mystique and awe that history has bequeathed them.

All of the brands are registered as trade marks across the world and are rigorously protected. Royal Crown Derby is the oldest brand in the Royal Doulton portfolio, dating back to 1748. It achieved early success with royalty when King George III gave the company permission to incorporate the British Crown in its backstamp. Minton china, with its gold leaf decoration, was created 45 years later. Royal Doulton was first made in 1815 and quickly developed into a wide giftware range. Royal Doulton has set up sourcing and licensing arrangements for glassware, textiles and kitchen products, allowing the company to exploit its technical, design and brand strengths.

Royal Doulton is a name imbued with pedigree and tradition, ensuring a plentiful supply of customers for its still-expanding range of china, glassware, textiles and kitchen products.

SAINSBURY

Sainsbury made its first mark as a British retailer in 1882, when a store in North London began smoking and selling its own bacon. The range of cooked meats grew to include sausages prepared in the store's own kitchens and, from the 1920s, Sainsbury expanded across all packaged foods. After World War II, Sainsbury became Britain's leading own-brand maker, winning plaudits for its simple design. The range grew to include vegetables and household goods, and eventually wine through in-store off-licences.

Sainsbury's advertising has never failed to stress its strong brand differentiation in a highly competitive UK retailing market. In the 1980s, for example, its slogan ran, "If it isn't better, or cheaper, or different, it isn't Sainsbury's."

The company has recently developed a number of sub-brands in a bid to challenge dominant proprietary brands. Among these is a range of household detergents called Novon (now the fifth largest UK detergent brand) and Classic Cola, which claims a national market share of some 13 per cent. Classic Cola is an example of a highly successful sub-brand that has been designed to replicate some of the design characteristics of the manufacturers' brands, and that has led to friction between the brand owners and the retailer.

Sainsbury has been a leader in the own-brand revolution in the UK, posing a long-term challenge to the brand owners which they have yet to meet successfully.

Despite increasing competition from arch-rival Tesco, Sainsbury remains the UK's most profitable supermarket chain and a byword for good quality at reasonable prices.

SAMSON

Samson roll-your-own tobacco is produced by the Dutch company Royal Theodorus Niemeyer and has carved a world niche as the youthful alternative to the branded cigarette. The Halfzware taste and consistent premium quality, coupled with strong imagery, have made this a powerful brand. The company has kept the price low enough to ensure strong loyalty among the less well-off.

When Samson started to strike a chord with the youthful generation of the 1960s and 1970s, the brand was associated with feelings of freedom, individuality and nonconformity. In recent years, Samson has expanded its tobacco range by adding Mild and Extra Mild taste versions to supplement the now familiar Halfzware taste.

Mass-market pricing combined with a niche marketing strategy and a non-conformist image have allowed this evergreen roll-your-own tobacco brand to maintain its youthful appeal.

SAMSUNG

Lee Kun-Hee, the chairman of Samsung, did an extraordinary thing in 1993. First, he spent two months talking to 1800 executives at the company about every aspect of its operations. Then he set about writing a small book encapsulating a radically new philosophy to sustain the Korean industrial giant well into the twenty-first century.

Distributed in 1994 to Samsung's 180,000 employees in 59 countries, the book is an extremely unusual piece of corporate creativity. It shuns jargon and 'management speak' and talks instead about the pressing need to rid Samsung of "selfishness" and "authoritarian attitudes". One chapter is entitled: "Humanism, morality, manners and etiquette."

Chairman Lee describes the sleepless nights he has endured contemplating the crisis facing his company. It has become a "life or death" situation requiring "change, no matter what the cost." The most immediate result of all this navel-gazing was the launch of a new corporate identity and corporate philosophy. The new image features white lettering on a blue ellipse background. The blue equates to "stability, reliability, warmth and intimacy", while the ellipse shape reflects "dynamism" and a sense of the world moving through space. The new philosophy talks of contributing to a better global society, where the old mission statement alluded only to national prosperity. More concrete evidence of change includes a shorter working day to encourage a stronger sense of family life among Samsung employees and a recruitment drive to bring more female personnel into senior management positions.

Founded in 1938 by Lee's father, Lee Byung-Chull, Samsung was rated the fourteenth largest company in the world in 1994 by *Fortune* magazine, with net sales of $51·3 billion. With interests in engineering, electronics, chemicals and financial services, Samsung is aiming to quadruple its sales within the next decade. Lee seems less interested in profits. Currently ploughing most of them back into the corporate restructuring, he writes in his book: "Profits without humanity are worthless."

With its inspirational chairman, electronics to financial services giant Samsung is charging into the new millennium with an even more innovative outlook.

SAN MIGUEL

The San Miguel brand of beer had its one-hundredth birthday in 1990 and the brand's heritage and familiarity is, for the Filipino drinker, its key point of difference.

Even though San Miguel was the first beer to be brewed in the Philippines there are now 13 beer brands produced locally and a further ten imports are available in major supermarkets. San Miguel, however, dominates the medium to high price segment as a result of quality, distribution, promotion and constant innovation – recently, for example, San Miguel Super Dry and San Miguel Non-Alcoholic beers have been introduced. The company has also put much effort into dealer aids, for example electric coolers and signage, a powerful factor in a market like the Philippines.

San Miguel beer is brewed and marketed under licence in Papua New Guinea, Indonesia, Western Samoa and Nepal: there is also a major San Miguel brewery in Hong Kong. In addition, San Miguel is exported to major overseas markets such as the United States, Australia, the United Kingdom and Japan where it enjoys a reputation for high quality.

Sara Lee, which began life as a cake brand and ended up as a corporate name denoting a hugely diverse product portfolio, is a great example of just how far strong branding can go.

SARA LEE

Branding the corporation can be overlooked in a company's search for product branding and marketing, but the Sara Lee Corporation has not made that mistake. The American company, which makes a vast range of foods and domestic items, exchanged its accurate but boring title, Consolidated Foods, for the much more friendly one of Sara Lee to develop expressive branding values. In seeking to relate to shoppers, the company took the route taken much earlier by Betty Crocker – finding a name that excited some common values and memories with the customer in the hope that the corporate name will reflect the product values.

The Sara Lee did not come out of thin air, of course. In 1956 Nathan Cummings, the company's founder, acquired the Chicago-based bakery kitchens of Sara Lee, securing a strong position in the frozen baked foods sector. However the company name remained Consolidated Foods. In fact, despite massive diversification into completely unrelated markets such as white goods (Electrolux) and apparel (Gant, Country Set and Canadelle), it was not until 1985 that the name was finally changed to the Sara Lee Corporation.

Today, with 140,000 employees and revenues of $15·5 billion (1993–4), Sara Lee owns brands such as Douwe Egberts, Bali, Playtex, Mr. Turkey, Ball Park, Endust, Behold, Hillshire Farm, Jimmy Dean and, of course, Sara Lee. Its products range from shoe polish to packaged meats, from bras to bubble baths, from desserts to insecticides, from coffee to hot dogs, from household products to hosiery (of which it is the world's largest manufacturer).

SCALEXTRIC

Along with Hornby trains and Meccano, Scalextric is a ubiquitous childhood memory. Seeking to update his clockwork cars, Scalextric founder B. Francis made modifications, such as inserting electric motors and devising a track system for them to operate on. The success of this resulted in the launch of Scalextric in 1957.

The brand saw unrivalled growth over the next two decades, thanks to its painstaking attention to detail and constant innovation. It was not all plain sailing, however. A much-hyped design gimmick called "You Steer", did not create the huge sales expected. For a while in the early 1970s, the company's future looked uncertain. But things were soon back on track. A sister company, Hornby Hobbies, took over all Scalextric production and refocused the brand positioning. With an injection of new technology, Scalextric managed to reclaim its position as a toy market leader. It even survived the onslaught of the home computer in the 1980s. Still a forerunner in its market, Scalextric today is proving adept at keeping up with the ever-increasing demand for higher quality and more realistic children's products. The latest racing car models have working brake lights as well as rear and front headlights.

A ubiquitous childhood memory, the continuously updated Scalextric has survived the onslaught of computer games and remains as compelling as ever.

The world's leader in mixer drinks.

SCHWEPPES

Jacob Schweppe was a Swiss entrepreneur who emigrated to London in the late eighteenth century and quickly set up in business selling pure, bottled waters to wealthy London society. And the market was huge – drinking water was almost all polluted and it was recognised (even if it was not proved until some fifty years later) that much disease originated from the appalling water supply.

Mr Schweppe was blessed with a delightful, onomatopoeic name (would he have prospered had he been named Reifenhauser or Uithoff?) and Schweppes soft drinks are now famous world-wide. Curiously, Schweppes has always found it difficult to compete internationally in the pop drinks sector against such brands as Coca-Cola, Pepsi and Seven-Up (though in many countries the company acts as distributor or joint venture partner with these brands). Schweppes' heartland is in the mixer drink area and even though the production and distribution of such drinks is identical to that of pop drinks, clearly the culture of branding in the two market sectors is quite different – whereas mixer drinks are adult, sophisticated and 'special occasion' and also require a wide range of flavours, pop drinks are younger, informal and more closely focused on a single product formulation.

SCOTCH TAPE

Invented in 1930 primarily as a seal for perishable food in cellophane wrappers, Scotch Tape is now one of the top selling office products in the USA.

The brand became obsolete in its intended market following the introduction of a heat-sealing cellophane process, but the Great Depression gave Scotch Tape an unexpected boost. The new-found need to be economical provided many uses for which it had not been intended – repairing torn book pages, ripped clothing and torn bank notes, for example.

Brand improvements over the next few years ensured ease of use and growing popularity. In 1932 the first heavy-duty tape dispenser was designed and marketed. Thirty years later 3M engineers perfected the tape, to prevent it from yellowing and oozing excess adhesive. Scotch Tape today is used in a vast span of human activity, from fixing schoolbook covers to sealing bottles of wine.

With its foundations in the Great Depression of the 1930s, adhesive tape brand Scotch Tape is the marketing success story par excellence, turning

SCRABBLE

There are not many board games which can claim to have a following as fanatical as that of Scrabble. Created by New Yorker Alfred Butts in the 1930s, the game now comes in 31 different languages and even features Braille and computer versions. It is sold in over 120 countries worldwide, including the recently selected markets of the Czech Republic, Hungary and India.

There are national and world Scrabble championships. In Thailand the game is so popular that there is a daily column devoted to it in the national press. The highest ever word score achieved in competition is 392 points, by a Dr Karl Khoshnaw of Twickenham, UK. He achieved this incredible feat with "Caziques", the plural form of a word referring to a West Indian chief.

Scrabble is the world's best-selling word game. J.W.Spear & Sons, now owned by Mattel, bought the UK distribution rights in 1954 and the worldwide rights outside Australia, Canada and the USA in 1969. Under its new ownership, the Scrabble phenomenon should continue to spread across the globe, harnessing new converts with its unique blend of frustration and reward.

Scrabble is one of the few board games to inspire a fanatical following, and new global licensing deals should ensure even more devotees.

SEARS

Sears represents the cream of US retailing, offering a vast range of items to its predominantly middle-market, female clientele.

SEARS

Today the Sears Corporation is one of the world's largest retailing and mail order operations, an American brand name of unparalleled power and width.

But Sears' origins are humble indeed. Richard Sears was a telegraphist on the railway in Minnesota in the 1880s when he began to dabble in selling watches. The business had greater prospects than the telegraphy and he advertised for somebody who understood watches. He gave the job to Alvah Roebuck. The partnership set up their mail order business, aimed mainly at farmers, in the Chicago area, eventually taking the name Sears, Roebuck and Co.

They expanded their catalogue list out of jewellery and sold almost every available consumer product. The business boomed on the strength of new and untried systems for mail order management, rigorous product quality control (in the "Sears laboratory") and a spare tone to its catalogue writing. In the mid-1920s, Sears launched its first shop and by 1931, it was selling more goods by retail than through mail order. Today there are more than 800 Sears department stores across the USA, and 1,800 smaller shops.

Sears aims at what it calls "middle market" customers, and it says its typical customer is a woman aged between 25 and 54 whose household income is about $37,000: "She is the chief purchasing agent for her household for everything from apparel to appliances, electronics and furniture. More than half of all purchase decisions are made by women." Sears franchise lines, Kenmore appliances, Craftsman tools and Dietland batteries, dominate the marketplace and are leading American brands.

SEGA

SEGA, the multi-million dollar entertainment corporation, has gone from strength to strength since it pioneered the home video games market in the early 1980s. SEGA's continuous investment in research and development (approx 8% of total sales revenue), combined with its creativity in bringing ideas to life, have given consumers millions of hours of enjoyment.

Such has SEGA's impact been on popular culture that Sonic the Hedgehog, SEGA's most famous character, has now been added to the archives of the British Film Institute. Not content with this, SEGA have launched their latest attraction, Segaworld, the first virtual-reality theme park of its kind. Based within London's Trocadero complex in Piccadilly Circus, the centre spans seven floors, covering an area bigger than the Albert Hall! SEGA is undoubtedly a vibrant, dynamic brand, prepared to push technology and creativity to the max. As the SEGA saying goes..... creativity is life.

© Sega Enterprises Ltd. 1991/1992

As SEGA says, 'Creativity is life'.

SELLOTAPE

Sellotape, introduced in 1938, swiftly became a market leader and still holds that position today. It is currently recognised by over 90 per cent of the UK population and even has an entry in the *Oxford English Dictionary* – an acknowledgement of its usage as a generic term for clear adhesive tape.

In 1995, in a bid to free the brand from its generic image and to allow an extension of the product portfolio into new market sectors, its owner changed its name to the Sellotape Company. This paved the way for a £2 million "Rediscovery programme". The first area of operations to be affected by the change was the Office and Commercial division, with new lines marketed under the "Sellotape Office" brand. Another aspect of "Rediscovery" is the new across-the-range packaging. The brand seems well placed for continued dominance well into the twenty-first century.

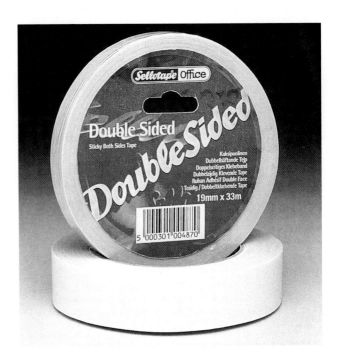

Sellotape has recently taken radical action to revive its flagging fortunes and associate the famous sticky tape name with a host of new and innovative products.

SEVEN SEAS®

The national institution for fish oil supplements.

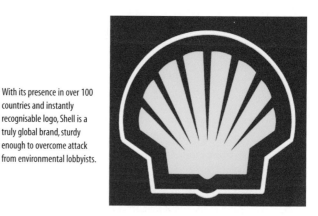

With its presence in over 100 countries and instantly recognisable logo, Shell is a truly global brand, sturdy enough to overcome attack from environmental lobbyists.

SEVEN SEAS

Seven Seas is a national institution. How many people were 'dosed' with cod liver oil as a child and still buy Seven Seas healthcare products today?

From the company's pre-war beginnings in Hull, when a group of trawlermen formed a co-operative to refine and market cod liver oil, Seven Seas has increased in size and reputation to become the leading brand in the dynamic health supplement market – a market which has recorded such impressive growth over the past decade that it is now the most valuable of all over-the-counter sectors.

Seven Seas' leadership has been crucial to the growth of this market and, as a result, it is currently the most successful positive healthcare company in the UK.

Over the years, Seven Seas has demonstrated commitment to research and has fought to achieve the pharmaceutical and medical recognition that has fuelled consumer belief in product benefits. Its heavyweight advertising, promotion and consumer education programmes and investment in product development have succeeded both in creating new markets and in attracting new users to established products.

In addition to cod liver oil, which continues to outperform all other health supplements, the Seven Seas portfolio includes evening primrose and starflower oils, multivitamins, single vitamins, minerals and a range of supplements such as ginseng and garlic. Seven Seas also markets leading healthcare brands, New Era, Pulse, Hofels, Minadex and Haliborange.

Seven Seas sets the pace in the health supplement market, yet it has never forsaken its healthy heritage. It has successfully married traditional values with contemporary aspirations and style to dominate a fast-moving market without losing consumer confidence or trust.

In 1994, Seven Seas was granted the Royal Warrant.

SHELL

Few brands extend to cover as vast an empire or employ so positive a branding policy as Shell. Today the Royal Dutch/Shell Group is one of the world's largest businesses, operating in more than a hundred countries. It has about one-tenth of world oil and natural gas, outside the former centrally planned economies, and has interests in nearly all aspects of the oil and chemical business, plus substantial investments in coal and forestry.

Yet one brand is closely managed to cover all this enormous operation. Shell sees its brand, conveyed by the Shell emblem (the pecten), the word "Shell" and the Shell colours, red and yellow, as one of its most important assets, and manages it in such a way that it is as far as possible seen as a constant. That brand can mean the Royal Dutch/Shell Group itself or the individual company with responsibilities for oil, gas, chemicals, coal and so on. It can also signify the Shell retail automotive network; or be the recognisable brand on thousands of widely diverse products; or services such as fuel cards and customer care, or be the corporate name and marketing brand of new businesses and new products.

Whatever the context, the brand aims to be seen as a guarantee of quality and reliability, and also to communicate a sense of added value, strength and an identity as part of the community with its own character and personality. The company sets out its brand goals in a table of values which stress commitment to the environment (which sometimes comes up against conflicts of interest), leadership in product quality and service standards, and technological improvement.

The Royal Dutch/Shell Group was formed in 1907 by the merger of the Royal Dutch Petroleum Company and the Shell Transport and Trading Company, which agreed to retain their separate identities. Both had roots in the nineteenth century: Marcus Samuel (later Lord Bearsted) founded Shell in 1897; the Dutch company began even earlier, in 1890.

SINGAPORE AIRLINES

Singapore Airlines is a leading competitor in the airline industry, alongside leaders like British Airways and Cathay Pacific, but it also embodies many of the branding values that typify the small island from which the company takes its name. Singapore Airlines offers high-quality customer service, up-to-date aircraft, cabin and airport suite design and military-type precision. The airline actively promotes Singapore as the tourism and business location of the twenty-first Century, a destination which the world's leading economies need to visit.

Singapore Airlines has won many awards and accolades for the quality of its products and services. During 1994–95, the airline was named Best Airline for Long Haul Business Flights (Business Travellers UK's reader poll); Best Airline (for the fifth consecutive year – Business Traveller Asia-Pacific's 1994 Business Travel Awards) and Best Airline (Zagat Airline Survey, USA).

Singapore Airlines belongs to the SIA Group, the largest private sector employer and third largest publicly listed company in Singapore.

SKF

With 90 factories, 7,000 distributors, and 41,000 employees in over 130 countries, SKF is the world leader in the production of bearings and has been so for nearly a century. Did you know that one out of five rolling bearings (excluding China and the former Comecon) is made by SKF?

For those who thought bearings were a simple product, SKF produces over 22,000 different types of roller, plain, hydrostatic, slewing, gas and ball bearings at a rate of over 227,000 per hour. The company has developed an unrivalled reputation for the quality of its products and its leadership in research. These products are incorporated into a diverse array of items, from the world's largest telescope to everyday objects such as washing machines and cars. As SKF says, "We reduce friction to help you move the world forward".

The world's leading manufacturer of bearings.

SMIRNOFF

Vladimir Smirnoff was the sole member of the family appointed to supply vodka to the Tsar to survive the ravages of the Russian Revolution. He established a distillery in Paris in a bid to bring his family craft to the West and make a modest living. In fact his vodka recipe was a triumphant success and, in 1934, he was able to sell the US rights. The rights were bought in 1939 by GF Heublein for a derisory $14, 000 plus royalties. By 1988 today's owner, Grand Metropolitan, had valued the brand on its balance sheet at £588 million.

The world's leading vodka brand mixes ancestry and authenticity with decidedly off-the-wall ads to keep the attention and loyalty of its growing army of fans.

Smirnoff is now the world's leading brand of vodka and the second largest spirits brand. Heritage, authenticity and ancestry are the brand's predominant characteristics, but the company has given a distinctly zany feel with some innovative advertising which uses optical illusions to disorient and surprise.

Smirnoff has become the first western vodka to be produced in Poland – in a sense, a return to its territory – and it has recently been launched in India. A sub-brand, Smirnoff Black, is produced in Russia and is currently undergoing tests in other world markets, including the UK, Australia, Singapore and Ireland.

SNICKERS

Snickers is owned by the Mars Corporation. It is a chocolate confectionery bar containing nougat, caramel and peanuts. First introduced into the US market on 4 February 1930, the product took its name from a favourite horse of the Mars family. The brand's values are those of an energising snack between meals. It has a youthful exuberance and has recently acquired sporting connotations via its advertising and most recent sponsorship of the 1994 Football World Cup held in the USA.

The brand was originally known as "Marathon" when introduced into the UK market in 1967. To bring it in line with the parent company's aim to make a truly global brand, the brand name was converted to Snickers in 1990. In what could have been a marketing disaster in terms of sales, the company had carefully planned the name changeover in stages: first having the sentence "Internationally known as Snickers" printed under the brand name banner; then having the words, "The new name for Marathon", printed under the new Snicker banner upon the renaming. As a result, the careful and informative approach by the brand-owners actually saw the product sales increase dramatically over this period.

Snickers is available worldwide and has a variety of brand lines to meet the local market requirements; for example, in the USA there is a peanut butter variety of Snickers.

Snickers has survived a name-change and mounting competition from new chocolate snack bars to become a global brand which is well adapted to the individual tastes of different markets.

A compelling cocktail of old-world charm and youthful trendiness, Southern Comfort has survived the rigours of a mature market to remain the pre-eminent bourbon from America's Deep South.

After stagnating somewhat over the last decade, Sony is now a revitalised company, determined to dominate the digital revolution just as it dominated the electronic revolution.

SONY

There are many ways of achieving brand identity, but the ultimate must be when a company or brand name becomes the generic term for a type of product, preferably written with a small letter: 'hoover', or 'technicolor', or, above all, 'walkman'.

The Sony Corporation is, of course, much more than personal stereos. Founded in 1946, the company has long been at the forefront of technical innovation in its field. The word 'Sony' – short, distinctive, international, and with allusions to both 'sonus' (Latin for sound) and the term of endearment 'sonny' – appears in bold capitals on a whole range of electronic sound and visual products. Notable firsts include the home video system (1975), CD player (1982) and camcorder (1983). Recently the company has also moved into entertainment 'software' with its acquisitions of CBS Records (1988) and Columbia Pictures Entertainment (1989).

Behind Sony's success lie a number of policy factors: concentration on its own brands and a refusal to act as subcontractor for other companies; clear focus on a single product area, electronics; technical research and innovation; an early focus on world markets and, later, a policy of 'global localisation' by bringing manufacturing bases closer to consumer markets; and a clearly defined corporate structure giving considerable independence to individual divisions and branches.

But the Walkman is special. People use 'walkman' to describe personal stereos whoever the manufacturer is. But, by dint of careful advertising, Sony has ensured that 'Sony Walkman' remains a fixed and familiar word combination. So anybody who finds the term 'personal stereo' cumbersome and uses 'walkman' instead is giving Sony an implicit plug. As promotion goes, this is cheap and extraordinarily effective.

Ironically the Walkman was treated with considerable scepticism before its launch in July 1979. The marketing men at Sony feared that consumers would find the headphones annoying and object to a cassette player that could not record. The decision to go ahead was finally taken by Akio Morita, the company's founder and chief executive. The scepticism extended to rival companies, giving Sony a year's start on its potential competitors. This lead has been maintained and Sony still commands 40% of the world market in personal stereos.

SOUTHERN COMFORT

In a sense, Southern Comfort has a problem of contrasting brand images. On the one hand there is the logo and name, harking back – quite justifiably – to a gentle age of Mississippi paddle steamers and the Old South. On the other, it is the drink of the brash young set, classless America and the cocktail bar.

There are also problems at international level. Southern Comfort, for better or worse, is viewed as a very American drink. Bourbon whiskey, and even more so a sweet liqueur based on bourbon whiskey, has none of the kudos of Scotch whisky. Even so, its popularity outside America has grown steadily since the 1930s, in part as the drink of GIs serving abroad, in part as the favoured slug of the hard-bitten hero of a thousand Hollywood movies.

Southern Comfort was first perfected by a New Orleans barman in the 1860s and remained in his family's hands as late as 1979. Now part of Brown–Foreman Beverages Worldwide, it is marketed in over 70 countries and is one of the top 50 spirits brands in the world.

The number one performance swimwear brand.

SPEEDO

Owned by the Pentland Group, Speedo is the number one performance swimwear brand throughout the world, manufacturing products such as swimsuits, goggles, hats, pool shoes, nose clips and ear plugs. Although Speedo is ultimately a performance brand targeted at professional swimmers it is increasingly moving into the fashion arena. Its ability to meet the fashion demands of the swimwear market – whilst not losing sight of the needs of competitive swimmers – will effect the success of such a strategy.

STEFANEL SPA

Stefanel's success has been built on distributing high-quality, factory-made knitwear through its own tightly linked chain of outlets. The shops succeed in combining the two concepts of a "boutique" and a "high street store". Over the years, as well as expanding its own network of shops, Stefanel has also broadened its range of merchandise, originally limited to clothing for men and women, to include the Stefanel Kids brand for children's clothes.

To ensure that the brand values of Stefanel clothes are maintained, the positioning of the brand has shifted from the concept of designers and fashion shows to the broader and more marketable concept of clothes that are "fun to wear". To this end, press and TV advertising adopts the strategy of associating Stefanel items with an evocative and enchanting natural landscape or with a significant and decisive emotional moment in the lives of its wearers.

Begun in 1959, when Carlo Stefanel started a business producing knitwear, Stefanel today is a solid, internationally known group, with a turnover of more than 500 billion lire – approx. £0·2 billion – and over 1,500 sales points throughout the world.

Fashion brand Stefanel has built a high-street presence and fun image without deserting its boutique, high-fashion roots or its commitment to quality.

Faced with stiff competition in its native New Zealand, Steinlager has turned successfully to sports sponsorship in a bid to rejuvenate its image.

STEINLAGER

Steinlager is the flagship brand for Lion Breweries New Zealand, having won many international awards for taste and quality. The beer is a market leader in its native country and an imported premium bottled lager of varying success in foreign markets. With intense competition in this market, the brand has struggled to maintain its prominence. Indeed it has been relegated to a marginal beer brand in many countries.

Steinlager has an extremely close association with sport: it is a sponsor of the New Zealand All Blacks national rugby team and the New Zealand yachting team, a recent winner of the prestigious America's Cup. This victory has yielded great results for Steinlager. The rejuvenated brand should, with careful, innovative marketing, be able to rebuild its position as a major contender on the international front.

STEINWAY & SONS

Craftsmanship and big business are rarely to be found in harmony, but piano manufacturer Steinway & Sons has managed to achieve this difficult balancing act. It has been acknowledged as a producer of the world's finest pianos since 1853.

Founder Heinrich Steinweg emigrated from Brunswick, Germany, to America in 1850, 14 years after building his first piano in his kitchen. Wisely he waited three years to assess the market and American business practices before setting up his own company in a New York loft. Expansion came quickly and in under 10 years Steinway & Sons had built the world's largest piano factory, with 350 people making 35 pianos a week.

The business passed on to sons Theodore and William after their father's death in 1871. While Theodore brought in technical innovations and developed the modern grand piano, his brother William concentrated on shrewd marketing and promotion. He placed bold advertisements in the *New York Times*, singing the company's praises, and then started to gather endorsements from leading composers and pianists for what became known as the "Instrument of the Immortals".

He also proved prescient by anticipating the global economy with a second Steinway factory in Hamburg and a London showroom. Back in New York, Steinway Hall, opened in 1866, became the centre of the city's musical life and featured many virtuosi from Europe. This roll of honour came to include such diverse talents as Rubinstein, Horowitz, Irving Berlin and John Lennon (who gave Yoko Ono a white Steinway grand as a birthday present).

The brand name has remained unsullied, despite potentially lucrative offers during the hard times of the Depression for lending the name to help sell refrigerators and other household goods. Still blending craftsmanship and quality with new technology, Steinway produces only 5,000 pianos a year (compared with up to 200,000 a year from competitors such as Yamaha). Still supremely unassailable, Steinways are the centrepiece of 90 per cent of all piano concerts performed today.

Sold to CBS Broadcasting in 1972, and then John and Robert Birmingham in 1985, Steinway now employs 800 people worldwide.

The Steinway brand has been a byword for the world's finest pianos for over a century, helped considerably by its owner's refusal in times of hardship to sign illogical licensing deals.

STUBBIES

Stubbies was launched in 1973 as a range of men's shorts. To date it has sold 40 million pairs of the original Stubbies shorts. It is a no-nonsense, down to earth brand, which has outstanding recall among Australian consumers.

Known to be a brand which provides consistent quality, good fit and value for money, Stubbies has become a prominent player in Australia's booming discount retail sector.

Notable advances in the Stubbies offering include wrinkle resistant trousers and shorts, and the addition of jeans and schoolwear.

STUBBIES®
J E A N S

Stubbies is a no-nonsense Australian clothing brand offering excellent value for money and maintaining its popularity through constant innovation.

SUBBUTEO

Created in 1947, Subbuteo is based on arguably the world's most popular sport: football. Today, like the real game, Subbuteo has a global following, but the brand has humble origins, beginning life as a small mail order company in south-east England. The name 'Subbuteo' derives from the Latin for hobby hawk, the favourite bird of the game's inventor, Peter Adolph.

It originally consisted of two cardboard teams, a cellulose ball and wire-framed goals with paper nets. The players had to mark out their own pitch, using the piece of chalk supplied and the ex-army blanket (in plentiful supply during postwar years). Today it is a rather more user-friendly affair, with a vast array of optional extras and a total of 800 different teams. A massive 300,000 Subbuteo games are sold worldwide each year. The brand has become synonymous with good entertainment and has been awarded the title of Top Action Game for almost 50 years by the National Association of Toy Retailers. It was also proclaimed Game of the Year in 1988 by toy manufacturers – the industry's most prestigious award.

Like football, Subbuteo has its own association, the Federation of International Subbuteo Table Football (FISTF), which organises worldwide tournaments and oversees play regulation. The seventh Subbuteo World Cup was held in Chicago, USA (a week before the Football World Cup) and drew entrants from 23 countries. The association takes its "football" very seriously. Not only does it organise the European Subbuteo Championships, it has applied to the International Olympic Committee for the game to be included as an Olympic sport.

Subbuteo is much more than a football game – it is a way of life – which is why the brand retains its integrity despite a dazzling array of very lucrative extension activities.

SUNKIST

Citrus fruit was once a luxury. Sunkist, the Co-operating Citrus Growers of California and Arizona, claim to be largely responsible for turning it into a household staple. Sunkist, they say, first advocated "drink an orange" and started the entire American orange-juice industry; first promoted the benefits of vitamin C and its abundance in citrus fruits; convinced people that tea was good with lemon juice; recommended a squeeze of fresh lemon on fish; introduced oranges as a garnish; and advised putting a fresh lemon slice in every water glass.

Sunkist Growers Inc., with more than 6,500 growers throughout California and Arizona, is one of the oldest, best-known agricultural marketing organisations in the world. Formed to develop and maintain stable markets for its members' fruit, gain the best possible returns for their produce and supply consumers with top-quality fresh citrus and processed citrus products at reasonable prices, it is a strong, well-established international brand.

Strong brand promotion coupled with aggressive and creative marketing techniques and an attractive logo have made it a hallmark for fresh, succulent, health-giving citrus fruits and citrus products.

Orange juice brand Sunkist used shrewd marketing to turn what was once a luxury into an everyday convenience product at an affordable price.

SWAN VESTAS

That buyers consistently ask for Swan Vestas by name – true of no other brand of match – is evidence of its status as a strong, well-established brand. The UK's best-selling match since the 1930s, Swan Vestas today has a market share of 27 per cent.

Successful branding can be attributed partly to the easily recognisable green, red and yellow pack design featuring the royal swan on the unique long, flat container which has changed little over the last 100 years. The distinctive bright pink match head which can be struck on any rough surface is another plus factor, appreciated by smokers and making Swan Vestas the pipe-smoker's first choice.

The brand has been extended to a range of other smokers' accessories, including Swan cigarette papers, lighter flints and fuel, Swan slimline filter tips, Swan pipe cleaners, the Swan hand-rolling machine and, the latest addition, Swan hand-rolling tobacco.

The UK's best-selling match is noted for its distinctive packaging, which has remained virtually unchanged for the past 100 years, and for its resilient match heads.

SWATCH

Swatch was launched in 1983 as part of a rearguard action by the Swiss watch industry in response to increasing competition from Japan. Japanese technology, production and marketing methods looked set to topple the Swiss watch industry from its pedestal. But the Swatch brand proved a potent weapon and rapidly brought Switzerland into the late twentieth century.

An inexpensive quartz watch with half the moving parts of standard models, it came in endless colour and design variations. By the mid-1980s, Swatch had established itself as a formidable fashion accessory. The brand is showing promising signs of longevity: its snappy, irreverent name, relatively low price and trend-setting advertising have seen it cruise comfortably into the 1990s.

Recent brand extensions, such as the incorporation of a paging device within the watch, are admirably innovative. Swatch also has a joint venture with Mercedes-Benz, developing a "micro-car" specifically designed for the city streets of the future.

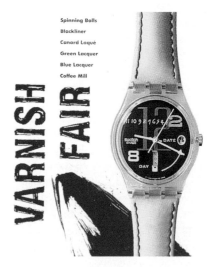

Spinning Balls
Blackliner
Canard Laqué
Green Lacquer
Blue Lacquer
Coffee Mill

VARNISH FAIR

A youthful watch brand that single-handedly saved the Swiss watch industry, Swatch now looks strong enough to extend successfully into cars, pagers and all manner of innovative new products.

TABASCO

It is ironic that Tabasco saw no problem in lending its famous diamond-shaped logo to such unlikely items as T-shirts, aprons, ties and boxer shorts well before it decided to launch a green jalopeño version of its famous red pepper sauce.

But then the launch of the original Tabasco was itself steeped in irony. With his family's sugar-cane fields and salt works destroyed by the Civil War, New Orleans banker and *bon vivant* Edmund McIlhenny was forced to experiment with the apparently worthless red peppers which had survived the general devastation. Adding some local salt and French wine vinegar, McIlhenny blended the first Tabasco sauce in 1868 on Avery Island, Louisiana.

He selected the Tabasco name (Mexican Indian for "land where the soil is humid"), labelled bottles and sent out samples to 350 wholesale grocers. The next year orders poured in for thousands of bottles at one dollar a time, and in 1870 McIlhenny obtained a patent for his unique recipe. Two years later the company opened a London

office to cater for European buyers. Today sales of Tabasco in over 100 countries generate more than $50 million a year, with the famous label printed in some 19 languages.

A family business in its early years, the McIlhenny Company was formed in 1907 with a view to protecting its increasingly desirable trademark. Other Tabasco products today include a Bloody Mary mix and and 7 Spice Chili Recipe, and New Orleans Style and Caribbean Style steak sauces. The green pepper jalopeño sauce was launched in 1995.

The original red pepper sauce has flown into space with NASA astronauts, served with the troops in Vietnam and the Gulf War, and is even said to be a favourite of George Bush and the Queen Mother. Though production continues in Avery Island, now also a bird sanctuary and wildlife park, the company also owns pepper farms in Mexico, Honduras, Venezuela and Colombia.

The Tobasco logo has been carefully controlled over the years so that its recent brand extension activity reflects the unique positioning of the original red pepper sauce from Louisiana.

TAG HEUER

Within eight years TAG Heuer has been transformed from a marginal player with struggling sales, verging on the brink of bankruptcy, to Switzerland's fifth largest watch-maker. A complete re-assessment of the Tag Heuer brand and an overhaul of its marketing strategy have played a fundamental role in this significant change in fortune. Firstly TAG Heuer identified a niche market segment, unserved by other luxury watch-makers – young achievers between the ages of 25 and 40. A youthful, athletic image was developed to reflect both the target audience and project the values of the brand.

TAG Heuer is now the world-wide leader in professional sportswatches. They remain inextricably linked with elite sporting competition, including Formula 1 motor racing, World Cup skiing and Americas cup sailing. The international advertising campaign "Success. It's a mind game" further emphasises TAG Heuer's close sporting associations by focusing upon those moments of total concentration before a personal best sporting performance.

TAG Heuer, from the brink of bankruptcy to Switzerland's fifth largest watch-maker.

TAMPAX

Tampax tampons – 'sanitary protection worn internally' – were launched in 1936 at a time when feminine protection was considered such a confidential subject that few magazines would accept tampon advertising. Despite such difficulties, the brand prospered both in the US and abroad. It is now the world's leading brand of tampon and commands in many countries a dominant market share.

Tampax is near-synonymous with tampons and still dominates the market despite determined efforts from competitors.

TANGO

Owned by Britvic Soft Drinks since 1986, Tango did not reach its current position as the UK's top non-mixer carbonate until the extremely successful and popular "You know when you've been Tango'd" advertising campaign, which began in 1992. The ad agency responsible for this, Howell Henry Chaldecott Lury, helped develop Tango's brand personality by building on its core values of irreverence, humour, Britishness and a streetwise attitude. The resulting campaign succeeded not only in entertaining its audience but also in clearly communicating its taste attributes – the "hit" of real oranges. The ad's fun scenarios of "being hooked on Tango", have been extended into other promotions, notably one which allows the largely teenage customer base to get hold of their very own Tango voodoo doll.

Tango was given a striking redesign in 1992, ensuring its exalted status in the 1990s and achieving an enviable prominence on-shelf. Sales volumes in 1993 were three times higher than in 1987. Now firmly marketed as the "hard, soft drink", Tango has reached its highest-ever market share of 5·3 per cent. The drink is available in apple, blackcurrant, lemon and orange flavours. A still version was relaunched in 1995.

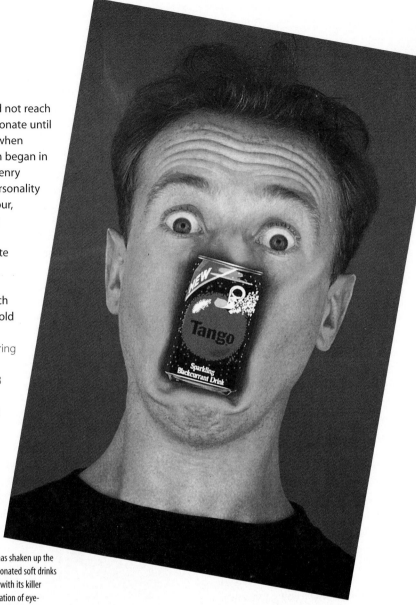

Tango has shaken up the UK carbonated soft drinks market with its killer combination of eye-catching packaging, "in your face" advertising, opportunistic PR and hyperactive brand extension.

TARMAC

Invented in the Industrial Revolution by the celebrated road builder 'Tar' MacAdam, Tarmac is now in world-wide use. The company that bears its name has developed from road construction into a major international company involved in massive construction projects. The 'Tarmac' name is probably one of the most richly evocative in the building industry. It is now the leading construction company and almost certainly one of the best-known corporate brands.

TEFAL

PTFE – polytetrafluoroethylene – is the technical name for the non-stick substance which dates back to the 1930s. It was in 1953 that a French scientist discovered a way of bonding the substance to aluminium, leading to a revolution in cookery and the creation of a global brand.

Now a subsidiary of the French SEB Group, Tefal introduced the world's first non-stick frying pan in 1956 and has been a market leader in cookware ever since. Tefal – it acts as both company name and brand name – is also innovative in the area of kitchen-based electrical goods: it pioneered cordless kettles, electric fryers and irons which feature an ultraglide soleplate.

Best known for its widely acclaimed non-stick pans, Tefal has also moved successfully into the manufacture of kitchen electrical appliances.

TESCO

Claiming to be the largest supermarket and superstore group in Britain and a pioneer in the field, Tesco serves eight million customers a week in over 500 stores. These are not only the vast Tesco superstores but also "Compact" stores, offering the same range of products on a smaller scale, the "Metro" branches with a range selected to attract town centre shoppers, and the "Express", combining a petrol forecourt and convenience store.

The brand name was born when, in 1924, a market trader, Jack Cohen (later, Sir Jack) bought a job lot of tea from a tea importer, T.E. Stockwell. His initials and the first two letters of Cohen's surname marked the label of Tesco's first branded product. Since then Tesco own-label lines have grown continually: in 1995, 2,500 were introduced, including 500 health and beauty items made for Tesco in Switzerland and France. These own-label products aim to be as good as, if not better than, main-line brands. The range is constantly reviewed and caters for all customers, whether they use premium goods, basic lines or both. Currently Tesco is the largest own-label wine retailer.

The leader of price wars and price slashing, Tesco aims to offer the customer the best value for money and the most competitive prices, backed up by an effort to meet her/his needs by constantly seeking and acting on her/his opinions on innovation, product quality, choice, store facilities and service.

Hundreds of special offers on a whole range of products every week are supplemented by 'New Deal' pricing, keeping prices down on about 100 staple products, including big brands such as Nescafé and Kellogg's cornflakes, as well as key fresh food lines like milk and apples. In addition the distinctively packed Tesco Value Range offers lowest possible prices on over 100 family basics such as bread, toilet rolls and baked beans. A quality guarantee means the customer's money is refunded with no questions asked if any Tesco product falls below standard, while a One-in-Front check-out service reduces queuing at the cash desk. A Clubcard gives regular customers a discount based on the amount they spend.

Tesco is the toast of UK retailing, with its highly innovative customer loyalty schemes helping it surge past Sainsbury to become number one in the UK supermarket wars – in turnover, if not in income.

TETLEY'S

Tetley's is a national UK beer brand that plays heavily on its regional character. Brewed in Leeds, Tetley's is the best-seller in the draught bitter ale market in the UK, shifting a head-spinning 23 pints every second during pub opening hours. It outsells its nearest rival by more than 20 per cent.

Joshua Tetley formed the Tetley's Brewery in 1822 with a product line of four beers. The ales were so successful that by 1850 he was brewing 17 different products. Today the brand has made big concessions to the burgeoning off-trade market. It is now available in cans as "Draught Tetley". Tetley's is currently benefiting from its sponsorship of the England cricket team (a deal which lasts until the year 2000). This exposure has introduced the brand name to a wide international audience.

There is no danger, however, of Tetley's losing touch with its roots as a traditional Yorkshire pint: its huntsman trade mark, dating from 1920, is a forceful reminder of the brand's unique heritage.

Tetley's, the very traditional draught bitter brand, manages to appeal to new generations of beer drinkers through its innovative packaging and high-profile sponsorships.

TETRAPAK

Invented in the 1950s by Ruben Rausing, Tetrapak can be found in virtually every fridge in the world. Owned by the Swedish packaging and machinery group Tetra Lavall, the Tetrapak brand holds a dominant market position in the packaging of liquid and semi-liquid products, and supplies the containers for major fruit-juice manufacturers such as Del Monte and Gerber. Whilst the brand name may not be as well-known as its other Swedish counterparts such as Volvo or IKEA, the brand has a presence in 117 countries and employs over 16,000 people.

Tetrapak holds a dominant market position in the packaging of liquid and semi-liquid products.

 Tetra Pak

TEXACO

Texaco is engaged in the exploration, production, refining and marketing of oil, gas and petroleum products througout the world, operating in some 150 countries. Its largest affiliate outside the US is in the UK, where its presence has been felt for more than 75 years. Employing around 28,000 world-wide, Texaco have some 2000 people in locations around the British Isles. The company owns and operates one of the most advanced oil refineries in Europe, based at Pembroke in South Wales.

UK sales and marketing activities supply fuel, gas, motor oils and lubricants, a broad spectrum of industrial, commmercial and domestic markets, as well as marine and aviation fuels to international markets.

In an increasingly competitive petrol retail market, where supermarkets are taking their toll, Texaco has become increasingly customer focused to gain competitive advantage. Award-winning service station designs incorporate customer-led initiatives like 24 hour service, well-lit forecourts, clear signage and glass-fronted shops selling famous-brand food-snacks and convenience products. Proud of their CleanSystem® fuel and Havoline motor oil products, Texaco aim for clarity, consistency and integrity in their brand communications.

The Leading US oil company.

The French fast train.

TGV

The TGV (Train Grande Vitesse) is the world's fastest revenue-earning train service. It was established in 1981 at which time it provided a service between Paris and South-East France at speeds up to 270 km/hr (almost 170 mph) and since then the network has been extended to the Atlantic Coast and to the south-west and operating speeds have increased to a maximum of 300 km/hr (almost 190 mph).

TGVs are highly sophisticated, comfortable trains which perform best on specially designed and designated track. As Europe's airspace and airports become increasingly crowded and as, too, the problems involved in journeying to airports, checking in and clearing security become more acute, it seems certain that high-speed rail travel will grow steadily in popularity and will become increasingly important in solving long-distance travel needs. The TGV gives France a major lead in this area.

THOMAS COOK

The modern travel industry was almost single-handedly created by one man – Thomas Cook. From the humble beginnings of a successful one-day rail excursion at a shilling a head from Leicester to Loughborough in 1841, his company has built an international organisation and launched innovations which have become standard practice.

Thomas Cook today is one of the most widely recognised and respected brands in the world. The name implies quality, value, trust, innovation, response and proactivity. TC is also a major financial services group. It is owned by Westdeutsche Landesbank, Germany's third largest bank. With three core business lines – Leisure Travel, Foreign Exchange and Travellers' Cheques – Thomas Cook has a network of over 1,300 wholly-owned and representative offices in over 100 countries. The company employs 12,000 staff worldwide and serves around 20 million customers each year.

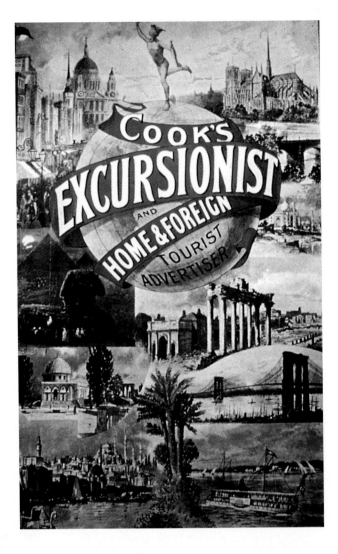

Like the holidays it sells, Thomas Cook is a brand that travels well, a name which signals quality, trust, customer service and good value.

TIGER BEER

Malayan Breweries Ltd established its first brewery in Singapore in 1931 and has been producing Tiger Beer ever since, though in 1990 the company changed its name to Asia Pacific Breweries to reflect its regional standing better. Today Tiger is the national beer of Singapore, with an international presence in over 50 countries.

The brand is associated with a "premium quality gold medal beer" and Tiger has won some 23 international gold medals for quality in Paris, Geneva, Rome, Lisbon and Madrid. *The Asian Wall Street Journal* rated it "the best among 18 brands"; *The Sunday Times* praised its "balance, clean taste and aroma"; and the *Washingtonian Magazine* voted Tiger "positively the best beer in the world".

Singapore's national beer, Tiger is also a big hit abroad, thanks to its multi-award winning brewing technique.

TIME

Time is the creation of two Yale students, Henry R. Luce and Briton Hadden, who launched the first issue on 3 March, 1923.

Today *Time* is one of the world's best-known and most widely read publications, distributed in over 190 countries and territories around the world. It has a total readership of around 30 million and is customised to suit national and regional interests.

Time Magazine puts into perspective the events and issues of the day, by organising the news in a compelling manner, anticipating trends and keeping readers on the cutting edge of changes in the world around them. The magazine analyses important issues, challenging readers to confront them and reach their own conclusions using the detailed information given.

One of the world's most popular news magazines, *Time* has prospered in its many markets by thinking global while acting local.

TIME

TIMEX

"Timex, it takes a licking and keeps on ticking", the advertising slogan accompanying a torture-test commercial in the 1950s, made Timex watches an international brand. The company, which created the original Mickey Mouse watch for Disney in 1914, is today one of the world's top watchmakers and a brand leader in the USA. UK Time, a wholly-owned Timex subsidiary, is a major player on the UK market, with a portfolio of 15 different watch brands, sub-brands and licensers, including distinctive fashion names.

Timex's current success comes from clever brand development, product ingenuity and market diversification. Timex took a licking when, in the mid 1970s, the quartz crystal revolution outdated its mechanical watches. It kept on ticking by reducing the size of the company and altering the single mass-market focus of its products as well as focusing on the burgeoning sports watch market. Timex now has about 2,000 styles (compared with the 300 sold in 1970) covering a wide range of price points and fashion bases. "We're covering many segments of the market with a multi-brand strategy," says Timex CEO C. Michael Jacobi.

The introduction of Indiglo, a patented watch-face lighting system giving uniform bright light at the push of a button, and of Data Link, the PC-to-watch wireless communication system, developed in conjunction with Microsoft Windows, takes Timex comfortably into the twenty-first century.

Watchmaker Timex demonstrates the importance of maintaining a diversified product portfolio in a fast-changing market.

TIPP-EX

The Tipp-Ex company was founded only some thirty-five years ago, in Frankfurt-am-Main, Germany. Its original product was coated correction strips for typing errors, but the Tipp-Ex trademark is now closely associated with correction fluids.

The popularity of correction fluids is due in large part to the more widespread use of photocopiers, but the use of Tipp-Ex correction products has now expanded from the office workplace into homes, schools, etc.

The success of Tipp-Ex is based on an original product concept, the rapid establishment of a powerful, international distribution network and strong branding.

Innovative products which help make our lives a little easier will always have appeal. Tipp-Ex correction fluid is one such product.

TOSHIBA

Toshiba, the consumer electronics company, is perhaps best known for the manufacture of televisions, camcorders and associated home entertainment. It is however involved with a far broader spectrum of activities ranging from semi-conductor technology to visual communications and power generation. Despite hefty competition Toshiba maintains the dominant market position in the production of portable computers, taking 41.8 per cent of the market share in the first quarter of 1996.

TOYOTA

"Before you say you can't do it, try it!" was the sales pitch that accompanied the first-ever Toyota car, the 1937 AA. It had six cylinders and a 3·4 litre engine. The company's founder, Kiichiro Toyoda, was the son of a famous Japanese industrialist. He used the family name for his own company but slightly amended it. There were two reasons for this: first, to make pronunciation easier and, second, because Toyota in Japanese has eight character strokes, which is considered lucky.

In the difficult postwar period, Toyota successfully launched a series of small cars to compete with the large 'gas-guzzling' American models. In the 1960s, it launched the Corona and the Corolla in the USA. The latter went on to become the world's best selling car in the 1970s and 1980s. Toyota demonstrated the flexibility of its brand when it entered the sports-car market in 1984 with the MR2. Later it brought out the Celica and the Supra. 1989 saw Toyota's most ambitious brand extension yet, with the launch of the top-of-the-range Lexus. It marked a move into dangerous new terrain, the luxury car market, and Toyota was keen to inject its new model with a very distinct personality and branding of its own. This approach could be seen in the effort that went into establishing a completely new dealer network, devoted exclusively to the Lexus, across the USA and other key markets.

Toyota has become increasingly interested in the concept of a world car, which is how it describes its latest version of the Corolla. But this does not mean that all Toyotas will start to look identical across the globe. In fact Toyota is determined to localise the look of its cars as much as possible and to cater to regional or national tastes. By 'world car', Toyota means a vehicle which can be manufactured with the utmost efficiency from a variety of locations in different countries.

With its luxury Lexus range, car-maker Toyota has shown the way for mass-market manufacturers to launch highly credible up-market sub-brands.

TUBORG

The Tuborg brand epitomises the characteristics of its Danish creators. The brand is very informal and relaxed, yet innovative and true to the basics of high quality lager.

Tuborg aimed at the international market from the start. Founded in 1873, the Tuborg Brewery was built by the sea. It had its own harbour to simplify shipping its export trade. Tuborg never lost its international focus and, although it quickly became popular in the home market, that was seen as a bonus, and its brand message and management goal were always to provide a global market.

Tuborg and Carlsberg joined forces in 1970, forming what today is known as the Carlsberg group inside Anheuser-Busch. The merger of the two arch-rivals has created the base for the company's rapid international expansion. Today Tuborg is brewed in the company's breweries around the world, making export Tuborg available in well over a hundred countries.

Danish beer brand Tuborg manages to combine a relaxed and informal image with a highly innovative and aggressive marketing strategy.

This Japanese coffee brand inspires passionate loyalty in its home market, and looks set for continued dominance with its inventive brand-extension activity.

UCC

As well as being famously fanatical about golf and electronic gadgetry, Japan is also pretty passionate about coffee. The coffee culture began in the 1920s and today the chances are high that you will get a better cup of coffee on the streets of Tokyo than in Bogota or São Paulo.

Founded in Kobe in 1933, UCC is a purveyor of fine coffees and now dominates its domestic market as the result of some far-sighted new product development. Its path to the number one position became clear when, in 1969, it launched the world's first ready-to-drink canned coffee. While this might have damaged the company by calling into question its pursuit of the finest coffees, in fact it became an instant hit and the company thrived.

With coffee estates in Hawaii and Jamaica, UCC is also known internationally for its Blue Mountain and Hawaiian Kona brands. UCC has 2,800 employees and annual sales (in 1993) of ¥191 billion (approx. £1·1 billion). Today UCC is developing lines of coffee-flavoured foods and opening UCC cafes both domestically and abroad.

UNCLE BEN'S

According to folklore, the real Uncle Ben was a rice farmer known in and around Houston for consistently delivering the highest quality rice for milling. So great was his reputation that other rice growers would use him as a yardstick, claiming theirs was "as good as Uncle Ben's".

Uncle Ben's did not become a brand name until the late 1940s, when Converted Rice Inc. commercially marketed the high-quality rice they had been supplying to the armed forces during World War II. Within eight years the rice had become so successful that the brand reached the best-selling position in its market. Recognising Uncle Ben as an appropriate symbol for the brand, Converted photographed a good friend of his (Ben himself had died some years previously) and incorporated his image into the packaging. This portrait is still used today, highlighting the enduring quality and trust the consumer has come to associate with the brand. Today Uncle Ben's is available in over a hundred countries.

Uncle Ben's confirms the power of branding: before the adoption of the legendary rice farmer as a key motif on the packaging, the product had a much lower profile.

Uncle Toby's has harnessed the power of national identity to boost its "Australian made, Australian owned" cereals brand.

UNCLE TOBY'S

Uncle Toby's has advanced from being a niche product to an Australian power brand, spanning more than 50 broadly based cereal and healthy snack products, with a turnover in excess of $360 million per year.

From humble beginnings as a porridge oats brand, The Uncle Toby's Company started to produce Muesli Bars, Wrapps, Le Snak and Roll Ups in the early 1980s. Later it launched cereal products such as Litestart and SportsPlus. Uncle Toby's also started to sponsor sports including the Ironman, the Australian kayak team, All Star Basketball and Olympic and individual swimmers.

Now a subsidiary of the foods combine, Goodman Fielder, the Uncle Toby's Company has strengthened and enhanced its brand values. It is recognised as healthy, sports-minded, a responsible corporate citizen and, above all, Australian. Below its logo are written the words: "Australian Made. Australian Owned".

UNITED AIRLINES

United Airlines' high proportion of owner-employees ensures strong teamwork and helps project a responsible and responsive brand image.

In 1994 United Airlines provided cargo and passenger transport to 152 airports in 30 countries and five continents. Its goal now is to be recognised worldwide as the airline of choice, a company committed to safety and service.

Claiming to be the largest company in the world, with a majority of its stock owned by employees as a result of an employee-ownership transaction in 1994, it projects a brand image of dedicated owner-employees, reliable and responsive to every individual customer, taking pride in a tradition of teamwork and trust.

The brand is in the process of repositioning to combine the previous policy of cost-cutting with concentration on consumer satisfaction. With the aim of offering the service the consumer wants, whatever the day, whatever the destination, United plans to develop different products for different markets. Its Shuttle service already provides a few-frills, reliable service at low cost for short-haul flights. At the other end of the scale, it intends to boost its first-class and connoisseur service for businessmen on international flights.

VASELINE

A refined petroleum jelly, Vaseline dates back to 1858 when Robert Chesebrough, a Pennsylvania chemist, first noticed oil workers treating cuts and burns with a residue from the oil pumps. Impressed by its medicinal properties, he began marketing the substance as Vaseline in 1877. Today, it is mainly used for the prevention of friction during sport, for nappy rash and for healing chapped skin.

Vaseline owes its success to two factors: first, its personality – honest, pure, safe and utterly dependable; and second, its loyal customer base in the medical profession. Vaseline has been used as a core ingredient in British skin care treatments for well over one hundred years.

The power of the Vaseline name has helped spawn a successful sub-brand: Vaseline Intensive Care, launched in 1970, now includes Derma Care Lotion, UV Lotion, Overnight Lotion and, from 1995, a range of anti-perspirants. Vaseline has shown how a well-established brand can not only extend into related sectors of the same market but can also expand into completely new areas.

VEGEMITE

Vegemite, a Kraft brand, is the Australian first cousin of Britain's Marmite and, like Marmite, is considered by those uninitiated into its subtle appeals to be every bit as 'strange'.

Vegemite is quintessentially Australian and as much part of modern Australian heritage as kangaroos and cricket. It is extremely widely distributed and is available not just in food stores and supermarkets but also in hotels and restaurants. The use of individual-sized catering portions has provided opportunities for trial over a very broad sector, thus expanding the customer base even further.

Vegemite has been available since the 1920s and is carried by Australian expatriates to all corners of the world. It has also given Australia an unofficial national anthem, the "Happy Little Vegemites" jingle, which continues to be extremely popular.

The Vaseline brand, denoting a refined petroleum jelly, has recently shown impressive signs of life for such a well-established name, extending into a range of related skincare sectors.

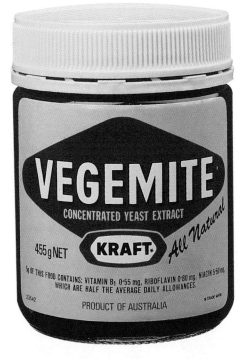

Like Marmite, Vegemite is a love-it-or-hate-it food brand, but one which it is impossible to ignore in its native Australia.

Vidal Sassoon, a brand which travelled a long way on the back of its eponymous founder's flair for publicity, is internationally associated with high-class haircare products.

VIDAL SASSOON

Vidal Sassoon started life as a hairdressing salon in London. Vidal Sassoon himself gained a reputation both nationally and internationally in the 1960s and 1970s for fine hairstyling. His talent for publicity and home products soon made him the favoured hairdresser of the rich and famous.

Recognising a good product and potential money-spinner, Procter & Gamble bought the brand and developed the Vidal Sassoon range to its present broad, international level. Despite this change of ownership, Vidal Sassoon has managed to maintain its reputation for excellence.

VIRGIN

Virgin's owner, Richard Branson, may be considered a maverick, an unpredictable operator who chanced upon an amusing company name, but the reality is that to build a brand as powerful as Virgin takes considerable planning and discipline.

One of the UK's largest private companies, with sales of £1·5 billion in 1994, Virgin began life as a mail order operation in 1970. The first Virgin record shop opened in Oxford Street, London, a year later, but it was the launch of the Virgin record label in 1973 that really set the company on the path to brand superstardom. Mike Oldfield's *Tubular Bells*, which became one of the biggest selling albums of the decade, was the engine for Virgin's expansion.

By 1977 the company had also established a music publishing operation, and the next year saw the opening of the first Virgin nightclub. The company started to diversify in the early 1980s: Virgin Vision was formed to distribute films and videos and to give Virgin a foothold in TV and broadcasting; Virgin Games, a computer games software publisher, was launched in 1983; and 1984 saw the quantum leap into airlines (see Virgin Atlantic). Virgin Holidays followed in 1985.

In 1992 Branson sold his music interests to Thorn EMI. The cash windfall allowed him to accelerate his drive into new markets,

Virgin boss Richard Branson has ambitions to turn his rapidly diversifying company into one of the most powerful global brand names of the twenty-first century.

such as radio stations and multi-media, and to expand the Virgin Megastore chain. But perhaps the most important milestone for the Virgin brand is one of the most recent: 1994 saw the formation of the Virgin Trading Company, whose sole purpose was to identify FMCG (Fast Moving Consumer Goods) opportunities to extend the Virgin name.

So far, this has resulted in Virgin Cola, Virgin Vodka, Virgin PC and Virgin Direct Personal Financial Service. The rapidity of these brand-licensing deals has left the marketing world reeling. It is, quite simply, unprecedented for a company to move so boldly and hastily into such totally unrelated areas. But, so far, Branson appears to be confounding his critics. His Cola, in particular, has caused a stir in the UK drinks market by achieving wide distribution and impressive sales. Branson is determined to repeat this domestic success internationally.

The power of the Virgin brand, and the reason why it may be able to conquer such foreign territory, is its potent mix of vitality – the young, unconventional upstart – and heritage. It has, after all, been around for a quarter of a century. It is radical but familiar.

virgin atlantic

VIRGIN ATLANTIC

Virgin Atlantic seems to be both young and old at the same time: young in that it still plays up to its 'new kid on the block' image, which gives it a more dynamic personality than some of its more established rivals; but old in that the name seems to have been around for longer than its 11 years, such have been its achievements in this relatively short space of time.

When he launched the brand, Richard Branson was famous as a leading light in the world of pop and rock music. Cynics, who included his fellow Virgin directors, saw his move into the airline business as a foolhardy stunt which would undoubtedly backfire. But Branson was convinced his knowledge of the music business would also prove valuable with airlines – after all, both were consumer-led industries.

Although the early Virgin Atlantic service was restricted to the London–New York route, Branson immediately began forming what was to become the most distinctive brand in the skies. He restricted seating to two classes only – business and economy – and ensured that the basic level of service would be sufficient to make other economy classes sit up and take notice. Over the years, his independent-minded approach has seen the addition of many unorthodox creature comforts. These include on-board telephones and faxes, Sony video walkmans, individual TV screens, interactive video entertainment, video gambling and mail order.

The Branson formula has proved phenomenally successful. With a clutch of industry awards behind it (particularly for what has now been renamed Upper Class), Virgin Atlantic now flies many long-haul routes (including Hong Kong, Los Angeles and Tokyo). It has also entered into partnerships with other airlines, such as Delta, Malaysian Airlines and British Midland. In 1992–3 it had revenues of £400m. By 1994 Virgin Atlantic had carried 1·7 million passengers

Virgin Atlantic has grown from a frivolous young upstart into a hugely respected airline, well positioned to take maximum advantage of the world's increasingly open skies.

VISA

Visa International is a credit and debit card payment system operator. Its major rival is the MasterCard network and the two brands are now in fierce competition for the global leadership of the plastic-card payment market. The market, however, is a complex and rapidly changing one: success depends not just on product and brand quality but on widespread distribution through participating banks and financial service organisations and on availability of the service at point of sale.

The increase in electronic banking, changing alliances between banks and payment system operators, the launch of value added sevices (such as gold and debit cards) and the entry of retailers into the fray are all tending to create a kind of 'brand soup' which experts understand but which is often confusing to the consumer. In such a situation the reassurance provided by the powerful brands such as Visa will be of increasing value.

Locked in fierce combat with arch-rival MasterCard, Visa has managed to remain aloof from the flood of new entries into the credit and debit card market.

The UK-based Vodafone has correctly anticipated consumer demand for mobile phone services and looks strong enough to cope with new competition on the home front while it expands abroad.

VODAPHONE

December 1994 marked a turning point for Vodafone, the UK-based mobile phone firm established in 1985. The company was the happy beneficiary of what it describes as "an unprecedented pre-Christmas boom" in sales to the all-important consumer market; 115,000 subscriptions were sold, mainly for the LowCall service. Designed for emergency and occasional use only, this service was pioneered by Vodafone and has since been widely emulated.

With a combination of luck and foresight, Vodafone timed its entry into the UK mobile phone market to perfection. The yuppie boom of the late 1980s made its products much sought-after by business users. The subsequent recession coincided with much deregulation in the UK telecommunications industry and the recovery brought with it a more mobile and self-employed workforce.

Vodafone is now, like arch-rival Cellnet, in the process of switching from an analogue system to one that is fully digitalised (it is keenly aware of the new domestic competition from Orange). There are now 1,800 Vodafone digital base stations around the UK and the company plans to have 3,500 in place by the end of 1996. It is also forging links with telecommunications companies across the world, from Fiji to France and from Sweden to South Africa. Vodafone has offered access to international calls since 1991.

Meanwhile there has been frenetic expansion on the home front, with 50 new Vodafone retail centres opened in 1994 and a total of 640,000 new subscribers in the same year, almost doubling the total customer base to 1·5 million. The Vodafone sub-brands have been expanded to include two different business tariffs – BusinessWorld and BusinessCall – and three consumer ones – MetroWorld, PersonalWorld and LowCall.

The massive investment in infrastructure that Vodafone has made in recent months has eaten into profits (up 2 per cent to £371 million in 1994) although turnover is rising significantly (£1.15bn in 1994, compared with £851 million in 1993). And despite the increasing competition, Vodafone is confident of maintaining a strong position in this burgeoning market.

If only everything in life was as reliable as a Volkswagen brand.

VOLKSWAGEN

The British soldiers who commandeered the Volkswagen factory at the end of World War II oversaw the production of two hand-made VW Beetles. But because the cars received a lukewarm reception from automotive experts, the Brits decided not to take long-term control of the manufacturer. These oddly-shaped cars, they reasoned, had little chance of commercial success.

In fact the "People's Car", designed by Ferdinand Porsche in 1934, was destined to become the world's most popular model, overtaking the Ford Model T and notching up almost 21 million sales before it ceased mainstream production in 1978 (it is still manufactured in Mexico, and there is constant talk of a revival in Europe and the USA).

The name 'Beetle' was first used – unflatteringly – by *Time*, but it stuck. It was when the other world-famous Beatles were getting into their stride that VW's ugly duckling was transformed in the eyes of youthful US consumers into a highly desirable swan. The Beetle's advertising messages played to its maverick strengths, but they also began to establish the VW trademark of safety and reliability. The Passat appeared in 1973 and the Golf in 1974. The latter, which has comfortably passed the 10 million units mark, also ranks as one of the car industry's biggest sellers.

The VW Group today encompasses fellow German car brand Audi, Spanish car marque Seat and Czech manufacturer Skoda. It is the world's fourth largest car company (its Wolfsburg plant is the size of Monaco), producing 12,000 vehicles a day and employing 250,000 people on four continents. It had sales of DM 80 billion (approx. £34·8 billion) in 1994.

Although badly wounded in the last recession and by an early 1990s scandal alleging industrial espionage, the company is pressing ahead with a radical restructuring programme designed to introduce lean production techniques. It is also working hard to establish a presence in emerging markets.

VOLVO

Seen by Swedes as Sweden's industrial flagship, Volvo is one of few carmakers perceived worldwide as a specialist manufacturer offering more in the upper mid-class range than most global car manufacturers. Although one of the smallest mainstream car producers – in 1994, 361,500 Volvo cars were sold – Volvo is one of the largest volume manufacturers in this upper segment of the market.

A powerful brand name based on safety, reliability and concern for the environment, Volvo is strong in the larger family car market. But heavy competition and the backlash of the company's divorce from Renault are driving Volvo to expand its brand image to attract more pre-family and post-family buyers by projecting greater driveability, with more emphasis on performance. In 1994, working from a product range concentrated on only three families of cars, a new Volvo 960 and a special version of the Volvo 850 Turbo were introduced and the Volvo 400 series supplemented by a diesel engine. To achieve greater flexibility, Volvo has also joined forces with TWR, the UK automotive engineering group, to develop and produce small-volume niche products, initially a cabriolet and a coupé.

The brand's reputation as the safest car in the world began when founders Assar Gabrielsson and Gustaf Larson said, "Cars are driven by people; therefore our fundamental principle ... must always be safety." Larson sketched his first designs for a passenger car in 1924; three years later the first vehicle appeared, the OV4, affectionately called "Jakob" and ultimately named Volvo, the Latin for "I roll".

The UK's third largest grocery brand.

WALKERS

1996 has been a successful year for Walkers crisps who are currently the UK's third largest grocery brand. Its current branding campaign 'No More Mr Nice Guy', starring the football hero Gary Lineker, made history in the snack industry with sales of the Salt and Vinegar variety rising by 60 per cent when renamed "Salt and Lineker". Having been voted brand of the year by *Marketing* magazine and with annual sales of over 269.5 million, Walkers has established itself as a vibrant and dynamic brand. Not bad for a brand that started life as the offshoot of a pork-pie manufacturer!

VOLVO

Renowned for its safety and solidity, Volvo is now showing great courage and marketing flair in attempting to inject a more dynamic and sporty image into the brand.

WALL STREET JOURNAL

The Wall Street Journal was first published on 8 July 1889 in the United States and has since developed into a leading US national newspaper. Today paid circulation is in excess of 1,800,000 (the highest circulation of any daily in the US apart from USA Today) and such has been its success that a sister title, The Asian Wall Street Journal has been established. The Journal has been awarded no less than 18 Pulitzer Prizes and can be noted for the quality of its columnists.

WARSTEINER

With its easily recognised bottle featuring the words: "Eine Königin Unter Den Bieren" ("A Queen Among Beers"), Warsteiner is a leading beer brand in Germany. Its success is warranted by its high standards of quality, ingenious marketing strategies and a company philosophy that lays special emphasis on teamwork.

Founded in 1753, the Warsteiner brewery has remained firmly in family ownership and has continuously increased both productivity and sales. In 1994 it had a turnover of DM1.1 billion (approx. £0·5 billion), with one brand alone – Warsteiner Premium Verum – exceeding 6 million hectolitres. Warsteiner's three product lines, Premium Verum, Premium Light and Premium Fresh, are available in 35,000 hotels, bars and restaurants in over 40 countries.

German beer Warsteiner attributes its success to teamwork, lateral thinking in the marketing department and, of course, a very high product quality.

WATERFORD

The incomparable purity of colour and the distinctive, deeply cut patterns that shatter light into brilliant dancing shards are the hallmarks of Waterford crystal. Despite the slow upturn in worldwide crystal demand, strategic repositioning of the brand and higher marketing reinvestment have increased worldwide sales of Waterford Crystal by almost 50 per cent since 1991.

Repositioning to meet changing consumer needs, Waterford has adapted to a role in which its products are sold globally and in which it must match today's mobile life-styles with more flexible cost and styling. In parallel with the classics, new collections, such as the Marquis range, offer the finest crystal in contemporary designs and more affordable prices to suit modern living. In future, Waterford crystal will not only be a prerequisite of the world's grandest homes but also bring in previously excluded new customers.

During 1995 Waterford introduced 196 products, including the gold banding of some of Waterford's most successful stemware lines, a new high-end collection, the Waterford Crystal Designers' Gallery, two new stemware suites (Mourne and Newgrange, designed specifically for the Irish market, where Waterford holds a 65 per cent share

Although Waterford is renowned worldwide for its fine crystal products, the brand has invested in marketing to ensure it stays on top of changing consumer needs.

of the premium crystal market) and Waterford Crystal's Nocturne collection, developed specifically for the UK market.

In the competitive US market, the total Waterford brand share climbed in the five years from 1990 from 27 per cent to more than 35 per cent. The company continues to develop close working relationships with store groups and is also studying new distribution opportunities and potential for brand extension. The Waterford Society of brand collectors of Waterford crystal was launched in 1994 to enhance consumer loyalty and generate fresh sales.

Founded in Waterford, Ireland, in 1783, Waterford products are found, not only in private homes, but also in many great public buildings of the world. To commemorate Westminster Abbey's 900th anniversary in 1965, Waterford Crystal created 16 pendant chandeliers, while other examples can be found in in Waterford Cathedral, the Kennedy Center in Washington DC, and Dublin Castle.

WATERMAN W PARIS

Fountain-pen brand Waterman has managed to retain its commitment to beauty and quality while simultaneously pushing ahead with radical advances in technology.

WATERMAN

In 1883 Lewis Edson Waterman developed the capillary action fountain pen and it immediately became the standard for the writing instrument industry. The Waterman pen has undergone many changes in technology and style over the years, but the Waterman commitment to beauty

and quality has never changed. For more than a century Waterman has dedicated its research to making handwriting a pleasure.

Waterman offers a full line of luxury writing instruments that are known for their elegant sense of style. Waterman, which is based in France, was acquired by the Gillette Company in 1987.

WEDGWOOD

A brand name which evokes visions of heritage, elegance and gracious living, the quality and rich tradition of Wedgwood fine bone china has taken it to a leading position in world markets. In the UK the Wedgwood group has 38 per cent of the high-quality fine china and 10 per cent of the fine earthenware markets.

Recent changes in consumer needs and competition from imports have dictated repositioning of the prestige brand to bring the luxury of fine china within the reach of less formal living. More moderately priced additions to the informal tableware range in 1994 were the Home Collection – a first in fine porcelain for the Wedgwood brand – and Embassy, directed at the important and very competitive US market. In Japan, where Wedgwood has established a position as the ultimate luxury brand in imported tableware and giftware, brand extensions into tea, coffee and quality textiles score successes.

In 1995 the company celebrated the bicentenary of the death of Josiah Wedgwood, "Father of English potters", who in 1759 founded Wedgwood in Staffordshire,

home of English pottery. Wedgwood's first big success came with fine cream-coloured ware, named Queen's Ware by consent of Charlotte, wife of George III. He went on to develop a brilliant green glaze and to produce Black Basalt, a fine black stoneware formed into thousands of classical vases. His most enduring creation was his Jasper Ware, an unglazed vitreous fine stoneware suitable as a background for white classic reliefs or for portraits. Today it is one of the most valued and sought after ranges of ornamental ware in the world. Legendary commissions included the Frog service of 952 pieces for Catherine the Great, and the bone china service of 1282 pieces for the White House during Theodore Roosevelt's presidency. Decorated in gold, the service inspired the long-running Wedgwood Colonnade design.

The marriage of art and industry, an essential element of Wedgwood philosophy for 200 years, is reaffirmed today in innovative projects which bring together the finest contemporary artists and ceramic craftspeople.

While maintaining its carefully crafted image of heritage, elegance and gracious living, Wedgwood has managed to appeal to today's less formal consumers.

WEIGHT WATCHERS

Weight Watchers was the creation of Jean Nidetch, a New Yorker who lost 72 pounds through an innovative weight loss diet and started selling the formula. In 1963, together with business partner Al Lippert, Nidetch founded Weight Watchers in a room above a cinema. She charged two dollars to attend, the same price as a movie ticket. The aim was to encourage controlled eating in a supportive environment. It was an immediate success and the idea was soon franchised to other diet specialists.

The Weight Watchers International trademark was registered in 1968 in the USA and 26 other countries. Brand extension began in earnest when the company engaged food companies to

produce Weight Watchers products. A highly successful Weight Watchers magazine was established, and a series of Weight Watchers diet books were published. Today Weight Watchers is the world's largest weight-loss programme and claims 40 per cent of the market. H.J. Heinz bought the business for $100 million in 1978, anticipating synergies between its food products and the Weight Watchers' Foodways sub-brand.

Weight Watchers has not lost touch with its roots and still organises meetings for which there is no shortage of customers. And the brand appears just as relevant – if not more so – today as when it was launched: no fewer than 34 per cent of Americans were said to be overweight in 1994, up from 28 per cent in 1980. The brand clearly has a giant future.

WELLS FARGO

The famous Wells Fargo stagecoach is still used by Wells Fargo & Co, now a major banking group in the western United States, as a symbol of dependability and drive and of service to communities throughout the West.

Wells Fargo's history extends back to Gold Rush California – the company provided banking services, transportation of bullion and carried passengers, and even had a shipping service for agricultural produce – as early as 1856 Wells Fargo shipped cabbages, onions, vegetables and potted plants down to Sacramento to be distributed by the newly opened railroad and by 1893, 5000 tons of produce a year was being carried by Wells Fargo to the Southern Pacific Railroad for shipment to Arizona, New Mexico and Texas.

Wells Fargo still benefits from its romantic past and from a brand image which is both exciting and differentiated. Now, however, Wells Fargo's world is not that of stagecoaches, cowboys and settlers but of loan portfolios, leveraged transactions, liquidity management and capital adequacy ratios.

The world's best-selling pet food brand, Whiskas' huge range of varieties and sizes as well as in-depth market research has kept customers purring with pleasure.

WHISKAS

Whiskas cat food, introduced in 1959, is today the best-selling pet food brand in the world. In the UK, the brand outsells its nearest competitor by nearly three to one. The advertising slogan, "Eight out of ten owners who expressed a preference said their cats prefer it", has become one of the most widely known.

The extensive Whiskas range, featuring an array of different varieties and sizes, has been central to the brand's success. There are now over 30 different Whiskas products, ranging from specially made food for kittens to Select Menus – a number of selected meals in plastic pots. A programme of continuous communication with the consumer through TV, press and media campaigns, as well as extensive feeding tests and market research, has kept the brand up-to-date and encouraged brand loyalty.

Winston, the second largest cigarette brand in the United States.

Wrangler has managed to change with the times, launching fashion and women's lines, without sacrificing its core brand value of rugged American authenticity.

WINSTON

Winston cigarettes were introduced at a time when smokers were ready for an innovative new product: filter-tip cigarettes. In 1951, vice-president R.J. Reynolds returned from a vacation trip to Switzerland with surprising news that filter-tip cigarettes were popular in that country. There was some hesitation on the part of Reynolds to react, however, because at that time to a tobacco man in the United States a filter was like ketchup to a French chef. In addition, the bland filter tips of the period accounted for only a minuscule share of the market. Reynolds finally concluded, nevertheless, that smokers might opt for a filter cigarette if it was blended properly. The company set its experts to work, but it wasn't easy. The Reynolds test panel smoked about 250 versions of the trial Winston over two years before someone took a puff of blend number 736 and cried, "This is it!"

Winston went on sale in March 1954. In the first nine months 6·5 billion units were sold, and by 1956 Winston was the top U.S. filter brand, with sales of 31 billion cigarettes. Ten years later it became the best-selling cigarette in the nation. Advertising played an important role in the cigarette's success … particularly a jingle that aroused smokers and non-smokers alike: "Winston tastes good, like a cigarette should." This simple slogan became the keystone of a phenomenally effective campaign. Purists objected strenuously to the use of "like" as a conjunction, and the publicity it generated was invaluable. Grammarians argued on television, on radio and in print. Probably the most famous incident occurred when the jingle was discussed, pro and con, for 20 minutes on a TV panel show. John Mason Brown, the noted author and critic, ended the discussion by declaring that the jingle gave him "physical pain". With that, he pulled out a pack of Winstons, lit one right on camera, and added, "But I think the cigarette is great".

Today, Winston remains the United States' second-largest premium cigarette brand and is one of the world's 10 best-selling international brands.

WRANGLER

A brand which has changed positioning in line with the fashion market, Wrangler today is a powerful international name, as jeans have moved from a role as the workclothes of cowboys to everyday wear for large sections of the population.

Wrangler's "authentic western jeans" were launched on the American market in 1947, long before the jean culture became widespread. The brand image then was of the toughness and quality that made Wrangler the preferred jeans of cowboys and cowgirls everywhere. A famous tailor, Rodeo Bill, who personalised garments for media cowboys like Gene Autry and Roy Rogers, was hired to develop Wrangler's early styles and professional rodeo cowboys were enlisted to wear-test the jeans and endorse the Wrangler brand name. As recently as 1974, the Pro Rodeo Cowboys Association endorsed Wrangler jeans and shirts.

In the last 20 years Wrangler, owned by the enormous VF Corporation clothing conglomerate, has diversified in line with the boom in jean popularity. In 1979 the Rustler brand, a basic jean that could be sold through mass merchandising, was introduced, and five years later the Wrangler America brand aimed at mass merchandisers with fashion jeans tagged "The Most Comfortable Jean Known to Man". The 1990s saw the Timber Creek by Wrangler line launched to capitalise on the growing casual wear market, and Wrangler America for Women, featuring classic-styled jeans in proportional fits designed to feel and look "just right".

Wrigley's focused marketing and distribution strategies have given the leading chewing gum brand a global presence equalled by few.

WRIGLEY'S

Wrigley's is one of those rare companies whose brand name has become synonymous with the market in which it operates. Think of chewing gum and chances are you think of Wrigley's.

A remarkably focused company, it has not been tempted to stray too far from its familiar territory, but has concentrated instead on brand extension. The Wrigley's line-up today includes Wrigley's Spearmint, Doublemint, Juicy Fruit and Orbit Sugar-Free. The company has backed its brands with strong advertising, promotions and distribution. It is one of the most widely available FMCG (Fast Moving Consumer Goods) brands in the world, helped by the fact that it requires a relatively low investment by the retailer to ensure a good stock of Wrigley's products.

Wrigley's future looks promising, given the rapid development of brand-hungry new markets, and the dramatically increasing sales of sugar-free chewing gum in the developed world.

XEROX

Xerox is such a well-known trade mark that in many countries – particularly the USA – it has become a generic term for photocopying. It is used as a verb in the same way that 'Hoover' is used to mean "vacuum" in the UK.

Taken from the ancient Greek words for "dry" and "writing", the first xerographic image was invented by Chester Carlson in 1938. But it was not until 1948, with developments at the Haloid Company, that the first Xerox copier was introduced into the market. Its arrival signalled the start of the continuing trend towards ever-greater office efficiency. The late 1950s saw the introduction of the first automatic office copier to use ordinary paper.

The Xerox corporation today develops, manufactures and markets the widest array of document-processing products and systems in the industry, supplying more than 130 countries from its worldwide customer operations. The company describes its philosophy as "meeting the needs of the present, without compromising the future generations' ability to fulfil their requirements". Indeed the company's commitment to providing its customers with innovative products and services that fully satisfy their needs has led to international recognition, with the securing of prestigious awards in many countries.

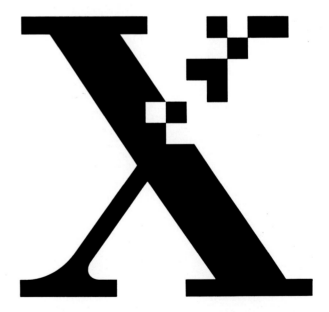

Xerox has become a generic name for photocopying, such is the brand's reputation as a pioneer and innovator in this market.

YAKULT

In 1935, researchers at Yakult Honsha Co Ltd. found a way to culture and utilise the special lactic acid bacterium which survives and is beneficial in the human intestine. Since then the company's mandate has been to promote preventive medicine through the use of beneficial micro-organisms.

Yakult, a brand of milk products containing lactobacillus casei Shirota, a strain of lactic acid, is today a brand leader in Japan, dominating the lactobacillus dairy beverage market. More than 12 million bottles and packs of Yakult are consumed daily in Japan and the brand has become a generic for all lactobacillus products.

The Yakult name has been extended to juices, soft drinks, health foods, cosmetics and pharmaceuticals and is now expanding globally. Yakult products are currently manufactured and sold in 12 other countries.

A global marketing push is now set to make milk-based health drink Yakult as popular internationally as it is in its home market of Japan.

YELLOW PAGES

Good old Yellow Pages! The message of an inspired advertising campaign concentrated attention even further on an already well established international brand, enhancing the image of a friendly, reliable, authoritative and impartial source of information. The registered trademark, the Walking Fingers, and the slogan, "Not just for the nasty things in life", encapsulate precisely the function of the product.

Used worldwide to describe the listings of trades and professions, businesses and services classified under easily identifiable headings and published most often at a local level, Yellow Pages and its registered trade mark are generally owned on a national basis; in the UK, Yellow Pages is part of British Telecom. There is no overall international owner. Although the same name is used for a concept originating in the USA in the 1960s, the history of the brand and its market position differ from country to country.

"Not just for the nasty things in life"... Yellow Pages

Italian white goods manufacturer Zanussi is renowned for its cutting-edge technology and stylish designs.

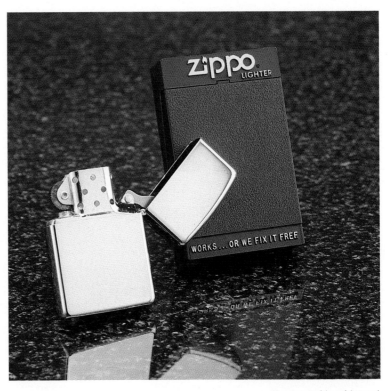

Zippo is powerful proof that good design sells products – the simple, rugged Zippo lighter is a classic.

ZANUSSI

Based in Italy, Zanussi is a global brand leader in household appliances. Named after its founder, Zanussi was established in 1916 and originally known as REX in its home country. It was elevated to iconic status with the launch of its hugely successful fridge in 1956.

Zanussi is widely acclaimed in the industry for its innovative designs and for making technologically advanced products which are both stylish and foolproof.

ZIPPO

The uncomplicated, rugged Zippo lighter is an icon of the American way of life, or at least of the American way of life of the 40s, 50s and 60s as portrayed by Hollywood.

A Zippo lighter is a simple machine: a petrol soaked wick with a flint ignition system. It is robust, reliable and remarkably satisfying to use – the lighter is pleasant to hold, fits snugly in the pocket and using it can become an art form – you throw back the cover and spin the.wheel with your thumb in one fluent movement.

ZURICH INSURANCE

Zurich Insurance Group is one of the longest-established players in the global insurance market, and currently has a presence in all five continents. As such, it is perhaps one of the few genuinely global financial services businesses, although the use of affiliated companies and co-operative partners means that there are many variations in the way that the Zurich name and brand is used.

ZURICH INSURANCE

Zurich, one of the longest established players in the global insurance market, with a presence in all five continents.

Today 4711, the original eau-de-Cologne, is not just a fragrance product but also a source of refreshment.

4711

4711 – the original eau-de-Cologne – takes its highly individual name from the original Cologne Production site: Glockengasse 4711. The subsequent two hundred years have established it as a powerful brand, with distinctive packaging and a familiar blue and gold label that ensure strong brand name recognition and popularity. However 4711's success as a fragrance product does create some anxieties for its owners, Muelhens of Cologne, who have initiated an "enlightenment campaign" to extol the brand's refreshment benefits through the use of slogans such as "We need cool heads again" and "The fresher you are the better you feel".

The brand's history began on 8 October 1792 when a Carthusian monk gave William Muelhens of Cologne a wedding present: a secret recipe for making an aqua mirabilis, so called because of its refreshing, invigorating and curative properties. It was marketed as a medicine until, in 1810, Napoleon ordered all secret recipes for such products to be disclosed. The company, anxious to preserve its secret (the exact ingredients and recipe of 4711 are still carefully guarded), changed the brand's image and started to sell the product as a toilet water for external use.

Today 4711 is exported to more than 60 countries. The brand has also been extended to meet the modern consumer's needs for new forms of application. The result is 4711 shower gel and a full range of body care lines, including body lotion and deodorants.

3M

3M started out as the popular nickname of the Minnesota Mining & Manufacturing Company, a business formed at the turn of the century to mine ore in Northern Minnesota. But when it discovered that the ore deposits were not as rich as expected, 3M turned to the manufacture of abrasives, adhesives and related products.

Today it is a world leader in this field. The company has a powerful corporate culture, central to which is a respect for innovation and technical excellence, and a focus on relatively small working teams, embracing manufacturing, marketing and development functions. One of 3M's best known brands is Post-it – see page 136.

3M is a world leader in the manufacture of abrasives and related products.

7-UP

7-Up was the inspiration of one C.L. Grigg, who hailed from St Louis, Missouri. Grigg's Howdy Corporation began making the famous soft drink in 1929, after testing 11 other formulas. Although the drink was launched just two weeks before the stock market crash of that year, and carried the extraodinary name Bib-Libal Lithiated Lemon-Lime Soda, it quickly found favour with the local market. But when Grigg changed the name to 7-Up – a name derived from the drink's seven flavours – sales grew rapidly and, by the late 1940s, it had become the third largest soft drink in the world.

The 7-Up Company took on the might of the cola giants in 1968 with an advertising campaign whose slogan was "The UNcola" and it later built on this message with a campaign stressing the drink's freedom from caffeine. In the late 1980s, 7-Up extended into the cherry drinks area with the launch of Cherry 7-Up and Diet Cherry 7-Up, two further drinks for the youth market. The company, based in Dallas, Texas, is now owned by a private investment group linked with the Dr Pepper company.

From its beginnings in 1929, 7-Up has grown to make the brand the world's third largest soft drink.